THE TRAGIC PLANE

The Tragic Plane

H. A. MASON

CLARENDON PRESS · OXFORD
1985

Oxford University Press, Walton Street, Oxford OX2 6DP

Oxford New York Toronto
Delhi Bombay Calcutta Madras Karachi
Kuala Lumpur Singapore Hong Kong Tokyo
Nairobi Dar es Salaam Cape Town
Melbourne Auckland

and associated companies in
Beirut Berlin Ibadan Mexico City Nicosia

Oxford is a trade mark of Oxford University Press

Published in the United States
by Oxford University Press, New York

British Library Cataloguing in Publication Data

Mason, H. A.
The tragic plane.
1. English drama (Tragedy) – History and criticism
I. Title
822'.0512   PR633

ISBN 0-19-812843-6

Set by Grestun Graphics, Abingdon
Printed in Great Britain at
The Alden Press, Oxford

PREFACE

When an author looks back on what he proposed to do and compares that with what he has actually performed, the disproportion may induce a fit of self-abasement. To have made, in the course of these pages, so many claims, in my various attempts to present a *tragic plane*, that my central thesis is *original* may have exposed me to the charge of either ignorance or presumption. Perhaps it would have been enough distinction to say that I differ from my predecessors in the extent to which I abandon normal modes of definition, that more than others I have come to see Tragedy as Hamlet saw the Ghost:

> Thou com'st in such a questionable shape . . .

Certainly in supposing that I was meeting the *real* when I opened my mind to some of the world's best tragedies I shall appear absurd in my finding that 'real' a tissue of *contradictions*. Yet in so doing I tread common ground with many respected contemporaries. It would not be hard to name fellow-travellers and associates who share my belief that, if in reading the greatest tragedies we are asked to rise high above our ordinary selves and begin to think and feel on a plane we do not habitually frequent, our difficulties lie just as much with the necessity to confront terrors and desires we think of as belonging rather to our heritage from the distant days when our ancestors had not yet emerged from the jungle. Again, it is commonly recognized that every account of Tragedy must accept the truth of two contradictory propositions: 'Tragedy must be religious' and 'Tragedy cannot be religious', or 'Tragedy is an affair of men' and 'Tragedy is the concern of the gods'.

One undoubted difference, where I part company with many who are as convinced as I am of the fundamental ambiguity of *Greek* tragedy, is in taking the best Greek plays to be *normative*. Those who are deeply immersed in Greek literature and 'thought' commonly regard the short period during which the great tragedies were composed as marking a stage which the Greeks rapidly left behind. The tragic dilemma, which presents the hero in his tragic act as both innocent and guilty, is thought by them to be a position that became untenable as soon as Greek philosophers got to work. My claim is that the very inadequacies of the common Greek vocabulary for handling ethical discussion enabled the composers of tragedies to be true to 'reality' in appropriate dramatic terms in such a way that the few great tragedies are as 'true' now as ever they were. I even go so far as to suggest that Homer may still be drawn on to help us and to force us to face the true facts.

This is only possible, I would argue, if Tragedy is ultimately a *mystery*, a unique phenomenon which cannot be classified under any of the heads used in the discourse of philosophers, theologians, psychologists, Marxists, structuralists, or post-structuralists. The burden of my book is therefore a plea for a change in common ways of thinking about Tragedy. I think the time has come to substitute an acute sense of the precarious nature of any attempted definition of the tragic. For this reason I have been careful to restrict myself to a few 'constituents', as I have called them. By this word I do not mean that if they are present Tragedy *must* be there also, but that they make *for* Tragedy, in that when they are present Tragedy is possible, and when they are absent, Tragedy will not be found.

Readers who have not come across an earlier work of mine entitled 'Shakespeare's Tragedies of Love' may be surprised and even irritated by two features of the present book. Both are in fact *re*-appearances of two features in this earlier work. The first is the choice of Tyndale's 1534 translation of the New Testament to quote from rather than the Authorised Version of 1611. My object was to compel a sharper attention by offering words both like and unlike those with which readers will long have been familiar from their own bibles. A similar motive accounts for the appearance in quotations of a largely unedited Folio Shakespeare when recalling some of the best-known passages in the tragedies rather than any modernised text. Readers are invited to open their own copies of Shakespeare's plays, to savour the differences and the challenge to make up their own imaginary acting version from the comparatively unhelpful lay-out of the Folio. In general, my objects, I thought, would always be better served by a *reading* than by an acting version of any quoted play.

CONTENTS

1
THE UNITY AND AMBIGUITY OF TRAGEDY

The theme of this first chapter is well summed up in its title. If by 'ambiguity' is understood the property of being now one thing and now another, such a theme must sound like a logical impossibility, for if Tragedy is always one and only one thing it cannot be more than one. Nevertheless my case falls if it is not found necessary to assert at one and the same time both the unity *and* the ambiguity of Tragedy. This theme will first be put forward in this chapter as a hypothesis, which, if granted hypothetical entry into a reader's mind, will have to work its passage hard if it is ever to become part of his own thinking. It will be my aim to hammer home the necessity of accepting this theme, which will be the subject of debate down to the last page of this book.

I open in such an apparently absurd way because this whole book will fail of its purpose if it is supposed that tragedy can ever be satisfactorily defined in the terms in which a proposition in law or science may be advanced and considered. It is of the essence of Tragedy that there can be no such cut and dry propositions made about it. That is why there is no book in existence which has been able to define Tragedy in such a way that the reader can by means of the definition discover which plays are truly tragic and which are tragic in name only or at best mediocre specimens. If this be so, the first question would naturally become, what sort of talk about tragedy suits tragedy, once we give up hope of cut and dried definitions? But the first answer to this will come as a disagreeable surprise to all readers who expect to be *informed* or *instructed* about Tragedy as they might legitimately expect to be if they were reading a treatise on points of law or elements of accepted scientific facts. Nothing useful about Tragedy has ever emerged from starting with the false supposition that the *facts* about Tragedy are of this order. I myself was for many years such a reader, and shared the false supposition until I was fortunate enough to be placed within earshot of F. R. Leavis declaring 'tragedy is something you will have to *invent* for yourselves'. It was many years before I recovered from the suggestions of anarchy and uninhibited subjectivism in this quip, and could digest the kernel of truth in it, and come out with the formulation, 'You cannot reach the tragic unless you have in some sense pre-imagined it.' Tragedy *is* a public reality − 'out there', as Leavis used to say − but it can only be perceived if it arouses ideas slumbering in the reader's or spectator's mind. So with this little book: the reader's subjectivity must be called on to challenge the author's. And there is a hard truth about Tragedy which may not be blinked. If that slumber is too deep for a Prince Charming to give the awakening kiss, it does not matter how many plays you may study, Tragedy will not be found.

If I appear to have been warning the reader of the difficulties of coming to terms with Tragedy, I am also aware of an opposite impulse, which I hasten to bring forward now before gloom sets in. If it is a hard truth that coming to possess a knowledge of Tragedy is only possible where the mind itself is in a process of growth and development, it is cheering to be told that the study of tragedy does not properly belong to people endowed with any form of special knowledge or linguistic equipment. Tragedy speaks to us all in so far as we are human, and the fuller the better. And if my sole aim is to define certain constituent elements of Tragedy, although my opening pages may be found baffling, I hope eventually to be found reaching a point where all these elements may be severally grasped and understood to be essential constituents of Tragedy by any mind sufficiently roused, sufficiently curious, sufficiently obstinate, and sufficiently humble and self-critical.

A necessary preliminary part of my self-imposed task of defining the tragic plane by way of these constituents is to clear the path by removing obstacles and obfuscation. It will be my contention that the modern study of Tragedy got off to a bad start in the nineteenth century, and, consequently, many things which were confidently put forward as wisdom in the early years of this century may now be seen to have been delusions. On a later page the reader will find me giving reasons for dropping the word *Fate* from discussions of the world's greatest plays. The nineteenth-century insistence on this word is only one instance of the blocking effect of thrusting on plays notions that have no place there. To prepare for the exposition of my first 'constituent', it will be necessary to get out of the way the notion so prevalent in the nineteenth century, and persisting down to the present day, that what chiefly gives unity and meaning to the study of Tragedy is the fact that *Tragedy develops*, that Tragedy is to be regarded primarily as providing a connected history of a literary genre, beginning with the primitive and showing regular stages of progress towards the complex and the sophisticated.

This is a view I held with great confidence throughout the period from 1930 to 1950. Although I can now see that part of the blame for my deluded self-confidence should rest on Aristotle's treatment of the topic of development in his fragmentary lectures on Greek tragedy (if that is what he has left us in his so-called *Poetics*), I was taken in by a theory I inherited from my schoolmasters. This theory I now judge to have been an illegitimate take-over from ideas made popular by Charles Darwin and his successors and *vulgarisateurs*, and applied to the origins and evolution of drama. I can draw immediate attention to the two main ideas by recalling the titles of the two most influential works, *On the Origin of Species*, brought out by Darwin in 1859, and Samuel Butler's *Evolution, Old and New*, published just twenty years later.

On the question of origins, the supposition was that enquiry into what preceded the first Greek tragedy throws genuine light on the essence of tragedy. The truth is, however, that if a student of literature searches for enlightenment on what preceded the first extant Greek play by Aeschylus, he immediately becomes aware that there is nothing for him to rest on which could be called hard evidence. The lack of real literary knowledge had to be made good by turning to the speculations of anthropologists. The apparent absurdity of relying on such people for *literary* expertise was masked because in the nineteenth century these Greek plays were taken to be immediate products of *religious* speculation. But the nebulous quality of the evidence for anything deserving to be given such a dignified name in the years between Homer and Aeschylus drove historians of the religion of those years out of the field in favour of others who were happy to plunge much further back into the mists of antiquity. The question of origins became a favourite topic among Germans who offered accounts of goings-on in the Teutonic *Urwald*, which were somehow linked with speculations about fertility-rites in various parts of the world. One great name has survived of this anthropological *fureur*, that of Sir James George Fraser, whose first volumes of *The Golden Bough: A Study in Comparative Religion* began to appear in 1890.

The learned in our universities by and large succumbed to the combined influence of Jane Harrison, whose *Themis: A Study of the Social Origins of Greek Religion* appeared in Cambridge in 1912, and of Gilbert Murray, who contributed to this volume *An Excursus on the*

Ritual Forms Preserved in Greek Tragedy. Students of English literature
in Cambridge caught a particularly virulent form of this disease, which
contributed to the establishment of the study of Tragedy as part of
the Tripos there. A notable victim, who never recovered, was F. R.
Leavis, who was not ashamed to advocate reading the bogus anthropology of Bertha Philpotts as a means of grasping the significance of
Shakespeare's *Hamlet*, as any reader may confirm by turning to the
following passage from the Clark lectures for 1967: 'Miss Phillpotts'
book (I wonder it is not more used by literary students) establishes that
there was a second ritual origin of tragedy in the North, and that a
continuity of dramatic tradition runs down through the Middle Ages
to Shakespeare, who, therefore, is at the point of intersection – or
junction – of the two lines.'[1]

Such a serious and yet totally uncharacteristic lapse calls for an
extraordinary explanation. It was not, however, exceptional among
men brought up in England in the early years of this century. It would
take me too far away from the scheme and scope of the present book
to describe the deepest causes for this general interest in the origins
of Greek tragedy. My summary diagnosis would be that the error, if I
may bluntly call it that, arose primarily from the projection of a deep
wish on to a world of meagre fact. Because of the depth and the intensity of the wish, these men were not careful to observe where the facts
failed to substantiate the desired image. We have here a cultural
phenomenon which was not confined to England. What is nowadays
called a *crise d'identité* was throughout the nineteenth century a deep
disturbance caused by severance from the body of orthodox Christian
belief. The most serious minds consequently began to look to Greek
tragedy with a new interest, and raised it from a status of minor
importance to the supreme literary genre. Yet it seems to me strikingly
significant that in this elevation Greek tragedy was regarded more as an
anthropological object than as a literary phenomenon. I believe that the
reason was that Greek tragedy had to support a religious craving which
could not be satisfied by formal Christian religion.

It would, however, be quite improper to constitute myself judge and
jury on this topic. Rather than refer any further to the reading I undertook on the origins of tragedy and of Greek tragedy in particular, I
offer the conclusions of two French scholars, who made a decisive
breakthrough in 1973, when they published a book entitled *Mythe et*

[1]   *English Literature in our time and the University*, pp. 162-3.

tragédie en Grèce ancienne. This will not be my last reference to a valuable aid, and valuable, too, for tragedy in general. One of the authors, J. -P. Vernant, there stated categorically: *'Le problème des origines est . . . un faux problème'* (p. 13), and his collaborator, Pierre Vidal-Naquet, wrote in another book published in 1973:

Il n' y a pas d'autre origine de la tragédie que la tragédie elle-même. Que le protagoniste sorte du Chœur qui chante un 'dithyrambe' en l'honneur de Dionysos, qu'un deuxième (avec Eschyle) puis un troisième acteur (avec Sophocle) viennent s'ajouter à lui dans l'affrontement du héros et du Chœur, ne peut s'expliquer en termes d'"origines'. Et on n'expliquera rien de plus en disant que le mot 'tragédie' signifie peut-être: chant déclamé à l'occasion du sacrifice du bouc (*tragos*). Ce ne sont pas des boucs qui meurent dans la tragédie mais des hommes . . .[2]

The Frenchman is here drawing on a few statements made by Aristotle, who does not appear to have had any substantial evidence to go on. I give a free and easy translation to suit the opening stage of the argument:

Tragedy itself must account for its own origins, nothing else can. No 'origins' can explain the emergence of a protagonist from the Chorus singing a dithyramb in honour of Dionysos, the addition of a second actor in the plays of Aeschylus or a third in those of Sophocles. Nothing about tragedy is made clearer by saying that the word 'tragedy' may originally have meant 'a song sung at the sacrifice of a goat' (*tragos*). Tragedy presents us with the death of men not goats. . .

The habit of regarding literature and art as fundamentally similar to a biological organism which develops through minute changes in an ordered progression from comparative simplicity to comparative complexity, set in well before Darwin began to affect literary criticism. An influential course of lectures on European drama was delivered by A. W. Schlegel in 1809. But once again I am obliged to resort to short cuts to present matters over which we as non-scholars have little control. The fundamental scheme governing the thought of these last 150 years is quintessenced in a few sentences of Theodor Mommsen's *History of Rome.* The passage is made apt for our purposes by the total confidence with which the conviction is presented as something so obvious as not to require argument in its defence. His topic was the effect on the Roman theatre of the plays of Euripides. His key-word,

---

[2] *Sophocle: Tragédies*, 1973, p. 13.

Individualisierung, was chosen to create a line of development for tragedy culminating in a Shakespeare seen exclusively as a creator of *character*:

> Das tiefe Wort, welches sittlich wie poetisch die Summe aller Tragik zieht, daß Handeln Leiden ist, gilt freilich auch für die antike Tragödie; den handelnden Menschen stellt sie dar, aber eigentliche Individualisierung ist ihr fremd. Die unübertroffene Großheit, womit der Kampf des Menschen und des Schicksals bei Aeschylos sich vollzieht, beruht wesentlich darauf, daß jede der ringenden Mächte nur im ganzen aufgefaßt wird; das wesenhafte Menschliche ist im Prometheus und Agamemnon nur leicht angehaucht von dichterischer Individualisierung. Sophokles faßt wohl die Menschennatur in ihrer allgemeinen Bedingtheit, den König, den Greis, die Schwester; aber den Mikrokosmos des Menschen in seiner Allseitigkeit, den Charakter bringt keine einzelne seiner Gestalten zu Anschauung. Es ist hier ein hohes Ziel erreicht, aber nicht das höchste; die Schilderung des Menschen in seiner Ganzheit und die Verflechtung dieser einzelnen, in sich fertigen Gestalten zu einer höheren poetischen Totalität ist eine Steigerung und darum sind, gegen Shakespeare gehalten, Aeschylos und Sophokles unvollkommene Entwicklungsstufen.[3]

Greek tragedy forms no exception to the rule that all Tragedy, whether regarded as literature or as moral truth, may be summed up in the profound remark, *doing is suffering, praxis* is *pathos*. But though the Greeks in their plays presented human beings as doing, they made no attempt to show them as individuals. Aeschylus has no rival when he brings Man and Fate into conflict, but his success was due to his broad, general treatment of each of his opposing powers. What is essentially human in *Prometheus* and *Agamemnon* is only faintly coloured by those touches of individuality the true artist brings to his work. So with Sophocles. Although he includes all the main features of human nature when he offers us a king, an old man, or a sister, not one of his *dramatis personae* brings before our eyes all the facets of humanity in that microcosm of mankind we call the individual *character*. These two poets reached a high level in their art, but not the highest. A superior form of art is attained when the totality of humanity is encapsulated in properly rounded and self-contained characters, and these individuals are woven together by poetic means to form a whole greater than the individuals who together make up the cast. That is why we must describe the tragedies of Aeschylus and Sophocles as merely stages in

---

[3] *Römische Geschichte*, Drittes Buch. Kapitel XIV. Band I s. 910–11 (9. Auflage, 1902).

a development which reached its climax and perfection in the works of William Shakespeare.

Fortunately, to fill the gap of our ignorance of the detail of the history of this 'heresy' about tragedy as essentially development, there was published in 1965 an essay by O. B. Hardison Jr., which makes it unnecessary for us to look any further. This essay, the first of a series collected under the title *Christian Rite and Christian Drama in the Middle Ages*, and entitled 'Darwin, Mutations, and the Origin of Medieval Drama', can be read as a separate item. We can also safely extract from it Hardison's account of the standard work entitled *The Mediaeval Stage*, brought out by E. K. Chambers in 1903, and use that account as exemplifying the prejudices which have governed the study of Tragedy down to recent times. Hardison makes it clear that Chambers was responding to the general desire to make the study of literature *scientific*. To this end Chambers adopted the principles which were thought to make the study of *history* scientific. This had one advantage, an immense respect for facts as such. But this advantage was cancelled out, says Hardison, by a grave defect:

... the 'main line' traced by Chambers does not emerge in classical empirical fashion 'from the data themselves,' but is assumed before the data are discovered and thus serves as an unconscious criterion for the selection. A circularity commonly associated with naive empiricism is evident. Having been selected on the basis of evolutionary theory, the data can hardly fail to illustrate the theory when assembled. (p. 9.)

Nineteenth-century scholars, he says, formed their conception of literary evolution by a synthesis based on an analogy between culture and biological organisms. Literatures, literary periods, and literary types were compared to living creatures. For instance, a continuous history of English drama was thought to illustrate three phases, 'growth', from the so-called 'germ' of liturgical drama to Marlowe, 'maturity', in the works of Marlowe, Shakespeare, and Ben Jonson, and 'decadence' in the Jacobean drama down to 1642, when 'dissipation' set in. Chambers himself, however, although when dealing with the medieval period he occasionally tampered with chronology in his attempt to preserve the idea of a gradual, uniform development from simple to complex, finally gave up the hope of finding continuity between medieval drama and the plays of Shakespeare. Hardison went on to discuss some of Chambers's successors and concluded with a figure of some importance in 1965, Professor Hardin Craig. One last quotation

from Hardison's essay will provide an epitaph on this failure of the
evolutionary theory:

Chambers had hoped for a history of medieval drama which would
'explain the pre-existing conditions which, by the latter half of the
sixteenth century, made the great Shakespearean stage possible.' The
failure of this ideal was inherent in his assumptions. Its epitaph is
Craig's observation that 'there is only the faintest possibility that there
was any tangible influence of the moral interlude on Shakespeare when
he wrote *Macbeth*. . . . It is not therefore a matter of the formal and
often thin thing called literary influence that makes Macbeth remind
one of Everyman, but a community of race and purpose that found
expression in the drama of two different though still closely connected
ages' (p. 25).[4]

To point the moral and adorn the tale, there is a little anecdote
which should be told to all beginners in the study of Tragedy. From the
time of Darwin down to 1952 it was generally held that a certain play
by Aeschylus must have been the work of a young man still fumbling
with an 'archaic' or 'primitive' form of drama.[5] Nobody in that time
had any reason to doubt that the *Suppliant Maidens* was an early work
because nobody doubted that tragedy had developed from a sort of
Cantata, and that the next evolutionary stage was a form of interplay
between one actor and the Chorus. And in this play, as all could see,
the Chorus was the protagonist and the single actors were comparatively
insignificant. The general frame of mind during this period is well
represented in a book first published in 1939, H. D. F. Kitto's *Greek
Tragedy*. In the 1950 edition of this work the reader will find the
Supplices of Aeschylus treated as the earliest extant Greek play, an
example of what Kitto called 'lyric tragedy'. If you open the 1961
edition of the same book, you will find that the author there confesses,
a confession made with the greatest reluctance, that the *Suppliant
Maidens*, so far from being an early play by Aeschylus, is in fact the
work of the mature tragic poet, a man in his sixties. What had brought
about such a painful reversal of judgement? Kitto, in a 'Note to the
Third Edition', called it, 'The discovery [in 1952] of about two square
inches of papyrus.' This recovery from the sands of Egypt is known to
the learned world as P Oxy.20/ No.2256 frg. 3.1b. The writing on it appears to date the play beyond question.

---

[4] *English Religious Drama of the Middle Ages*, 1965, p. 389.
[5] Cedric H. Whitman, in a book published in 1951, called it 'the earliest and
most austere monument of Attic drama'.

If the evolutionary theory does not fit the facts, and, worse, if it was never formed on a basis of fact, what conduct is imposed on us in any attempt to talk adequately about Tragedy? We might react against this mistaken emphasis on tragedy as a genre which develops in history by aping a procedure E. M. Forster allowed himself when making a similar protest on behalf of the Novel:

Now for a more important point, the proviso of 'period or periods.' This idea of a period, of a development in time, with its consequent emphasis on influences and schools, happens to be exactly what I am hoping to avoid during our brief survey. . . . Time, all the way through, is to be our enemy. We are to visualize the English novelists not as floating down that stream which bears all its sons away unless they are careful, but as seated together in a room, a circular room, a sort of British Museum reading-room – all writing their novels simultaneously. They do not, as they sit there, think 'I live under Queen Victoria, I under Anne, I carry on the tradition of Trollope, I am reacting against Aldous Huxley.' The fact that their pens are in their hands is far more vivid to them. They are half mesmerized, their sorrows and joys are pouring out through the ink, they are approximated by the act of creation.[6]

This step, however, threatens to lead us off the right path as far in one direction as the historical approach took us in the other. But merely to raise the supposition might provoke us to reflect on the principal offence of the evolutionary view of tragedy, namely, that its exponents were forced to rest their case so heavily on things we shall never know and at best can only posit or conjecture. We might therefore prefer to start with something we all know for certain. This is our actual response when exposed to plays one by one and plays of differing quality. We might try out the hypothesis that the world's best tragedies could be approximated by the nature of our response to them. For very little experience is needed to confirm the fact that when we are left to ourselves, and, above all, when we are totally innocent of any theoretical account of the nature of tragedy, our response is remarkably uniform. First, there is remarkable agreement that supreme tragedies are very few in comparison with the vast numbers of plays which are commonly given the name. Second, when we examine our response to what we consider the best plays, we normally establish it by a series of comparisons. The word 'tragic' is everywhere found to permit of degrees.

[6] *Aspects of the Novel*, 1927, pp. 18–19.

We may never acquire a cut and dried definition of tragedy, but we are always ready to say, 'this is more or less tragic than that', and we can often point to features which we think are causing us to prefer one play above another. I therefore concluded that the first natural step towards a definition of Tragedy would emerge from considering the small number of plays which are thought to constitute the supremely tragic, and by treating them as a class. The two main questions would be, 'have these plays any other features in common?' and, 'among the common features, are there any which are essential for producing the supremely tragic effect?'

The language I have been using of 'steps' and 'course' must not be thought of as an attempt to blind the reader to the inevitable resemblance of my approach to Tragedy to that made by the hero towards the Castle in Franz Kafka's novel, *Das Schloss*. I do not expect to be able one day to make the unity of tragedy triumph over its ambiguity. I shall consciously favour all apparent evidences of similarity in the chosen plays, but I do not expect to get very far towards unity for the very good reason that if anything characterizes the essence of tragedy, it is ambiguity. I therefore expect that the sense of ambiguity will only deepen as I proceed. All I can do is to try to face the facts — all the facts — and put up with the consequence of their contradictory nature.

There is another hypothesis which I shall consciously favour: that supreme tragedies exist to produce their own effect, and are not serving some other purpose. Such a hypothesis has many enemies, and perhaps the most insidious is to be found inside us. 'We are betrayed by what is false within', we are helpless victims of certain fears and desires which prevent us from allowing tragedies to be what they are, and force us into evasions and distortions of a painful truth. That is a remark which should either be suppressed or expanded, but I find it hard either to say less or to say more. If the reader knows himself all too well, and can without shame mention why he is unwilling or unable to face a tragedy without turning it into something else, all I need to say is that I share the reluctance and the inability. If a reader has nothing of this sort to declare, I can only say, consider some of the admissions made by the most eminent literary critics. How many distinguished figures have been unable to bear the pain of tragedy!

Let us take Shakespeare's tragedies, and recall Samuel Johnson's reluctance to read *King Lear* to the end: 'I was many years ago so shocked by Cordelia's death, that I know not whether I ever endured to read again the last scenes of the play till I undertook to revise them as an editor.'[7] A. C. Bradley is worth citing on this point. Here is part of the opening of his lectures on *King Lear*:

. . . this tragedy is certainly the least popular of the famous four. The 'general reader' reads it less often than the others, and, though he acknowledges its greatness, he will sometimes speak of it with a certain distaste. It is also the least often presented on the stage, and the least successful there. And when we look back on its history we find a curious fact. Some twenty years after the Restoration, Nahum Tate altered *King Lear* for the stage, giving it a happy ending, and putting Edgar in the place of the King of France as Cordelia's lover. From that time Shakespeare's tragedy in its original form was never seen on the stage for a century and a half.

Bradley did not wish us to return to Tate, but he thought Shakespeare would have avoided killing Lear and Cordelia 'had he taken the subject in hand a few years later, in the days of *Cymbeline* and the *Winter's Tale*'.

And what of Shakespeare himself? Did he not at times shrink from the last bitter drop that Tragedy required him to drink? Critics have never made good the contention that he composed *all* his tragedies *inuita Minerua*, against the grain, but surely there are signs that he occasionally pulled his tragic punches? I suppose that I shall never be allowed to get away with the following remark:

Humanly, of course, we can understand that a poet might not want to repeat the agony of pushing matters painfully home. We are so greedy for the supreme pleasure of tragedy that we overlook what it costs the poet to provide it. When I call this play a failure, I do not mean that Shakespeare tried for tragedy and failed: it seems to me he just did not try.[8]

'Cette page nuira plus d'une façon au malheureux lecteur' is a remark I have seen attributed to Stendhal. A feature of this book which will recur with maddening regularity in every chapter now intervenes to break off a promising thread of the argument. Just when I have succeeded in ramming home the thought that Tragedy is lost for many people because it is too painful, I have to make room for the opposite thought, that tragedy is more often lost because it is not painful enough. A concern for the facts about our common response to

[7] *Johnson on Shakespeare*, ed. Arthur Sherbo, 1968, vol. ii, p. 704.
[8] *Shakespeare's Tragedies of Love*, 1970, p. 270. 'Telling *versus* shewing in *Anthony and Cleopatra*'.

Tragedy forces me to admit that there is a strong disinclination in many
readers to accord pride of place in their system of thought to what after
all is only a piece of *fiction*. We have only to compare the feeling of
calamity and distress of a man who has just experienced an irreparable
personal loss with the feelings expressed by Keats in his sonnet 'On
sitting down to read King Lear once again':

> once again, the fierce dispute
> Betwixt damnation and impassion'd clay
> Must I burn through . . . .

and we all know which of the experiences it would be more painful for
us to re-experience. Tragedy is, after all, something which exists to give
pleasure. When such a comparison between art and life fills our minds
and we are asked to make our study of Tragedy start from our response
to *plays*, we may feel that we are being invited to take an inferior step,
a step down in the scale of value, just because for us the primary
meaning of 'tragic' applies not to certain plays but to certain events in
the 'real' world. Once a man has formed this habit, it becomes very
difficult even to allow as a hypothesis that the word 'tragic' applies
properly and only to literary fictions, and perhaps properly and only to
such literary fictions as could be performed in a theatre. It is common
to find such a man bypassing literature just because for him the 'tragic'
is an immediate property of 'real' events. He finds it natural to think
that what is tragic is not the play but those circumstances which make
up the human condition, and so to conclude that it is not literature
which is tragic but life, but existence itself, as human beings experience
it when they get deep into things.

   The main obstacle to this attempt of mine to establish the existence
of a *tragic plane* is that Tragedy is constantly being subjected to a great
number of assaults by those not primarily interested in Tragedy for its
own sake. They might all be described as forms of a take-over bid.
Everybody, philosophers, psychologists, theologians. Marxists, structuralists, post-structuralists, everybody wants to get in on the act, and it
is part of the ambiguity of Tragedy that it both invites and repels such
invasions by outsiders. From my vantage-point on the tragic plane I
fancy I see the contest between the two opposing parties each claiming
that Tragedy belongs to them, claiming, that is, on the one hand, that
Tragedy is *exclusively* literary, and, on the other, *exclusively* referring
to 'life', very much as a tussle like that which sometimes occurs when
two people find themselves under the same blanket. Each partner wants

more than his fair share. To claim that 'tragic' does not apply to literature at all seems to me a clear case of asking for more of the blanket
than is right. For some allowance must be made for the truth that
it is of the essence of Tragedy that it is *bearable*. What is generally
called 'tragic' in everyday life is often unbearable, too horrible for art.
We cannot bear to luxuriate in it, to let ourselves be penetrated by it.
Only under the conditions of art can the mind have the power and
leisure to see clearly and feel fully and deeply what is most daunting in
life. But the blanket is one: so we must also say, 'Only those capable of
feeling deeply what is thought to be tragic in life are going to be
capable of discovering what are the supreme triumphs of Tragedy in
plays.'

A radical doubt concerning the validity of this attempt to ground
the whole study of Tragedy on a reader's response haunts me and will
not be shaken off however well I eventually seem to bring off the
attempt. Can we pass so easily from what is essentially private to what
must be essentially public? The fact – if it is one – that all readers
respond in remarkably similar fashion to great tragedies cannot change
the intrinsic nature of a response, that it gives news exclusively of what
is happening inside a reader's mind, and has nothing to tell us of what
constitutes public tragedy which all may listen to or read. This haunting
radical doubt is vexing in one sense, yet it is perhaps reassuring in
another, if it reminds us what a delicate thing, how precariously poised
any attempt to talk adequately about Tragedy must be. It doesn't
get me off the hook to remind the reader that the fundamental issue,
how to make what is private become public, is the fundamental issue
for all discussions of literature and all discussions of what may be
broadly termed spiritual matters, matters in which people are concerned to communicate a sense of values and values which make a claim
to be the same for all people and the same for all time. It doesn't get
me off the hook, but it will help to open a discussion if I say that what
everything must begin from is a reader's *deep* response, the deepest
of which he is capable. The point of this use of 'deep' is to distinguish
sharply the shock of sensibility when first coming into contact with
a tragedy from the slow workings down into the mind of what is first
taken in more or less in a state of daze and bewilderment.

My contention, that is to say, is that, although all literature filters
through the mind gradually in this way, Tragedy reaches, in the tele-
vision phrase, areas of the mind which other forms of literature cannot
reach. But what is certain is that my investigation cannot get off the

ground unless the reader makes a response to tragedies which enables
him to give meaning to the spirit behind the lines:

> The Gods approve
> The depth and not the tumult of the soul,

unless he proves upon his pulses what Arnold was saying in his finest
poem:

> Below the surface-stream, shallow and light,
> Of what we *say* we feel — below the stream,
> As light, of what we *think* we feel — there flows
> With noiseless current strong, obscure and deep,
> The central stream of what we feel indeed.[9]

The specific crucial instance I had in mind where I thought it might
be possible to construct a bridge by which to cross the chasm (as it
seems) separating private experience from public lies in the almost
universal claim made in all ages that in responding to Tragedy we come
across a meaning for *truth* which seems to rival the most important
kinds of truth man can experience in all the other avenues open to him.
In the light of this, I wish to question one description of a response to
Tragedy which in many ways is for me a model. I have always thought
highly of the remarks on Tragedy dropped *en passant* by I. A. Richards
in his various books which deal specifically with literature. The following passage will be found on p. 246 of his *Principles of Literary
Criticism.* I hope to be ringing the changes on some of these observations
in my remaining chapters. (I might have invoked his name earlier, when
I was insisting on the small number of great tragedies. Richard breezily
dismissed most of the plays which are conventionally called tragedies
as 'pseudo-tragedies', in which he included 'the greater part of Greek
tragedy as well as almost all Elizabethan Tragedy outside Shakespeare's
six masterpieces'.)

It is essential to recognise that in the full tragic experience there is no
suppression. The mind does not shy away from anything, it does not
protect itself with any illusion, it stands uncomforted, unintimidated,
alone and self-reliant. The test of its success is whether it can face
what is before it and respond to it without any of the innumerable

---

[9] *The Cornhill Magazine*, Vol. XX. p. 608. Nov. 1869. 'Tell Fan that the lines
in my second *Cornhill* article, "Below the surface stream," etc., are my own, and I
think them good; I have seen them quoted in four places since.' (Matthew Arnold
to his Mother, 21 Feb. 1870).

subterfuges by which it ordinarily dodges the full development of experience. Suppressions and sublimations alike are devices by which we endeavour to avoid issues which might bewilder us. The essence of Tragedy is that it forces us to live for a moment without them. When we succeed we find, as usual, that there is no difficulty; the difficulty came from the suppressions and sublimations. The joy which is so strangely the heart of the experience is not an indication that 'all's right with the world' or that 'somewhere, somehow, there is Justice'; it is an indication that all is right here and now in the nervous system. Because Tragedy is the experience which most invites these subterfuges, it is the greatest and the rarest thing in literature, for the vast majority of works which pass by that name are of a different order. Tragedy is only possible to a mind which is for the moment agnostic or Manichean. The least touch of any theology which has a compensating Heaven to offer the tragic hero is fatal. That is why *Romeo and Juliet* is not a Tragedy in the sense in which *King Lear* is.

In his essay entitled 'Tragedy and the Medium'[10] Leavis both shows appreciation of this passage and points to what he calls 'Richards's essentially Neo-Benthamite ambition'. My own objection is slightly different in that I would rather claim that Richards was there yielding to the fascination of his interests as an amateur psychologist, and that, in any case, the impact of truth on us as we read a great tragedy is not to be measured *solely* in terms of inner harmony and a sense of balance. It feels like a real discovery, and what we think we discover matters more to us than the accompanying feeling of pleasure. What this feeling of discovery is like may be understood if we liken it to the impact of Truth on Mercutio in the play Richards too easily classed among his 'pseudo-tragedies'. It is the moment in *Romeo and Juliet* when Mercutio finds that he dies indeed, and turns on Romeo, who will not admit that the wound is serious:

No, 'tis not so deepe as a well, nor so wide as a Church doore, but 'tis inough, 'twill serue. Aske for me to morrow, and you shall find me a graue man. I am pepper'd, I warrant, for this world – A plague a both your houses! – 'Zounds, a Dog, a Rat, a Mouse, a Cat, to scratch a man to death! a Braggart, a Rogue, a Villaine, that fights by the booke of arithmeticke! – Why the deu'le came you betweene vs? I was hurt vnder your arme.

There would always be one special claim to be made for our response to tragedy in what it does *to* us and what it does *for* us. We need

10   Reprinted in *The Common Pursuit*, 1952, pp. 121–35.

not despise the effect a tragedy has on us just because it happens only
to us and is not communicable. The experience of tragedy would be
supremely valuable if its only function were to make us sum up our
whole lives, to make all our experience pass through the mind in a
drowning man's vision, and to compel us to see in a flash the difference
between earnest and game, between appearance and reality, and thus
learn what pain, suffering, horror, and death really are. But the tragic
experience is more than insight into how we have lived, and what are
the realities of our existence. An inseparable part of the experience is
of that spiritual world of value it is tragedy to frustrate or destroy,
through which we gain a deeper insight, insight into what ultimately
matters. The truth we discover on penetrating into this world begins by
being merely a truth for us and ends by turning into a public meaning.
We end with a vision of immense patterns forming, of things making
sense on a large scale.

But here I must, as on every topic where Tragedy is concerned,
contradict myself. I felt it right to blame Richards for forgetting that
we look out and beyond ourselves, and find a truth which in some sense
is 'out there', yet we very soon find ourselves making illegitimate claims
if we even slightly exaggerate the 'out-thereness' of our response to
tragedy. In the very act of writing the preceding paragraph I found my
pen wanting to run ahead, and put down phrases such as 'we end by
entering a tragic universe'. But in this act another voice pulled me up
and forced me to deny that the impression of *cosmic order* which may
then come over us carries with it a conviction that such an order has a
public existence. I am more inclined to say, borrowing (with a significant alteration) Richards's words, that if we exclaim after reading a
tragedy, 'All's right with the world', our real feeling is more likely to
be, 'All's right around our hearts'.

I am therefore bound to say that there seems to me to be a world of
difference in the quality of two distinct feelings which fill our being
when we are full of a good tragedy. On the one hand, we have the satisfaction we obtain from enjoying any great literary composition, that of
comparing what is offered as truth with all the available evidence in our
other reading and in our experience of the world. This is a joint contri-
bution of all we know of ourselves and all we know of others. In that
sense we may say that a great tragedy is true to all experience, and we
feel sure that the given tragedy will always have that amount of truth.
On the other hand, in a great tragedy we also seem to be receiving
intimations of a knowledge which extends beyond the sum of such an

all-inclusive experience. When we are thinking of transcendental truths, we need faith to claim that they are true although they can never be verified in ordinary experience. But even if we are sure that these truths are such that they can only exist to be perceived in tragedy and nowhere else, I would not therefore class them as exclusively private. I should feel that life as a whole had less value if we could dismiss convictions such as 'I saw Eternity the other night' as merely 'subjective'.

But it is vital not to extrapolate. We should observe a scrupulousness like that of T. S. Eliot in *The Dry Salvages*, where he wrote:

> But to apprehend
> The point of intersection of the timeless
> With time, is an occupation for the saint —
> No occupation either, but something given
> And taken, in a lifetime's death in love,
> Ardour and selflessness and self-surrender.
> For most of us, there is only the unattended
> Moment, the moment in and out of time,
> The distraction fit, lost in a shaft of sunlight,
> The wild thyme unseen, or the winter lightning
> Or the waterfall, or music heard so deeply
> That it is not heard at all, but you are the music
> While the music lasts. These are only hints and guesses,
> Hints followed by guesses;

The most valuable moments in our deep response to tragedy, I would argue, are moments only, and their virtue does not lend itself to extension. I therefore think that we should draw back whenever we are invited to convert the tragic vision into a metaphysical or theological *system*. It seems to me a wonderful fact about human beings that they can have visions, and that these visions can be transmitted down the centuries by means of literary fictions. It is also a wonderful fact of history that the course of events has been profoundly affected by people having visions and, as we say, 'seeing things' which are invisible to the rest of us. But I can sum up my conflicting feelings in a single judgement. It was fine of Ezra Pound to give Heracles a moment of vision in *The Women of Trachis*, and let him exclaim:

> SPLENDOUR,
>   IT ALL COHERES.

But it is just as necessary to recognize that the play as a whole is not backing him up. Do we not feel something similar when we take in the moment which comes to Edmund in Shakespeare's *King Lear*, and makes him say:

> The wheele is come full circle

and then contrast it with the truth we feel we finally possess at the end of the play? But I shall none the less be maintaining throughout this book that there are some moments which seem themselves to constitute the essence of Tragedy, in the sense that they contribute powerfully to our conviction that the whole play is tragic.

I hope that this outline will have prepared the reader for what I am about to put before him in the remaining seven chapters, and that he now knows that he is going to be invited to look on Tragedy as both one and not one; if one, never subject to a formula covering all tragedies, if not one, never so far reduced to disunity that the appreciation of one tragedy cannot help being heightened by contrast and comparison with another. Nevertheless my general line will not be neutral as between unity and ambiguity. I know I am lost if I simplify matters, but I shall constantly be trying to persuade a sympathetic reader that there are certain features occurring in all great tragedies which appear to contribute towards the impression of tragedy. My aim will be to devote each chapter to discovering how far I can go towards defining one essential constitutent of Tragedy. In Chapter 2 I propose to raise the question whether it is only when they come to see mankind in one peculiar light that great poets can make tragedies which deserve to be called deep because of the depth of the response they call out from us.

2
TRAGIC FIGURES

The simplest form my first question could take might run like this, 'What kind of people can Tragedy allow to enter into tragedies?' This formulation almost chose itself when I first came upon a review of George Eliot's novel, *Daniel Deronda*, which Henry James Jr., as he then was, contributed to the *Atlantic Monthly* in December 1876. James there had the happy idea of making a little play out of the arrival of the bound volume of the whole novel in a household containing some highly intelligent and extremely vivacious girls, who take up the pros and cons in a free and engaging manner. The critical discussion is so led on in a plausibly natural way until the character of the heroine of the novel, Gwendolen Harleth, is brought up for analysis, and we hear one of the girls proclaiming: 'Gwendolen is a perfect picture of youthfulness — its eagerness, its presumption, its preoccupation with itself, its vanity and silliness, its sense of its own absoluteness.' The tip for my formulation came in the girl's further remark: 'But she is extremely intelligent and clever, and therefore tragedy *can* have a hold upon her.' (p. 692.)

After our first natural observation, that there are no clever heroes in tragedies — for I have never been impressed by Hamlet's claim, or rather, the claim made on his behalf, that he is supremely or extremely intelligent, and Oedipus himself is the exception that proves the rule — we might turn to a more humdrum observation, that if we go through the *dramatis personae* of the world's greatest tragedies, the only common feature we can detect is that these figures are on the whole well-placed rather than lowly-placed on the social scale. Our next question, equally obvious, would be to ask whether poets had any good reason for selecting one end of the social scale in preference to the other or indeed for selecting any one segment (such as the *bourgeoisie*) to the exclusion of the others. Various people have given various answers, but all take for granted that the basic answer to the original question should be, 'Tragedy requires *personae* of a superior social status to figure in the chief roles, and especially that of hero or heroine'.

But this is not quite the answer we need to the query which arose from reading Henry James. What we need to know is, 'what effect has it on what is specifically tragic in a play to be given for principal agent or passive victim a person with a position which could be plotted as a high point on a social scale?' We can all feel something for the fall of princes, especially if we think of the prince as owing his position in part to divine intervention. There is a moment for all of us, even for those who rejoice to watch royal heads rolling in the gutter, when Duncan's murder is felt as a blow to the *social* fabric. But I appeal confidently to all who have read *Macbeth* or witnessed it, even in modern perform-ances, that the moment when Duncan is a social figure is overtaken when we hear:

> Most sacrilegious Murther hath broke ope
> The Lords anoynted Temple . . .

For then, in contemplating the death of this king, we are forced to think on the King of the Jews, and the primary event in human history for all Christians:

And when the sixte houre was come, darknes aroose over all the erth, vntyll the nynthe houre. And at the nynthe houre Iesus cryed with a loude voyce sayinge: Eloi, Eloi, lamasabathani, which is yf it be inter-preted: my God, my God, why hast thou forsaken me? And some of them that stode by, when they hearde that, sayde: beholde he calleth for Helyas And one ran and filled a sponge full of veneger, and put it on a rede, and gave him to drinke, sayinge: let him alone, let vs se whether Helyas will come and take him doune.

But Iesus cryed with aloude voyce, and gave vp the gooste. And the vayle of the temple dyd rent in two peces, from the toppe to the boottome.[1]

'*Cose note!*' the impatient reader may cry, 'why linger over these elementary considerations?' My desire was, before venturing on more hazardous ground, to have solid agreement behind us on two points, first, that while the *personae* in tragedies appear to be given a superior social position, it is not in virtue of that position that they become tragic figures, and, second, that many things which are necessary to the play as a whole are not necessary to that which makes us call a play supremely tragic — or supremely comic. For my ultimate goal is to turn

---

[1] Tyndale's version of *The Gospelle of S. Marke*, The .xv. Chap. in *The Newe Testament* of 1534.

the argument round, and end by saying that unless the *personae* have one particular characteristic they cannot enter into a great tragedy.

I did not open this chapter with George Eliot's novel and Henry James's review only to dismiss them without serious consideration. There is one class of readers, those nurtured on nineteenth- and twentieth-century novels, who would feel particularly impatient at my not drawing the (to them) obvious conclusion. The argument I seem to hear them putting to me runs like this, 'Why don't you come out into the open, and name that special characteristic here and now, and say that the *personae* must be *characters*? Why not admit that Tragedy is essentially an affair of psychology? The exact springs and motions of the heart are the main thing. The so-called action or plot is tragic only when we make out what it does to the hero in terms of psychology.' If I counter, equally bluntly, that Tragedy cannot arise directly from the realm of psychology, that you cannot cross from one realm to the other, I must not be taken to mean if we find the *personae* of a play arousing in us the interest we take in people we meet in everyday life, people who reveal by act or word that they possess some trait of character, that we ought to avert our eyes and treat the appearance of character as an illusion. I am not saying that we should walk blindfold through it or open our eyes only when we meet the truly tragic figure (whatever that turns out to be). No, we must believe that here, too, the playwright had our interests at heart, and that close attention to, and enjoyment of, any trait of character will bring us to the point where the tragic becomes visible.

That rather grudging phrase 'any trait of character', as it may appear when compared with the full-blooded language that we meet, for example, in A. C. Bradley's book on Shakespearean tragedy, where it is assumed that 'character' stands for a whole *person* more perfectly unified and mentally articulated than anybody we might meet outside the theatre, was my attempt to play fair, and not to try to get rid of psychology as an element in tragedy by exaggerating to absurdity the amount of psychology that can be worked into a play. But I applaud the whole tendency of people in the last sixty years to look very critically at the claim made for Shakespeare at his best that he creates whole people so successfully that we can safely say that we know what they are doing or saying when they have left the stage. (I have tried elsewhere[2] to define a sense in which we are all too eager to read 'character' into the personages of a play.)

---

[2] In *Shakespeare's Tragedies of Love*, 1970, pp. 61–5.

Nevertheless I do not for a moment wish to underestimate what can be brought off in a good novel. I therefore ask, 'What words are we to use to describe George Eliot's heroine, Gwendolen Harleth?' The author certainly thought she was applying the formula according to which tragedy occurs as a consequence of a flaw in a character who meets with adverse circumstances such that they bring on a disaster which would not have occurred at all but for the flaw. Who am I to deny George Eliot the right to call the result tragedy? Gwendolen's is a fearsome story, in which every successive step seems to follow necessarily from its predecessor. It is an inevitable journey, starting from a time when hope and the prospect of happiness flourished like conditions in spring, only to close in a drear, hopeless dead-end, with death as the only escape.[3] Because of the author's scrupulous attention to the development of plot and character, the story naturally universalizes itself until we feel that that is how life really is in this and all other cases where human nature exposes a weakness of character to the cruelty of chance.

I wish my words would convince a sympathetic reader that I was letting the largeness of the mind present in the tale expand to its true proportions[4] in my imaginative recreation, for I wish to make plausible what will seem a monstrous claim in the face of the greatest works of prose fiction. *The novel at its best is never tragic.* A formal critic might raise an eyebrow here, and say, 'why do you suppose it would be? The virtue of a certain kind of play called a tragedy is to be tragic. The virtue of a certain kind of narrative called a novel must be similarly bound up with its distinctive character as a novel.' But this argument will not do for us. If we are, as I have suggested, to measure the tragic by the response in the mind of an attentive reader, then there is nobody who has not been struck by the similarity of the deep response a good novel and a good tragedy call from us. Most of the terms I used just now when sketching the impression made on me by *Daniel Deronda* would be required when describing a good tragedy. If the tragic is to be confined to tragedies, it must therefore be in virtue of features I have yet to describe.

But before undertaking this perhaps impossible task, let me turn aside to an easier argument, that, if 'character' is the mark of a great

[3] That is to say, I am not persuaded by George Eliot's contrivance at the end of the novel.

[4] Constantius in the Dialogue is made to say, 'In whatever she writes I enjoy her mind – her large, luminous, airy mind.'

tragedy, there can be no great tragedies among the Greek plays. This problem was raised in the preceding chapter by a quotation from Mommsen. Here is a similar passage taken from a letter Schiller wrote to Goethe on 4 April 1797:

Es ist mir aufgefallen, daß die Charactere des Griechischen Trauerspiels, mehr oder weniger, idealische Masken und keine eigentlichen Individuen sind, wie ich sie in Shakespear und auch in Ihren Stücken finde.

It has struck me that the personages in Greek tragedies are more or less types, and stand for ideas rather than persons. They are not individuals like those I find in Shakespeare and in your plays.

Some people who come, like Schiller, from modern plays, or from modern novels, have gone even further in whittling down the element of 'character' in the *personae* of Greek tragedies. But a few instances will show to what lengths those scholars are prepared to go who are professional spokesmen for these Greek plays. H. D. F. Kitto in his *Greek Tragedy* wrote that 'Hermione is nothing but Spartan arrogance and narrow-minded cruelty.'[5] Gilbert Murray, in his excellent little book, *Euripides and his Age*, wrote of characters in the *Bacchae*, 'One might just as well call them — The God, the Young King, the Old King, the Prophet.'[6] If we listen to such voices, we are bound to protest, 'Come now, it's never so bad as that!' But we can easily slip into the error of supposing that the Greeks would have tried to rival Shakespeare, Goethe or Schiller himself, if somebody had shown them the way. The conclusion which I hope eventually to make good is that the personages in the great Greek tragedies have just as many traits of character as they need to become tragic figures. If the amount of 'character' were to be increased in a vain attempt to present individuals, the figures on the stage would cease to be tragic.

An exactly similar line of argument would be needed to dispose of the theory that tragedy flows from characters exhibiting *moral traits*. Some people think that a play becomes a great tragedy by exhibiting *poetic justice*. Here I side with the Goethe who thought that this idea was absurd, and that it was characteristic of tragedy to exhibit injustice and the giving of opportunities before they can be utilized, of crises occurring before their proper time: 'Die poetische Gerechtigkeit sei eine Absurdität. Das allein Tragische ist das injustum und praematurum.[7]

---

[5] p. 232.
[6] p. 119.
[7] From a remark Goethe made to Riemer on 3 Mar. 1809.

In both cases the conclusion I think we should reach is that tragedy lies *beyond* good and evil. But once again the onus lies on me to specify what precisely the area is which lies beyond good and evil, and once again I must defer my answer.

On the other hand, I hardly think I need to argue that no tragedy can arise if the personages in the play are not personages but walking Ideas. It is not my ambition to get rid of all philosophy in tragedies by denying dialectical debate a legitimate part in many of the plays we consider tragedies. All the great personages embody more than what is immediately suggested by their physical appearance on the stage, the sound of the voice, the social position, the kind of doing and suffering they are involved in. I could almost say, the more room for thought in the play the better, and I only draw back when I find philosophers, such as Hegel, trying to annex tragedy and assimilate it to philosophy.

The reader will now see that, if I could make it good, I would be saying to him, 'Out with psychology, out with philosophy, out with morality, if we wish to find what is specifically tragic in the tragic figures!' It is equally clear if I am to make *that* good I shall have to convince him that the essence of tragedy is to be found in what is left of the tragic figure when these three things are declared not to be of the tragic essence. Before I address myself to the difficult task of defining the specifically tragic in the tragic figure, the minimum condition for a figure to become such that 'tragedy can have a hold on him', I should like to be allowed to begin with a remark so simple that many armchair critics in their studies never make it. It is that we can never allow ourselves to lose hold of the primary impression made by actors on a stage. We can never give up what we think of them when we hear each personage using the first person pronoun in speech. The crucial question for me, therefore, is, 'what kind of "I" makes a tragic figure?'

The general line of my answer can be sketched by saying that the Hero becomes a candidate for Tragedy only when we are struck by some analogy between his relation to the whole world of his play and the relation of the Soul of Man to all that it is surrounded by in the Universe. More specifically, I would say that we judge a figure to be tragic by the attitude he takes up towards his world, how he 'struts and frets his houre vpon the Stage'. The tragic note lies between two extremes. If the hero regards himself as a mere puppet at the mercy of all that he calls his Fate or Destiny, then he cannot properly be called tragic. If he thinks he is in control of all his affairs, he is a deluded fool, and if the play as a whole supports him in his delusion, it does not deserve to be numbered among the world's greatest tragedies. I am not unaware of how much has been taken on board by introducing such big words as 'Fate', 'Soul', and 'Universe'. But it will not help to lighten the load by belittling these words in the hope of cutting them down to manageable size. So, as a preliminary step towards a real advance, it might not be poor strategy to introduce an exaggeration, an instance where everybody might agree that the poet has gone too far towards one of the extremes where the specifically tragic is lost.

I am proposing to put before the reader for a moment a now forgotten figure, William Ernest Henley (1849-1903), who in his lifetime commanded the admiration of his friends as being a man conquering circumstances which would have broken the hearts of the stoutest among us and reduced us to a whimper. (There is an unforgettable sketch of him in W. B. Yeats's *Autobiographies*.) My point would therefore be cheap and nasty if I appeared to be trying to score off a moral hero on easy terms. Henley, I shall be arguing, *has* crossed the line, and put himself outside Tragedy, but he has not strayed hopelessly far beyond the line. I could therefore wish the reader to hear the following lines read out to him as they were so often read to me in the twenties of this century, by an enthusiastic admirer, who would contest the verdict that this poem sounds the antithesis of the tragic note:

> Out of the night that covers me,
>   Black as the pit from pole to pole,
> I thank whatever gods may be
>   For my unconquerable soul.
>
> In the fell clutch of circumstance
>   I have not winced nor cried aloud.
> Under the bludgeonings of chance
>   My head is bloody, but unbowed.
>
> Beyond this place of wrath and tears
>   Looms but the Horror of the shade,
> And yet the menace of the years
>   Finds, and shall find me, unafraid.
>
> It matters not how strait the gate,
>   How charged with punishments the scroll,
> I am the master of my fate:
>   I am the captain of my soul.

1875[8]

[8] *A Book of Verses*, 1888, pp. 56-7.

This poem prompts in me the reflection that, while Tragedy requires heroes to assert their defiance of adverse circumstance, and in the process express their feeling of possessing an 'I' which confronts the universe, a play will not be tragic if the spirit of the whole resembles that which we associate with the Stoics, philosophers who thought of the ideal Hero as self-sufficing and independent of externals, unmoved by pain or pleasure.

My thought being large and simple can be expressed in a large and simple image. How should we picture the soul Henley was master of? I see a large metal spheroid floating in the void with no windows or port holes. No messages come into the sphere, no messages are sent out of it. Its movements resemble those of a 'dodgem' car, that is to say, the object moves in straight lines until it meets with another equally hard object. It then collides with a grunt and moves away. I don't mind if a reader prefers to substitute an image from the Seventh Canto of Dante's *Inferno*, where the sinful clergy with their opposite vice concerning possessions eternally bump and recoil:

> Percoteansi 'ncontro; e poscia pur lì
>   si riuolgea ciascun, voltando a retro,
>   gridando: 'Perché tieni?' e 'Perché burli?'
> Così tornauan per lo cerchio tetro
>   da ogne mano a l'opposito punto,
>   gridandosi anche loro ontoso metro;
> poi si volgea ciascun, quand' era giunto,
>   per lo suo mezzo cerchio a l'altra giostra.

They clashed together, and just at the point of contact they parted and rolled their weights back with one lot shouting, 'why are you so tight-fisted?' and the other riposting, 'why do you throw your money away?'. They struck up this insulting refrain once more as each retreated to the opposite point of his dark circle; and, once there, each turned and charged round his semi-circle to meet his opponent at the point of knightly combat.

And so the sphere rolls on until it meets with a force so much more powerful that it is crushed or annihilated. Then there is no more to say, for inside my – Dalek, I was almost going to call it – there was nothing but an ego. This ego, as time goes on, is progressively converted into pure self-affirmation, until it is in a position to say with Auguste in Corneille's *Cinna*:

Je suis maître de moi, comme de l'univers.
Je le suis, je veux l'être.

I am master of myself, as I am of the universe. I am and I will to be so.

Although I was not conscious of it when I formed this image, it is plain to me now that I was recalling some remarks by D. H. Lawrence which F. R. Leavis had made apt use of in the essay I mentioned in the previous chapter, when he was describing the spirit behind Russell's *A Free Man's Worship*. Lawrence's remarks bear on a still memorable episode in our cultural history, a wartime attempt he and Russell were making to find a foundation for truth and the good life. It seems to me now that Lawrence, in the act of attacking his opponents for support-ing 'Liberalism, Fabianism, and democracy', had hit on a general indict-ment of ordinary human nature:

I am so sick of people: they preserve an evil, bad, separating spirit under the warm cloak of good words. That is intolerable in them. The Conservative talks about the old and glorious national ideal, the Liberal talks about this great struggle for right in which the nation is engaged, the peaceful women talk about disarmament and international peace. Bertie Russell talks about democratic control and the educating of the artisan, and all this, all this goodness, is just a warm and cosy cloak for a bad spirit. They all want the same thing: a continuing in this state of disintegration wherein each separate little ego is an independent little principality by itself. What does Russell really want? He wants to keep his own established ego, his finite and ready-defined self intact, free from contact and connection. He wants to be ultimately a free agent. That is what they all want, ultimately — that is what is at the back of all international peace-for-ever and democratic control talks — they want an outward system of nullity, which they call peace and goodwill, so that in their own souls they can be independent little gods, referred nowhere and to nothing, little mortal Absolutes, secure from question. That is at the back of all Liberalism, Fabianism and democracy.[9]

Like jesting *Pilate*, we do not have to stay for an Answer to the ques-tion, 'Was Lawrence right?' For all my argument requires is that such people are disqualified from entry into Tragedy.

But if we are to begin to scale the heights of this argument, we need an instance of an equally aberrant view of the ideal tragic figure to match that presented by Henley, but one which, though I hope to persuade you to oppose, we can never expect to overcome. For it seems

---

[9] In a letter to Lady Cynthia Asquith, dated 16 Aug. 1915.

to me a law of Tragedy, or something through which we might guess
what Tragedy really is, to recognize that no one view about it seems
capable of *totally* excluding all others. This at any rate is my relation
to *George Santayana* (1863-1952), that illustrious Spaniard whose
writings were all in English. One of his great services to the humble
academic is that he has shown how such big words as we need when
dealing with our greatest works of literature must be deployed if we
wish to remain adequate to the heights and profundities of classic
masterpieces. I cannot do better than hand over to him for a minute to
allow the reader to learn how a master deals with the general position
or situation which makes a figure potentially tragic.

Those greatest poets by whose side we are accustomed to put
Shakespeare did not forego this advantage. They gave us man with his
piety and the world with its gods. Homer is the chief repository of the
Greek religion, and Dante the faithful interpreter of the Catholic.
Nature would have been inconceivable to them without the supernatural, or man without the influence and companionship of the gods.
These poets live in a cosmos. In their minds, as in the mind of their
age, the fragments of experience have fallen together into a perfect
picture, like the bits of glass in a kaleidoscope. Their universe is a total.
Reason and imagination have mastered it completely and peopled it.
No chaos remains beyond, or, if it does, it is thought of with an
involuntary shudder that soon passes into a healthy indifference. They
have a theory of human life; they see man in his relations, surrounded
by a kindred universe in which he fills his allotted place. He knows the
meaning and issue of his life, and does not voyage without a chart.
   Shakespeare's world, on the contrary, is only the world of human
society. The cosmos eludes him; he does not seem to feel the need of
framing that idea. He depicts human life in all its richness and variety,
but leaves that life without a setting, and consequently without a
meaning. If we asked him to tell us what is the significance of the
passion and beauty he had so vividly displayed, and what is the out-
come of it all, he could hardly answer in any other words than those he
puts into the mouth of Macbeth:[10]

Santayana then quotes a passage which over the years came to represent
for him Shakespeare's view both of what confronts the tragic hero on
the stage and what surrounds the Soul of Man in the Universe:

---

[10] *Interpretations of Poetry and Religion*, 1900, pp. 154-5, in an essay of
1896 entitled 'The Absence of Religion in Shakespeare'.

To morrow, and to morrow, and to morrow,
Creepes in this petty pace from day to day,
To the last Syllable of Recorded time:
And all our yesterdayes haue lighted Fooles
The way to dusty death. Out, out, breefe Candle,
Life's but a walking Shadow, a poore Player,
That struts and frets his houre vpon the Stage,
And then is heard no more: it is a Tale,
Told by an Ideot, full of sound and fury,
Signifying nothing.

My intention, however, remains polemical. Santayana, who shows himself to be so much at home with the great works of Western literature, is totally aberrant when he takes off the cap of literary critic and dons that of philosopher, while still pursuing the business of literary criticism. (I could say something similar about the Aristotle who composed the so-called *Poetics*.) My contention is that Santayana has failed, and failed *totally*, to understand what makes for tragedy in the best plays of the Greeks and of Shakespeare, and that he has gone astray exactly as Henley did in making the tragic hero a Stoic in a Stoic universe. The central issue in this contention turns on the question: 'what is the tragic attitude to the sum of things?' We catch Santayana's main drift in a casual remark made in an essay on *Hamlet*, first printed in 1908, where he exhibits all his enviable, sensitive *flair* for the poetic effect of Shakespeare's language in the play, and then says of him: 'How blind to him, and to Hamlet, are all ultimate issues, and the sum total of things how unseizable!' It was in an essay in *Scrutiny* (Mar. 1936) that Santayana affirmed most strongly that he felt that Seneca stood for the Great Tradition of tragic truth from which Shakespeare was aberrant. After requoting the lines from *Macbeth*, he went on:

Mr. Eliot says that this philosophy is derived from Seneca; and it is certain that in Seneca's tragedies, if not in his treatises, there is a pomp of diction, a violence of pose, and a suicidal despair not unlike the tone of this passage. But would Seneca ever have said that life signifies nothing? It signified for him the universal reign of law, of reason, of the will of God. Fate was inhuman, it was cruel, it excited and crushed every finite wish; yet there was something in man that shared that disdain for humanity, and triumphed in that ruthless march of order and necessity. Something superior, not inferior, Seneca would have said; something that not only raised the mind into sympathy with the truth of nature and the decrees of heaven, but that taught the blackest tragedy to sing in verse. The passions in foreseeing their defeat became prophets, in remembering it became poets; and they created the noblest beauties by defying and transcending death.

In Seneca this tragic philosophy, though magnificent, seems stilted and forced; it struts rhetorically like an army of hoplites treading down the green earth. He was the last of ancient tragedians, the most aged and withered in his titanic strength; but all his predecessors, from Homer down, had proclaimed the same tragic truths, softened but not concealed by their richer medium.

But let me return to the essay of 1896 for proof of the similarity of the language used to describe the Stoic Seneca and that used by Santayana for his own convictions:

Greek tragedy, as we know, is dominated by the idea of fate. Even when the gods do not appear in person, or where the service or neglect of them is not the moving cause of the whole play, — as it is in the 'Bacchæ' and the 'Hippolytus' of Euripides, — still the deep conviction of the limits and conditions of human happiness underlies the fable. The will of man fulfils the decrees of Heaven. The hero manifests a higher force than his own, both in success and in failure. The fates guide the willing and drag the unwilling. (p. 157.)

With the help of M. Vernant and others, I shall in later chapters attempt to show the *factual error* in this account of the role of Fate in Greek tragedies. I have done my best elsewhere to show that a sense for the cosmos did *not* elude Shakespeare. Each of my chapters will be an attempt to contribute to the thought that tragedy involves a conviction that the sum of things is for ever unseizable, and can be grasped only in the *fictional* world of tragedy.

But in the meantime the refreshing challenge provided by Santayana's essays inspires me to make a contrasting portrait of the truly tragic soul. It is almost entirely the opposite of the floating metal spheroid in every respect you could think of. First, it is rooted, but rooted in the universe — a phrase I shall try to make clearer in my next chapter, which will deal with the tragic bond. Second, it has no hard outlines of any sort. Third, it is like the chameleon in being responsive to all the winds and airs which move about in the world of spirit. The essential condition for this tragic soul is that it should be *porous*. I first introduced this apparently ludicrous epithet to distinguish the Homeric hero, when I saw how that hero's courage ebbed and flowed, came and went, and how generally exposed he was to all the moods of heaven. I shall return to this in a moment. But to bring out the force of tragic porosity, I shall imagine a voice emerging from my un-tragic spheroid more or less to this effect: 'You complain that I have no windows or portholes. If you knew how much heroic effort it cost me to block them up to stop the moods of heaven passing through me to destroy me, you would change your tune. You complain that I am all ego. If I had not struggled against these invading forces, I would have lost all sense of being an individual, and would have become as extinguished as Helen of Troy was when she was commanded into bed with Paris at the close of the Third Book of the *Iliad*.'

All great poetic minds have pictured Man as so exposed. Milton in Book Five of his *Paradise Lost* put into the mouth of Adam, who was trying to comfort Eve after a delightful yet horrible dream in which she thought she came upon the marvellous tree of forbidden knowledge and a heavenly form beside it plucked an apple and offered it to her, the following consolation:

> Evil into the mind of God or Man
> May come and go, so unapprov'd, and leave
> No spot or blame behind . . .

While this might be consoling to a pure soul like Eve's or Desdemona's, what consolation was that for an Othello whose soul had been destroyed by invading monsters?

A fanciful pictorial sketch of the tragic soul cannot carry us very far unless it is illuminating some known concrete facts. The general positions taken up by Santayana cannot be shown to be erroneous until we have ourselves experienced the potentially tragic features of the soul of a tragic figure. Ideally, therefore, we should now pass in review the chief personages of the few Greek plays that are universally considered to be great tragedies in order to discover whether they have common features, and, in particular, whether they are all tragic by virtue of a common structure or mechanism, and to find out whether it is a similar operation in the 'interior' of the soul which brings about the tragic act. Before we can undertake this research by direct inspection of cases, there are two necessary preliminary steps. The first is to take advantage of the fact that the best Greek plays are derived from Homer's epics. We can therefore find what is common to the plays by examining their Homeric source. The second is to consider the relation of this interior mechanism of the tragic soul to its surrounding circumstances from the most immediate to the furthest limits of the universe. Following this plan, my direct account of the tragic act will be found in Chapter IV, preceded by step two in Chapter III, where I give an account of what roots the tragic soul in the universe. Step one now immediately follows here.

It is my belief that the capacity for conceiving and creating tragic figures first came into the world with Homer's epics. It is also my conviction that you can better understand what is of permanent value in Shakespeare's intuitions about the self and the not-self and the way the one merges into the other by first seeing the problems writ large in Homer's epics and copied by the Greek tragic poets. So I thought it a piece of luck to have come across an excellent book by Bruno Snell, *Die Entdeckung des Geistes* (3rd Ed., 1955) (which for the want of a proper equivalent is known in England as *The Discovery of the Mind*) for it appeared to offer the chance of a better understanding of the tragic figures in Greek plays than any amateur rehash by me of the findings of classical scholarship. I still recommend the book even though I subsequently discovered that Snell is another ghastly evolutionary developer, and his book should rather be named *Die Entwicklung des Geistes, The Development of the Mind.* He did not think that Homer had developed far enough to create tragic figures. The phrase which opened my eyes to Snell's true views will be found on p. 51:

... bei Homer fühlt sich der Mensch noch nicht als Urheber seiner eigenen Entscheidung: das gibt es erst in der Tragödie. Bei Homer fühlt sich der Mensch, wenn er nach einer Überlegung einen Entschluß gefaßt hat, bestimmt durch die Götter.

In Homer's poems the heroes do not think of themselves as originators of their own decisions. We have to wait for Greek tragedies to find that happening. Homer's heroes think that any decision they come to after mature reflection was the work of the Gods.

Then, as I was fuming over this travesty of the facts, I was delighted to find that another German, Albin Lesky, had made a similar objection to this claim by Snell. His essay appeared in 1961 under the title *Göttliche und menschliche Motivation im homerischen Epos.* It was instantly acclaimed. If the reader consults the book by M. Vernant I recommended in my first chapter, he will find him referring to it favourably.

The great advantage of Lesky's essay for my argument is that the material he was writing about obliged him to come out openly on the characteristic which I think makes it possible for a figure in a tragedy to become truly tragic. In his analysis of the Homeric epics, Lesky dwells on the mystery of the collaboration of what he calls the human with what he calls the divine in every decisive act for which the actor feels responsible. I am inviting the reader to transpose what he says about Homer's heroes to all the great tragic figures. Tragedy, I would say, cannot occur on any other plane, although, once we leave Homer, it may be very difficult to give a clear meaning to 'divine'. Man is not truly serious unless he can say that what he does is as much divine as human. If we require of a tragic figure that he must be great, we do not want him to be a Superman. Nor should we equate him with the whole of humanity. Neither Oedipus nor Lear must be thought of as Everyman. The tragic figures are great because they cannot stir a stone without disturbing the universe of the spirit, the whole domain where we suppose that 'spirits' move about freely on their inscrutable business:

> Millions of spiritual Creatures walk the Earth
> Unseen, both when we wake, and when we sleep.[11]

Lesky has the happy knack of focusing on passages in Homer where we must not shrink from the difficulty of entering into a kind of double thinking, where the same moment in the mind seems to be both personal and supra-personal. He asks us to recall from the Ninth Book of the *Iliad* one of the great turning-points in the epic, where an appeal is made to Achilles to leave his wrath, emerge from his tent, and rescue the Greeks from disaster. Lesky asks us in particular to put ourselves into the position of Phoenix when he is trying in a long speech to soften Achilles and so break the deadlock by recalling childhood memories. In his last remark Phoenix begs Achilles not to persist in his refusal, and urges him to make the decision which will change the fate of the world. It is in this one sentence, ll. 600-1,

> ἀλλὰ σὺ μή μοι ταῦτα νόει φρεσί, μηδέ σε δαίμων
> ἐνταῦθα τρέψειε, φίλος.

that Lesky reveals the co-presence of the human and the divine in Homer's conception of the act of decision.

Although I am generally an advocate of Pope's version of Homer's *Iliad* for any reader who wishes to penetrate to the truth of *general nature* hidden in the particular ancient Greek manners, there are occasions when Pope's care for general truth hides the truly tragic moments in the epic. Nothing of the tragic nature of decision is to be found here:

---

[11] *Paradise Lost,* Book IV, 679-80.

Learn hence, betimes to curb pernicious Ire . . .

Lesky rightly asks us to look at the form of the Greek sentence, and
incidentally notes that it is characteristic of Homer to cast sentences
into two parts but to invite us to make our own whole from them
without specifying how it is to be done. This sentence certainly has two
parts. The first seems to be saying:

> Do not, dear friend, entertain such thoughts in
> your wits.

This part of the appeal sounds entirely modern, for it seems to presuppose that the decision must occur entirely enclosed in Achilles'
wits and in the thoughts he entertains there, as it were at a lonely
banquet. But grammatically parallel in the sentence is a second appeal
in which Phoenix begs Achilles:

> And do not allow *daimōn* to turn you in that direction.

What is this *daimōn* which has no definite or indefinite article before
it? Lesky claims, and I think with justice, that Richard Lattimore lost
Homer completely when he translated the second part of the sentence
as:

> Let not the spirit within you turn you that way.

Certainly all the mystery would go if the power leading to action were
totally 'within' Achilles, merely a verbal variant for his thoughts, part,
in a word, of a subjective mental experience. I think Lesky was right to
say that the basis of action, the centre of the force which might reach
Achilles and influence his decision, must be located outside Achilles
even if it succeeds in penetrating and, as it were, materializing itself
inside him as a 'thought'. But what is *daimōn*? Lesky does not let in
recent discussions which suggest that the best translation would be a
word with an affinity to 'chance'. He therefore rejects W. H. D. Rouse's
version: 'Let not fortune turn you into that path.' If we look at similar
uses of the word in Greek tragedies we can see that *daimōn* does not
lose its connection with the powers in the universe even though it may
be severed, unlike the principal rulers of heaven, I mean of Olympus,
from all that is *personal*. (I shall return[12] to another power which
affects all serious decisions when I come to *ātē* and its role in the tragic
act. It, too, is a power of the universe but has no personal form.) It is

[12]   In Chapter IV.

characteristic of our modern world that we cannot come out with a word for the dooming power. I can well imagine a modern speaker saying to an obstinate man: 'Don't let yourself drift into a fateful decision' because, as M. Sartre liked to demonstrate *ad nauseam* in his long-winded novels, we do not know what finally tips the scale when we make or refuse to make such decisions.

This small instance raises the largest possible issue. If it is of the *essence* of the epic that its heroes must be so intimately bound up with the powers that range through the universe, then we must describe the *Iliad* as, fundamentally, a *religious* poem. Lesky, it seems to me, forces us to take up a position opposed to the verdict which, I suppose, has the weightiest learned support. There can hardly be a weightier name in the study of Greek religion than that of Martin P. Nilsson. On p. 371 of the second edition of his *Geschichte der griechischen Religion* we find him declaring that the whole business of the gods in the *Iliad* is an outworn poetical fiction: 'Der Götterapparat ist ein poetisches Schema, das abgenutzt wird.' And a man whose insight into the *Iliad* seems more penetrating than that of most of us, Paul Mazon, is also on record as saying, on p. 294 of his excellent *Introduction à l'Iliade* (1928): 'la vérité est qu'il n'y eut jamais poème moins religieux que l'Iliade.' ('The truth is that there never has been a poem less religious than the *Iliad*.')

If I agree, as I do, with Lesky, that what makes us take the heroes of the *Iliad* seriously is that all the principal figures in the poem are bathed in a medium which is part of the universe in which the gods move and exercise their powers, and that the decisive acts of these heroes are somehow both human and divine, I nevertheless cannot forget the good reasons known to Nilsson and Mazon for refusing to allow the word *religious* to be used of the *Iliad*. But it is not our present business here to adjudicate between, on the one hand, Lesky and all those who see Homer's epic in religious terms, and, on the other hand, those who confine their attention to, or grant the status of 'real' exclusively to, the *humanity* of the fighting heroes. Our business is rather to discover whether this long excursus on decision-making in the epic has brought us on our way towards discovering what are the essential constituents of supreme tragedy in all ages.

A first conclusion might be that tragedy is only possible under Homer's conditions if there is an analogy between what the universe is supposed to be in his fiction and what we take to be the true facts outside the fiction. Here we must make a large concession that not all

Homer's fictions stand in this relation to what we take to be public
facts. Much in Homer has ceased to have the weight it carried in his
day. Much that Homer thought important does not seem to us to have
intrinsic importance. But if we keep our eyes only on those moments in
the *Iliad* that have never been rivalled, I would say that transposition
from fiction to fact comes easily. The great passages in Homer tell us
how things are generally and how they always will be. It is made clear
in those moments both that the universe contains more than men and
matter, and yet whatever is not these is not to be divided from man
when he reaches his full stature.

But how far have we got if we conclude that the figure on whom
tragedy can have a hold must be *religious*? We cannot retain the sense in
which for us to use the word 'religious' is to imply Christianity. What
are we left with if this hold is relaxed? It should be some comfort if
we can say that when we are exclusively concerned with the world's
greatest tragedies *Christianity never happened*. This is a point conceded
by Bradley when he allowed that a reader attached to Christian beliefs
'holds them in temporary suspension while he is immersed in a
Shakespearean tragedy'.[13] In this impasse it seems to me best to defer
an attempt to extricate myself until the argument has compassed all the
selected constituents of Tragedy. My 'last word' on this topic is therefore reserved for my final chapter. But in the mean time I can illuminate
the sense in which the tragic figure must be religious by returning to
things said by F. R. Leavis about D. H. Lawrence.

Although it would be malicious to say that Leavis attributed to
Lawrence every virtue under the sun, nothing could have made Leavis
back down from the claim that Lawrence in his writings had every right
to think of some of his intuitions as religious. Now if the conjunction,
the trinity, of Leavis, Lawrence, and Religion, is too much for him to
stomach, may I beg an indignant reader to perform a heroic act of
mental abstraction? For I am not here asking anyone to believe the
truth of any of these claims. I have one selfish aim: to induce a reader
to apply what Leavis says about the religious side of Lawrence to
Tragedy, the tragic figure, and the sense in which we may say that in
tragedy the human is inevitably entangled with the divine.

The two remarks I have in mind were both printed in 1932. Leavis
went on record in the September number of *Scrutiny* by affirming that
Lawrence was seeking among other things: 'a human naturalness,

---

[13] *Shakespearean Tragedy*, p. 325.

inevitable, and more than humanly sanctioned; a sense, religious in potency, of life in continuity of communication with the deepest springs, giving fulfilment in living, "meaning", and a responsive relation with the cosmos'. To the *Listener* of 5 October he contributed a review of *The Letters of D. H. Lawrence*, edited by Aldous Huxley, in which he wrote:

But those who know his work will admit that his constant preoccupation is fairly to be called religious, even if they are dubious about his 'God'. What he sought was a more-than-human sanction for human life, a sense of the life of the universe flowing in from below the personal consciousness: he sought, one might say, a human naturalness; he aimed at 'planting' man again in the universe.

But for the seeker after the essence of Tragedy literary critics are at best a minor help. The basic insights come from the great artists of the present who open our eyes to the greatness of the artists of the past. Two passages from Lawrence himself will illustrate the kind of help he can give us when we are thinking of a real meaning to be given to all that surrounds the Soul in the Universe:

I turn my face, which is blind and yet which knows, like a blind man turning to the sun. I turn my face to the unknown, which is the beginning, and like a blind man who lifts his face to the sun I know the sweetness of the influx from the source of creation into me. Blind, for ever blind, yet knowing, I receive the gift, I know myself the ingress of the creative unknown. Like a seed which unknowing receives the sun and is made whole, I open onto the great invisible warmth of primal creativity and begin to be fulfilled.[14]

This vocabulary is so vulnerable that it requires a protective context. Let me therefore give a more extended passage, which is the perfect pendant to the vituperation of Russell & Co., quoted above. Here we can feel the generosity of spirit in affirmation.

What man most passionately wants is his living wholeness and his living union, not his own isolate salvation of his 'soul.' Man wants his physical fulfilment first and foremost, since now, once and once only, he is in the flesh and potent. For man, the vast marvel is to be alive. For man, as for flower and beast and bird, the supreme triumph is to be most vividly, most perfectly alive. Whatever the unborn and the dead may

[14] From a piece first printed in the *English Review* for Feb. 1918, and reprinted in *Phoenix*, 1936, p. 696.

know, they cannot know the beauty, the marvel of being alive in the flesh. The dead may look after the afterwards. But the magnificent here and now of life in the flesh is ours, and ours alone, and ours only for a time. We ought to dance with rapture that we should be alive and in the flesh, and part of the living, incarnate cosmos. I am part of the sun as my eye is part of me. That I am part of the earth my feet know perfectly, and my blood is part of the sea. My soul knows that I am part of the human race, my soul is an organic part of the great human soul, as my spirit is part of my nation. In my own very self, I am part of my family. There is nothing of me that is alone and absolute except my mind, and we shall find that the mind has no existence by itself, it is only the glitter of the sun on the surface of the waters.

So that my individualism is really an illusion. I am a part of the great whole, and I can never escape. But I *can* deny my connections, break them, and become a fragment. Then I am wretched.

What we want is to destroy our false, inorganic connections, especially those related to money, and re-establish the living organic connections, with the cosmos, the sun and earth, with mankind and nation and family.[15]

To bring out the full force of Leavis's references to the religious side of Lawrence, I need to add some of Leavis's remarks on the religious side of *Wordsworth*. The point with which I wish to close this chapter will be found concentrated in an essay on Wordsworth which appeared in *Scrutiny*, December 1934. Here are two passages which might ease my passage from the topic of the tragic figure to that of the tragic bond:

The poetry . . . defines convincingly – presents in such a way that no further explanation seems necessary – the sense of 'belonging' in the universe, of a kinship known inwardly through the rising springs of life and consciousness and outwardly in an interplay of recognition and response:

> No outcast he, bewilder'd and depress'd;
> Along his infant veins are interfus'd
> The gravitation and the filial bond
> Of nature, that connect him with the world.

– 'Thank God I am not free, any more than a rooted tree is free.'[16]

---

[15] Taken from *Apocalypse*, 1931, pp. 306–8.

[16] For the readers of the magazine, the context of this remark could not help being a review of Eliot's *After Strange Gods* which Leavis had contributed to the previous number. It contained this remark: 'reviving what it may be crude to call the religious sense – the sense that spoke in Lawrence when he said, Thank God . . .' etc.

My chief point comes out in the claim made for Wordsworth, that his

. . . preoccupation was with a distinctively human naturalness, with sanity and spiritual health, and his interest in mountains was subsidiary. His mode of preoccupation . . . was that of a mind intent always upon ultimate sanctions, and upon the living connexions between man and the extra-human universe; it was, that is, in the same sense as Lawrence's was, religious.[17]

[17] This essay was reprinted as Chapter V of *Revaluation*, 1936.

3
TRAGIC BONDS

My picture of the tragic soul is still incomplete. I hope that it now floats before the reader as something like a beautiful flower — in fact, it would help if it could be thought of as resembling the soul W. B. Yeats imagined for himself:

> Though leaves are many, the root is one;
> Through all the lying days of my youth
> I swayed my leaves and flowers in the sun;
> Now I may wither into the truth.[1]

But so far, judging by what I have said, the reader would have every right to picture each flower soul as communicating *in solitude* with the divine, taking in influences from the outermost parts of the universe and breathing its odours into the universe very much as Baudelaire imagined it:

> Mainte fleur épanche à regret
> Son parfum doux comme un secret
> Dans les solitudes profondes . . .[2]

or, if words by Gray make a deeper impact:

> Full many a flower is born to blush unseen,
> And waste its sweetness on the desert air.[3]

If the reader is to have a complete picture, it is time to think more about the phrase I threw off loosely in the preceding chapter — 'rooted in the universe'. If the tragic figure is to have roots in the universe, it must first have a proper soil in a tragic society. It is easy for us, especially if we are inclined to think that Tragedy concerns individuals, to fall into confusion here. Because it so often happens in the best plays

---

[1] 'The Coming of Wisdom with Time', *The Green Helmet and Other Poems*, 1910, p. 7.
[2] 'Le Guignon.' (1852), in *Les Fleurs du mal*. 1857.
[3] Thomas Gray: 'Elegy written in a Country Churchyard' (1750).

that by the time the tragedy gets under way the tragic person seems to stand out as an isolated figure, we forget that there would be no tragedy if there were no tragic circumstances involving a whole society. In fact, it is due to the intrusive power of Christianity over our thought that we suppose that the gods of Tragedy, who, of course, know nothing of Christ, care first for the individual and only in second place for society. If the gods are concerned for a king, it is only because the king stands for the whole kingdom. It is due to the social theory sometimes called after Rousseau *le contrat social* that we think of individuals as existing before society and forming society by a wary bargain which preserves as many of the rights of those individuals as is compatible with public safety, etc.

If we wish to discover which social bonds are also tragic, we must clear our minds of cant and face the disagreeable fact that the sufferings and joys with which we as individuals are hourly, daily, yearly inflicted or blessed are not the sufferings and joys which concern Tragedy. Supreme Tragedy concerns itself with only one form of joy and sorrow, that which is embedded in human relations when man is seen as a social animal of a special kind. I think we hardly know what the precious bond really is which alone allows us to become human beings and so to be represented by tragic figures. When we are asked to picture the world of value embedded in human relations we fasten on trust, affection, sympathy, tolerance, and we bandy the word 'tragedy' about when thinking of breaches and breakdowns of such precious things. They are indeed precious acquisitions of an old civilization, in which brutality has gradually been softened down to something which makes a *dolce vita* a reality, but the tragic plane knows nothing of them.

To a reader who would not object to hearing a parody of something serious I could offer a glimpse of the mysterious bonds which concern Tragedy by showing them presented in an ironic or openly comic mode. To a reader already familiar with a novel by D. H. Lawrence, entitled *Women in Love*, I would only have to mention the scene with the two cats to recall the claim which the hero vainly makes that his love moves on a superior plane, and that he is enjoying a mode of being beyond ordinary love and affection. No harm will be done for anyone who does not happen to know this novel if I select out of Chapter XIII fragments from the conversation between a man and a woman who are about to enter into a lasting love-relationship. In fact, I feel fewer than the usual scruples one has in extracting phrases from a novel. The reason is this. Although I can well believe from the biographical record that Lawrence

had, as it were, been taught a lesson in his struggles with his future wife,
I get from this episode a strong impression that he had first worked out
his theory of two planes (which, for the moment, I shall call the all-
too-starry and the all-too-fleshly) and also of the lasting bond between
a man and a woman, and only afterwards had cast round for an appropriate setting for them. The dramatic enactment of the moral and the
illustration of the human argument in terms of the two cats help to
disguise from us the application of an *a priori* dialectical case, with the
full triadic form of thesis, antithesis, and synthesis.

The thesis comes forward when the dialogue opens, and the hero is
shown searching for something he calls 'final and infallible', and rejects
ordinary human love both as his own offering and as his own object.
He asserts that what he is looking for 'is something much more impersonal and harder and rarer'. For him ordinary human love does not
go far enough. Let me give a whole speech: 'At the very last, one is
alone, beyond the influence of love. There is a real impersonal me, that
is beyond love, beyond any emotional relationship. So it is with you.
But we want to delude ourselves that love is the root. It is not. It is
only the branches. The root is beyond love, a naked kind of isolation,
an isolated me, that does *not* meet and mingle, and never can.' The
heroine cannot take this in, which drives the man to more extravagant
language: 'there is a beyond, in you, in me, which is further than love,
beyond the scope, as stars are beyond the scope of vision, some of
them'. Very subtly, we become aware that the hero is overdoing it, and
that therefore the heroine's case will prevail in the end. The comedy is
still subdued, but already the warning for me and *my* thesis is plain.
Lawrence says his hero spoke 'in a voice of pure abstraction'. This is
the danger which befalls any attempt like mine which seeks to define
a tragic plane somehow above the ordinary human level. We can get a
similar warning from those little plays by W. B. Yeats which are all
'passion' and no flesh and blood. The trouble is, there are no tears
either, there is no anguish, there is no overwhelming impression of the
real. That is how Lawrence's hero strikes me in the following outburst:
'There is . . . a final me which is stark and impersonal and beyond
responsibility. So there is a final you. And it is there I would want to
meet you – not in the emotional, loving plane – but there beyond,
where there is no speech, and no terms of agreement.' It is true, the
hero is allowed one remark which might take us a long way: 'Only
there needs the pledge between us, that we will both cast off everything, cast off ourselves even, and cease to be, so that that which is

perfectly ourselves can take place in us. . . .' but in the end he remains
the prisoner of his own vocabulary, as in this remark: 'the world is only
held together by the mystic conjunction, the ultimate unison between
people – a bond'.

Then comes the antithesis, in the form of a dialogue (the hero speaks
first):

'One is committed. One must commit oneself to a conjunction with the
other – for ever. But it is not selfless – it is a maintaining of the self
in mystic balance and integrity – like a star balanced with another
star.'
    'I don't trust you when you drag in the stars,' she said. 'If you were
quite true, it wouldn't be necessary to be so far-fetched. . . . . . You
don't really want this conjunction, otherwise you wouldn't talk so
much about it, you'd get it.' He was suspended for a moment, arrested.
    'How?' he said.
    'By just loving,' she retorted in defiance.

I hope I am not bending the scene my way if I judge that the emerging
dialectical conclusion is one critical of *both* parties; both are pulling
too hard for what is ultimately in each case only one aspect of the bond
which creates eternal values, values which it is tragic to see destroyed.

But let me proceed more warily by returning to modern society.
I begin with a crass example of a society in which tragedy is impossible.
The example is crass, but once heard, it is not easy to forget. Here is
an extract from a beautiful prose poem, composed in 1847-8:

*Die Bourgeoisie, wo sie zur Herrschaft gekommen, hat alle feudalen,
patriarchalischen, idyllischen Verhältnisse zerstört. Sie hat die bunt-
scheckigen Feudalbande, die den Menschen an seinen natürlichen
Vorgesetzten knüpften, unbarmherzig zerrissen, und kein anderes Band
zwischen Mensch und Mensch übrig gelassen, als das nackte Interesse,
als die gefühllose 'baare Zahlung'. Sie hat die heiligen Schauer der
frommen Schwärmerei, der ritterlichen Begeisterung, der spießbürger-
lichen Wehmuth in dem eiskalten Wasser egoistischer Berechnung
ertränkt. Sie hat die persönliche Würde in den Tauschwerth aufgelöst,
und an die Stelle der zahllosen verbrieften und wohlerworbenen
Freiheiten die Eine gewissenlose Handelsfreiheit gesetzt. Sie hat, mit
einem Wort, an die Stelle der mit religiösen und politischen Illusionen
verhüllten Ausbeutung die offene, unverschämte, direkte, dürre
Ausbeutung gesetzt.*
    *Die Bourgeoisie hat alle bisher ehrwürdigen und mit frommer Scheu
betrachteten Thätigkeiten ihres Heiligenscheins entkleidet.*

My translation does not do justice to the original:

Centuries of accumulated sentiments and fine feelings, which had held together all feudal institutions, and all communities where the father ruled as the moral and political head of the extended family, have been swept away wherever large-scale industrialists and bankers have acquired political power. This hard-faced bourgeoisie has pitilessly wrenched open the tight-knit knots which tied men to their natural superiors in the wide spectrum of feudal social arrangements, and has left in their place no other bond between a man and his neighbour than naked self-interest and cash on the nail. The tremulous piety of the religious orders and their adherents, the chivalric idealism of the military classes, the maudlin sentimentality of the *petit-bourgeois* have all been choked to death in the icy waters of cold-blooded calculation. The *bourgeoisie* has converted personal worth into a commodity bought and sold on the Stock Exchange, and has abolished the thousands of commercial privileges extorted by great popular efforts over the centuries, and buttressed by charters duly signed and sealed, to make way for the one and only Charter, unprincipled *laissez-faire* — Free Trade! To put it in a nutshell, they have replaced a form of exploitation decently camouflaged by religious and political illusions with naked, blatant, direct, brutal exploitation.

The *bourgeoisie* has removed the last protecting shred of sanctity from all activities which up to that time had been regarded with pious awe as worthy of religious respect.

Karl Marx, in *Das Kommunistische Manifest*, spoke truer than he knew in that last sentence. What we have to face is the impossibility of having Tragedy so long as we live under a 'social contract'. If each soul in society is a well-protected metal sphere, entering into only selfish interests with every other metal sphere, keeping itself to itself, as we say, there can only be bumps or wars of extermination. Neither is tragic. To discover a society in which tragedy *is* possible, we have to return to Shakespeare and the Greek tragic poets. Not to their actual, historical societies, of course, for there exploitation and cruelty were as rampant as in the nineteenth-century world pictured by Karl Marx. What we should direct our attention to in the societies presented in their tragedies are the deep bonds underlying everything, bonds which create the value of human life, and, above all, we should attend to what Lawrence's hero called 'beyond', look through and past what Karl Marx called their covering of warm feeling. Then, I believe, we come upon something I was going to call 'cold', but only cold in the sense we have to use if we picture loving souls meeting in heaven. But perhaps with

Dante's *Paradiso* in mind, or the imagery of sun and snow in Eliot's
Little Gidding, we might rather think of a supernatural fire, or, as Yeats
put it, of 'flame that cannot singe a sleeve'.

But rather than flounder about in areas where one can easily lose
one's way, let me select one of the great underlying bonds, and with it
try to demonstrate how almost identical the deep meaning is in parts of
one Greek play and parts of one play by Shakespeare. It will immediately enact all I have been saying in this chapter if I may take the Greek
root *phil-*, the root we are familiar with in so many English words,
which in Greek enters into so many expressions involving ordinary love
and affection that it may strike one as an effort doomed from the start
to try to establish a meaning for the root *beyond* all such feelings.

It may be a boring intrusion of private experience to explain how I
came upon the conviction that the tragic plane is not merely human. As
a child is glad to place his small hand in the larger hand of an adult
whenever there is a threat of danger or a difficult step ahead, so, over
the years, being puzzled by so many things in Greek plays, I trusted to
various 'authorities' to help me to understand what was tragic in the
play by Sophocles entitled *Antigone*. Thus I became a meek student of
Jebb, of Hegel, of August Wilhelm Schlegel, and of a long list of
academics who printed the lectures they had delivered to undergraduates, until I came to an American journalist, Edmund Wilson.
He, too, I afterwards learnt, had followed a similar path of reverent
attention to the best that had been thought and written on this play
before, helped by an academic of his day, he was encouraged to bring
forward an explanation of what was tragic in the play.[4]

I shall not go into details here, but what took my attention in
Wilson's essay was his assurance in claiming that the explanation of
Antigone's behaviour towards one of her brothers was *psychological*,
and very up-to-date psychology at that time. Antigone, he claimed, had
a *fixation* on her brother, and this prevented her from loving her fiancé.
(M. Vernant is one of several modern writers who could provide us with
a much more plausible account of this tragic situation.) But when
Wilson wrote, there was no Vernant to be had, and I had to react to
Wilson as best I could. I made a valiant effort to pull myself out of the
Wilsonian error, which had me half won over for a while. But I eventually saw, or thought I saw, that the real direction of the play was

---

[4] I first came upon his essay in the *New Republic* some time in 1930. It was
reprinted in the volume of essays entitled *The Shores of Light*, 1952, p. 473.

toward the definition of a bond, and a bond not known to the professional psychologist. I also thought that Sophocles in attempting to
define this bond was obliged at the same time to define others. But my
efforts, though valiant, were vain, because I could not get beyond
psychological terms such as those Wilson adopted, terms which seemed
to be ordering me to define love as a mental commotion confined to
the interior of the metal spheroid but occasionally allowing two ego-
epidermises to make external contact.

I did not get any further out of the Wilsonian error until the happy
day when I was introduced to the volumes of Émile Benveniste. Nobody would guess from the title of his two volumes, *Le vocabulaire
des institutions indo-européennes*, 1969, that many of Benveniste's
pages deserve rather to be called 'the perfect introduction to the
essence of Greek tragedy by way of Homer'. My first, real introduction
to what was tragic in *Antigone* came from the fourth chapter in his
third book, entitled LES STATUTS SOCIAUX, which deals with several
social bonds. The reader's enthusiasm and curiosity may evaporate
when he also discovers that Benveniste takes us back into the remote
origins of the Greek words for the bonds. I can easily imagine an
objection in this form, 'What is the use of going back to the *origins* of
the Greek word *philos* and its related words? Surely we ought to confine ourselves to the *actual uses* in the years when the greatest tragedies
were being written?' The answer to this question will bring out one of
the senses in which we must call the best tragedies *mysterious*.

It has puzzled those commentators on Greek tragedy who think of
the three great tragic poets as men not only of their times but in
advance mentally and morally of most of their contemporaries to find
all three introducing into their plays what these commentators describe
as 'archaic Greek thought'. (I have noticed a similar disappointment in
English literary critics when they are unable to discover any 'advanced'
or 'progressive' thought in Shakespeare's best tragedies.) It seems to be
a law of great tragedy that, while it has to deal adequately with our best
thoughts in what, for shorthand, I shall call the daylight world, what
moves us profoundly in the plays is the emergence to the surface of
fears and joys which might be called primitive at first sight but are seen
on reflection to be the human normality buried like coal in the deepest
seams of race history. It clearly assisted the coal-mining to quarry for
plots in a body of (to the Greeks) inexplicable stories — I mean myths
which for them were stories *sans* everything that makes *us* call them
myths, but stories full of suggestions about the true nature of man.

Since the bonds are that which makes us truly human, what renders them precious is both that which originally forged them in the days when society itself was first forming and that which was forged as a result of formulating the words to carry the meaning of the felt bonds. It is therefore of great advantage to the literary critic who is trying to get below the surface of the plays to be able to draw on the findings of comparative linguistics to unearth the root meanings of the words for the great uniting bond. (Of course, this would be a pure waste of time if we could not discover anything of the sort in either Sophocles or Shakespeare.)

Fascinating as it undoubtedly is to dream about those unknowable, far-off times of which we have no written record, it would be untrue to suppose that what is hidden in our words does not give us *some* real knowledge of what must have been going on in those distant days. We are not reduced to *fancy* when we ask what underlies our various expressions for the *sanctity* of social bonds. Benveniste reminds us of a general truth concerning what is there visible on the page, on many pages, of Homer's poems: 'Pour comprendre cette histoire complexe, il faut se rappeler que, chez Homère, tout le vocabulaire des termes moraux est fortement imprégné de valeurs non individuelles, mais relationnelles. Ce que nous prenons pour une terminologie psychologique, affective, morale, indique, en réalité, les relations de l'individu avec les membres de son groupe' (p. 340). If I may put the gist of this passage in words suited to the present argument, we can only enter into Homer's meaning if we retrace the course of history and think first of men banded together in social groups, and only in the second place of the individual members of the groups and their individual feelings. Benveniste does not go on to say that what is there for all to see on the surface of the epics cannot be found in the tragedies until what is truly tragic in the action begins to declare itself. But when it does so emerge, we should, I suggest, greet it both as something *behind* our words for love and affection and, as the poor hero in Lawrence's novel kept wailing, as something *beyond* them.

The enormous advantage of Benveniste's book for the student of the *Antigone* became apparent to me when I discovered from it that the root meaning of *philos* and all related expressions was the very bond which I thought made personages in tragedy capable of becoming truly tragic figures. His pages on the bond enable us to discriminate between the Antigone who is a figure of *pathos* and the Antigone who is a figure of Tragedy. She did not die for love but for a bond. Any reader who himself found as he experienced the play that he had to make this distinction between pathos and the tragic will be cheered to learn from Benveniste that Antigone's feeling for the bond was an age-old possession of the race long before it found expression in tragedy. The most striking fact Benveniste discovers is that the noun, *philotēs*, was regularly used by Homer for a contract between *enemies*, enemies who have no intention of becoming friends. The fighting men use the word to describe an armistice made to give both sides fresh breath to resume mutual slaughter on the morrow. This usage confirms Benveniste in his general conclusion that the *phil-* words are not in the first place expressions of feeling but expressions of a contract comprising rights and duties for all the contracting parties.

I do not need to remind the reader that the society we enter in reading Homer's poems, simple or even 'primitive' as it appeared to seventeenth-century Frenchmen, is highly sophisticated. Since Homer rarely if ever peeps into the dark backward and abysm of time, we have to use our imaginations to present to ourselves what were the foundations which made his society possible. (I don't like to use the word *order* as it is so often borrowed from Shakespeare's vocabulary to describe what it is tragic to destroy. Perhaps I am being finicky when I say that for me the word 'order' smacks too vividly of the spiritual world of Charles Maurras, of right-wing combinations of religion and politics, and that we might all now have a different feeling for the word if the last world war had gone the wrong way, and we were living in a Europe with a New Order manufactured in Berchtesgaden. But although I don't like the word, it is plain that the Greeks did, and if a reader turns to M. Vernant, he will find him rightly singling out the Greek word, *nomos*, as both the key-term to which the two main characters in Sophocles' play appeal, and the word which gives us the very nub of the tragedy, *Antigone*.)

Since we are all ignorant in different degrees, the learned and the lay alike must use their imaginations. I trust that, this being so, it will not seem improper if I say how I help myself to feel my way into the original situation which caused the Greeks to build up the complex of words in *phil-*. Quite properly, I hope, I go back to the terrors of childhood. A particular instance is the terror which comes over nervous children when they first leave a small, comfortable, school, where they were little demi-gods, and confront the hundreds of hostile faces on the first day at their public or massive state school. The new boy instantly loses his identity. He has no place or station. There are no fixed marks to measure things by. Anything can happen. He has no protection. In fact, in this first sight of a new community there are no grounds for security whatever. The bottom seems to have dropped out of his world. I was just writing those words down when a friend called on me, who, after hearing me read them out, told me of an adventure she had had in New Guinea when she was taking a small cannibal out of his territory into that of a neighbouring tribe. The normally bold little chap turned back in terror when he saw the alien spears, the alien face-markings, and found nothing he could recognize. Death then had a thousand faces.

When we consider how the schoolboy acquires assurance and a fixed place at the bottom of the lowest class or in the outfield of the weakest house cricket match, we leave the primitive world behind, and once again must fall back on our powers of imagination to picture to ourselves the enormous length of time it must have taken man to enter into bonds of any kind, bonds which, as the word suggests, can feel like manacles as well as guarantees of safety. But to diminish the proportion of mere fancy in our imagination, it will be as well to return to Benveniste and consider one primitive survival which continued as a living reality into Homer's day. Homer's men, like us, were used to the thousand bonds which constitute a working society. But if one of the men ventured outside the safety of his own society, he fell into the void. He no longer had a place in the universe. He might be killed by the first man who detected that he was a stranger. Those of you who have looked into the faces of modern dwellers on the coasts of Cornwall can easily divine that the ancient inhabitants of those regions had no mercy on the poor devils wrecked on their rocky shores. To meet the needs of the traveller, the Greeks set up an institution which I cannot describe so well as M. Benveniste:

Il reste maintenant à dégager ce qui caractérise en propre le *philos*, ou le rapport de *philótēs*. Ce mot abstrait est plus propre à nous renseigner que l'adjectif. Qu'est-ce que la *philótēs*?

Nous ferons usage pour définir cette notion d'un indice précieux que nous fournit la phraséologie homérique; c'est la liaison entre *phílos* et *xénos*, entre *phileîn* et *xenízein*. Formulons d'emblée ce que cette liaison enseigne dans nombre d'emplois: la notion de *phílos* énonce le comportement obligé d'un membre de la communauté à l'égard du *xénos*, de l' 'hôte' étranger. Telle est la définition que nous proposons.

Cette relation est fondamentale, dans la réalité de la société homérique comme dans les termes qui s'y réfèrent. Il faut, pour l'entendre pleinement, se représenter la situation du *xénos*, de l' 'hôte' en visite dans un pays où, comme étranger, il est privé de tout droit, de toute protection, de tout moyen d'existence. Il ne trouve accueil, gîte et garantie que chez celui avec qui il est en rapport de *philótēs;* rapport matérialisé dans le *súmbolon*, signe de reconnaissance, anneau rompu dont les partenaires conservaient les moitiés concordantes. Le pacte conclu sous le nom de *philótēs* fait des contractants des *phíloi*: ils sont désormais engagés dans la réciprocité de prestations qui constitue l'"hospitalité".

C'est pourquoi le verbe *phileîn* exprime la conduite obligée de celui qui accueille à son foyer le *xénos* et le traite selon la coutume ancestrale. (p. 341.)

We are fortunate in having a means of defining the root meaning of the Greek word for friendship or love, *philotēs*, by observing its use in Homer in connection with the language formed to express reciprocal relations between 'guests' and 'hosts'. Here we come upon one of the fundamental bonds in Homeric society. When a Greek visits another country, he has no rights, no protection, no means of support. But he enjoys all these with one native, his opposite number, so to speak. The outward, visible sign of this sacred bond is the ring broken in two of which each contracting partner holds a part that fits when put together with the other half to make up the whole. The two parties are called *philoi*, friends. The verb 'love', *philein*, denotes full hospitality according to ancestral lore extended to the defenceless stranger.

And, to close this section on a delightful note, Benveniste offers an instance which, incidentally, alters the meaning of a sentence in the *Odyssey* in the very way I am hoping to alter the general prejudice, which sees this bond as primarily one of feeling. My aim is to provide evidence suggesting that this bond is primarily a divinely-sanctioned contract. I choose this particular instance because Benveniste confesses that long before Homer's day these bones of the skeleton of human society had been what Shakespeare called 'Corrall made', or, to express myself more naturally, had long been covered with the flesh and blood of affection and love. For example, although Homer's man may have known that his 'dear wife' acquired the epithet 'dear' because she had emerged from the darkness of some other society or large family, and had come to sit among the women of his own hearth, and consequently enjoyed all the rights and privileges which constituted his 'family', he nevertheless found her as 'dear' as the word implies when used to-day.

It is a wonderful luxury for a mere mortal to feel sorry for a goddess! But if ever a person deserved our sympathy it is the poor beauty who rescued Odysseus from shipwreck and lived alone in perfect bliss with him on her little island. True, the ideal man was given to walking down to the sea and looking out over the water. But until the gods ordered her to let him go, *Calypso* had every hope of faring better than Aurora with Tithonus, and turning Odysseus into an *immortal* husband. So we throb with her indignation when we read the opening lines of the Fifth Book of the *Odyssey*. Benveniste suggests that we should opt against the usual translation of one line (135):

τὸν μὲν ἐγὼ φίλεόν τε καὶ ἔτρεφον

in the passage which runs more or less like this: 'What, you begrudge me the man whose life I saved with my own hands when he was clinging to the keel of his capsized vessel. Zeus had split it with his thunderbolt, and all the crew had perished. When the wind and the waves drifted him near enough to fish out of the water, I' – and this is where most translators, except the German, Voss, say: 'I loved him and gave him something to eat . . .' Benveniste suggests that we translate the verb with *phil-* in it like this: 'I decided to perform the duties of one who accepts the position of a host to a stranger.'

Does all this help us to distinguish the tragic plane in Sophocles' play, the *Antigone*? Let us perform a little experiment. Let us go to a Greek play in the right spirit, let us listen to the first hundred lines of the *Antigone* as they have not been listened to for centuries, that is to say, by spectators who attend exclusively to what they find before them and whose minds are otherwise totally vacant. For it is fatal to have a programme in your hand setting out the 'Theban story'. But if we are starved of every scrap of illegitimate advance news, we shall be hungry to gobble up each crumb Sophocles lets fall in these first hundred lines. But what a lot of things *we* look for will not be provided! We shall never know what Anouilh is only too glad to tell us: 'Antigone, c'est la petite maigre qui est assise là-bas . . . la blonde, la belle, l'heureuse Ismène . . . .'[5] These may be vital statistics for the Frenchman, who may have wished us to have the conventional protective feelings towards the little dear (it is worth counting how often in the course of his play we hear the adjective), the little Piaf who has never filled out properly, and the conventional feelings gentlemen are supposed to entertain towards gorgeous blondes with fixed Hollywood smiles. But what may have been vital for the modern author would

---

[5] Jean Anouilh, *Antigone*, first produced 1944, first published 1946.

have been death to Sophocles, who could not afford to have his sharp, unforgettable point blunted by irrelevant details of age or physique.

But an even more striking absence will be noted if we contrast these opening lines with the similar opening scene in J. -P. Sartre's play about the return of Orestes to kill his mother, *Les Mouches*. The modern author has to paint a picture of the moral taint in his Denmark, if I may so express the fact that his Argos is visited by a plague of flies of an unusual size, a picture which requires this programme note by Jupiter himself:

> Jupiter (*qui s'était approché*).

Ce ne sont que des mouches à viande un peu grasses. Il y a quinze ans qu'une puissante odeur de charogne les attira sur la ville. Depuis lors elles engraissent. Dans quinze ans elles auront atteint la taille de petites grenouilles. (*Un silence.*)

They're only blow-flies — king-size, perhaps. A powerful stink of corpse flesh has been attracting them for the last fifteen years. Corpse flesh is fattening. Before another fifteen years are out, they'll come as large as little frogs.

If Sartre had undertaken to do for this play what he did for *The Trojan Women* by Euripides,[6] he might have opened his version of the *Antigone* like this:

— What a stench! It seems to stick to to the walls. I've washed my hair every night. I change my underclothes twice a day, but I still can't get rid of the Billingsgate odour.
— What can you expect, sister dear, with ten thousand Argive stiffs blocking the seven entrances to our town? When I look out of my bedroom window, I see nothing but slinking shapes moving quickly in and out of the packed masses of dead bodies.
— Look up into the sky. The birds appear to be giving the men all their attention.

Logically, all this information is relevant. If tragedy was really concerned to present a *tranche de vie*, it would be *necessary*. These are the events which immediately precede in time the first exchanges between Antigone and her sister, Ismene. But for Tragedy to make its proper impact we must get our knowledge in a non-temporal order. So the form my little experiment takes is to get the reader to say what he has been *exclusively directed to* in the first hundred lines of Sophocles' *Antigone*:

---

[6] As set out in a later chapter on Pathos (pp. 149-158).

— Ismene, my own dear sister, you know, don't you,
  What troubles Zeus has brought to pass on us,
  The last two left of our dead father's blood?
  All that could grieve us, that might bring disgrace,
  Dishonour, and could make us accursed, all
  That I have seen falling on you and me.
  And now this latest thing our General
  Has trumpeted, they say, to Thebes in arms,
  Have you heard a whisper of it, or don't you know
  That trouble is on the march for those we love?
— No news, good or bad, has come to me,
  Antigone, about our dear ones, ever since we two
  Lost our two brothers, dead on the same day,
  Two hands administering a fatal cut.
  I know that the Argive force has just withdrawn
  In the darkness, but since then nothing new
  Has come to make us happy or accursed.
— I thought as much, and that is why I've brought
  You here outside the yard gates by yourself.
— What's happened? I see you've trouble on your mind.
— I have. Burial! Creon has paid his dues
  To one dear body, but defamed the other.
  Eteocles, I hear, has had his proper rites.
  Creon has hidden *his* body away in earth, and so
  Has done what's wanted by the dead below.
  But poor dead Polyneices, as I hear,
  A different fate has been proclaimed for him.
  His corpse may not be buried or bewept.
  He must be left a morsel for the kites,
  As they spy him down below, their treasure-trove.
  That's what they're saying. That's what our dear Creon
  Has trumpeted for you and me, *me*, do you hear?
  And he's coming here to make it plain to all
  Who haven't yet heard the message. And the penalty
  For disobedience won't be mild: no less
  Than death by public stoning. So you see
  The choice before you. Show the world you are
  A true child of good parents, or a bad.
— Poor dear, if things are as grim as you make out,
  What do you expect me to do about it?
— Consider, will you work along with me?
— What ghastly risk are you planning to run now?
— Will you join hands with me to lift the body?

— You're not thinking of burying him when it's forbidden?
— My own! — and yours, whether you wish it or not.
— Will you say 'yes' when Creon says 'no'? Ah, sister!
— He has no call to come between me and mine.
— Sister, you must reflect. Our father,
    You know, died hated, with his glory darkened.
    When he himself discovered what he'd done,
    He tore out both his eyes with his own hands.
    And then his mother-wife, wife-mother — what
    Am I to say? — destroyed herself with
    A twisted noose. Then our two poor brothers
    By meeting on that fatal day brought on
    Their common death with fratricidal hands.
    And what of us two now that they have gone?
    A much worse death awaits us if we break
    The law, defy the tyrant and his powers.
    Think, sister, we are women, never meant
    By Nature to engage in war with men.
    We must obey our masters, both in this
    And in much worse things that are bound to follow.
    For all these reasons I shall ask the Spir-
    its down below to pardon me. I yield
    To *force majeure*, obey authority.
    To tilt against it were mere Quixotry.
— You need not bother, thank you, I would hate
    To have your help now even if you offered.
    Do what you think best, I shall bury him.
    Then 'twill be passing sweet for me to die,
    To lie close body to body in the grave,
    Doing right by doing wrong. I'd have to
    Be pleasing those below much longer than
    Those here, for I'll lie there for everlasting.
    Dishonour what the Gods prize as you will.
— I do them no dishonour. But it's not in me
    To go against the wishes of our folk.
— That's your excuse, keep to it. I leave you now
    To heap earth on my dearest brother's corpse.
— You terrify me. Don't you see your fate?
— Leave that to me and care about your own.
— Well, do it if you must, but do it so
    That nobody finds out, and I will help.
— No, no, proclaim it on the housetops. I shall hate
    You even more if you don't broadcast it.

— What a hot heart you bring to cold business!
— I'm pleasing those whom I ought to please most.
— Yes, if you manage it, but you won't succeed.
— I'll not give up until my strength gives out.
— But you ought not to try. It can't be done.
— No more of that or I shall hate you and
The dead will hate you, too, and you'll deserve it.
Leave me to my own foolishness and let me suffer
The consequence you dread. For I am sure
I shall avoid an ignominious end.
— Go on then, if you must, but rest assured,
Fool though you are, you serve your dear ones well.

The most vacant mind is now filled, I take it, with one conviction, that, whatever the main concern of this opening scene turns out to be, it has to do pre-eminently with a father, a mother, a brother, two brothers, in fact, and two sisters, that is to say, a group of people closely related by *blood*. (Creon is here only as the 'General'.) But to increase our conviction that we possess Sophocles' main point, we must in imagination turn from a poor English version to the expressive Greek. For it then becomes apparent that Sophocles is ringing the changes on two Greek roots, one being *phil-*, and the other *tim-*. And in time it will become equally apparent that we can only understand what Sophocles here means by *philos* when we discover the relation of *philos* to *timē*. Everything else is either subordinated or played down to allow our minds to focus on the blood relations as *philoi*, related by *timē*.

So what is this Greek root-word *tim-*, which appears so often in these ninety-nine lines both as noun and verb? If any reader has consulted an obscure book on Pope and Homer,[7] he may be heartily sick of hearing it served up again. Yet if we are to discover the tragic plane and distinguish it from the other planes in this play, we must understand what is meant by saying that *timē* is the name for the code governing the Greeks' practical religion. It corresponds to the shadowy yet powerful Christian feeling in Shakespeare's plays that every human bond embodies the divine, so that a parent or an employer offended God if he did not observe the duties of his station. *Timē*, then, is what Benveniste called a relational or situational word. It tells you about the rights and duties of all people in a bond. Each man looked to obtain it from his fellow-men. The gods exacted it from mortals, and

---

[7] *To Homer through Pope,* 1972, pp. 22–5.

occasionally paid it to mortals. *Timē* was always known to be present by some external act. It could therefore be measured both by the givers and by the receivers, and society could look on and estimate whether it was being justly exacted and paid.

We can now begin to understand the central fuss over the burial of one brother and the refusal to allow the other brother to be buried. Corpses have claims to *timē* in the shape of performance of certain ritual acts including burial and public lamentation. The opposite of *timē* for a corpse is to be devoured by scavenging animals, but it is also very bad to be seen and smelt rotting in the sun. Nor is the corpse the only one to be offended or pleased by the payment or withholding of *timē*. There are gods underground with an equal interest. A corpse may not gatecrash the underworld: somebody must pay dues for it. The chaps in the cellerage (οἱ κάτω θεοί) stood no nonsense. They were far more forces than they were persons. Ismene was expressing a very rash hope if she really thought they had forgiving natures. She should have known they hadn't.

What we must above all be clear about is that the claim to receive burial could only be satisfied by the corpse's blood relation, by all his blood relations. From this opening scene we learn that the name for these contractually related persons is *philoi*. What binds the family group is something more primitive than affection, for the tie could exist without cultivated feelings. It can best be understood in terms of the acts which have to be performed to satisfy *timē*. For Antigone, to give *timē* to a *philos* is almost automatic since she feels identified with her *philoi*, so close is the complex they form. We can go some way to finding a parallel in modern life, for we probably know of families not really very affectionate where a wrong done to one member is immediately resented by all. And if we asked a brother we knew disliked his sister why he entered a quarrel over her in which he hadn't a hope of winning, he might even to-day fall back on an answer like Antigone's, 'Why, she's my sister, isn't she?'

I can well believe that a disgruntled reader, properly impressed by the gravity of the subject, a gravity inherent in the very concept of Tragedy, might be all too ready to liken my manner of twisting and turning the argument to the scurryings of a hunted hare. Yet I persist in hoping that a full backward survey from the present page to my first would wring from him the concession that I also qualify for a likeness to the hunter who knows how elusive his quarry is, and must be, and that from the beginning the Chase always had a Beast in view; or, to put it in terms of a reader's feelings, that I have usually laid a generous paper-trail of phrases to guide him to the goal. Nevertheless I have to apologize for the unconscionable number of formulations in this chapter which appear to be floating in the air or at best only loosely tied down to a solid body of fact. One difficulty I could not get over is that the same paper clues which have to be laid down as markers to point the way are also promissory notes which cannot be redeemed until I have got further in and have explored other essential constituents of Tragedy.

It would be reassuring if *any* of the following winged words had come home to roost or had taken up a provisional lodging in a reader's mind:

— rooted in the universe
— the tragic figure requires a tragic society
— supreme tragedy concerns itself with only *one* form of joy and sorrow
— the ultimate unison between people — a bond
— the bond which creates eternal values
— when we attain the tragic plane we come upon something cold like supernatural fire
— fears and joys buried in the deepest seams of race history
— the sanctity of social bonds
— bonds which feel like manacles . . .

They were all stages on the way to altering the general prejudice which sees the tragic bonds as primarily bonds of feeling. My suggestion is that we should see these bonds as primarily part of a divinely-sanctioned contract. I do not think that, as regards the argument of this chapter, I have ever left it in doubt that the Beast I had in view from the start of the Chase was Shakespeare's *King Lear*, and that I was using thoughts stirred up by considering the Greeks to enable the reader to get beyond what I called 'the warm outer covering of love and affection' and so to discover what is potentially tragic in the violation of the bonds which hold together all families and societies, and emerge as an essential constituent of what is tragic in Shakespeare's play.

I shall therefore bid an abrupt good-bye to Sophocles' *Antigone* and leave for the moment all that in those first hundred lines was pointing forward to the emergence of Tragedy. I am reserving for the next chapter consideration of the tragic act here only threatened, and postponing elucidation of the guilt-in-innocence of the heroine, which is merely hinted at in Antigone's phrase, 'Doing right by doing wrong', which was my attempt to render the ὅσια πανουργήσασ' of l. 74.

Could we now take up the Cordelia who said:

> I loue your Maiesty
> According to my bond . . .

and the sisters, and the complex bonds that Gloucester mentioned: 'Loue cooles, friendship falls off, Brothers diuide. In Cities, mutinies, in Countries, discord; in Pallaces, Treason; and the Bond crack'd 'twixt Sonne and Father. . . .'? Or can I simply leave the rest of this chapter for the reader to complete? An author has a natural reluctance to reprint in one book what is available in another. But now that the first book is available only in *libraries*, there might be a case for breaking the rule. Yet if we concentrate on all that Shakespeare draws our attention to in *King Lear* about the bonds binding parents and children, I hardly think we need to consult books of commentary. What may still need to be added to the argument of this chapter is that the sacred bonds extend beyond blood relations to cover what the sociologists now call the extended family but what the Greeks and Shakespeare considered the normal family. A reader who may be reluctant to accept my suggestions about the bonds between fathers and children might perhaps be willing to consider the sanctity of the relations between master and servant, and the heinousness of breaches and abuses of this bond. Everybody has been disturbed by the non-dramatic, that is, the apparently dramatic irrelevance, of one outburst in *King Lear*: 'A Seruingman, proud in heart and mind, that curld my haire, wore gloues in my cap, serued the lust of my mistris heart, and did the act of darkenes with her, swore as many oaths as I spake words, and broke them in the sweet face of heauen . . .' which sends us off at once to *Timon of Athens*.

Whenever, as now, I feel an itch to mount the pulpit and preach the wisdom in this side of Shakespeare's thought, my two deflationary acts are, first, to remember that Erasmus' darling clown, Moria, has climbed up before me, and, second, to make *myself* the object of my scornful attack. So let me confess that I have been a child of my age in my reluctance to let service, the role of a servant, stand for a holy office. While there is a nobly romantic part of me which thrills to recall that the Prince of Wales still has *Ich dien* as a royal device, and I love to hear the story of the Black Prince who took *spolia opima* from the King of Bohemia on the field of Crécy in 1346 — princes were vassals

of the Emperor and the Emperor was the vassal of God, and the ladder
thus stretched gloriously down from the top of society to Herbert's
skivvy, 'Who sweeps a room, as for thy Laws' — there is also a sullen
child in me who still responds to the cold rebellion expressed in James
Joyce's *non serviam*.[8] So I am aware that Shakespeare has to pull hard
against a closing door when he offers Kent as the first representative
of the second great bond, that between master and servant. When
writing on this play, I thought he introduced 'a sacred note' which
Shakespeare was anxious that we should not miss in these lines:

> Royall *Lear*,
> Whom I haue euer honour'd as my King,
> Lou'd as my Father, as my Master follow'd,
> As my great Patron thought on in my praiers . . .

My parting self-quotation, however, concerns the scene in which
Gloucester is blinded:

Gloucester knows he is fallen among the damned, living bodies with
devils for souls like those in the *Inferno* (Canto XXXIII).[9] But the
action is interrupted for one of those little scenes that are of immense
depth for all their brevity. I see a world of meaning in the servants who
are forced to witness their masters behaving like devils. If anyone
ever doubted that service was one of the sacred values for Shakespeare,
a bond indispensable for the good life on earth, he might be converted
by listening and watching with care at this point:

> I haue seru'd you euer since I was a Childe:
> But better seruice haue I neuer done you,
> Then now to bid you hold.

Because of this my mind will for ever linger on a certain pile of rotting
filth and, among the putrefaction, on the remains of a life-long servant

---

[8] The rebellion which is described almost autobiographically in *Stephen
Hero* is given sharper expression in fictional form at the close of *A Portrait of the
Artist as a Young Man*.

[9] Fra Alberigo to Dante:

> . . . tosto che l'anima trade
> come fec' io, il corpo suo è tolto
> da un demonio, che poscia il governa
> mentre che 'l tempo suo tutto sia volto.
> Ella ruina in sì fatta cisterna . . .

As soon as a man turns traitor, as I did, a devil takes over his body and controls its
actions until that body has lived out its allotted span on earth. But the soul of that
man plunges headlong into the dreadful cesspit in which you have now found me.

in a noble house who paid the full price for an impulse of goodness, an impulse without which social man cannot persist.[10]

---

[10] *Shakespeare's Tragedies of Love*, p. 201.

4
THE TRAGIC ACT

In an earlier chapter I warned the reader that the work by Jean-Pierre Vernant and Pierre Vidal-Naquet, entitled *Mythe et Tragédie en Grèce ancienne*, was going to prove helpful at more than one point in my argument. It is particularly helpful when we come to analyse *the tragic act*. For many years I felt uncomfortably out on a limb in combating the then prevalent views on this topic, both as they dominated the criticism of Shakespeare's tragedies and most of the books I came across dealing with Greek Tragedy. The tribute I should like to pay to these two Frenchmen is to trace my own wandering steps before it came over me that the generally-held views about this tragic act must be radically revised. The following short excursion into autobiography will, I hope, be excused as a method of registering the shock to the established state of opinion delivered by this little French book.

Everybody knows the saying, 'The Devil knows how to quote.' But Jesus also knew how, as I am reminded when I look round for a way to express the astonishment I felt as it first came over me that I had spent my adult life looking in the wrong places for an account of what it is that makes an act tragic. The proverb we find Jesus quoting in the New Testament is still expressive, even in these days of delapidated high-rise dwellings: 'The stone which the builders refused is become the headstone of the corner.' The builders in my twentieth-century application of the proverb were the authors of writings on Shakespeare's play, *Macbeth*, who undertook to make clear to me the motives of each personage at each crisis of the play, and accounted for Macbeth's tragic act by invoking the motive of *ambition*. We certainly hear in the play that Macbeth is 'not without ambition', and he himself confesses:

> I haue no Spurre
> To pricke the sides of my intent, but onely
> Vaulting Ambition . . .

and there are many small confirmations to suggest that he really was

ambitious of becoming King of Scotland. But can anybody say that, as
we approach the decisive act of murder, the motive of ambition grows
in force, gets anything like the force required to account for the act?
My commentators thought that the tragic act ought to be explicable,
and they regarded it as a failure in Shakespeare's art that the motivation
was so clouded, if not totally absent. The aptness of the Biblical
proverb began to dawn on me when it became clear that it was just this
very absence of motive, or rather, the impossibility of there ever being
a clear motive which made the murder of the King a tragic act — 'a
deed without a name'.

It gives a false impression if we foreshorten into dramatic scenes
those decisions or revelations which we only learn years afterwards to
have brought about a complete change in outlook. So that I must not
say that this one discovery about Macbeth's act led at once to a complete revaluation of the play. The truth is rather that I did not appreciate what it was that I had found until I was able to generalize from this
one instance and grasp a law governing all tragic acts. And this did not
happen until I had recovered from the conventional account of those
passages in Aristotle's *Poetics* having to do with what in the original is
called *hamartia*, a noun, and *hamartanein*, a verb. This word, *hamartia*,
has virtually become part of the English language whenever tragedy
is under discussion. Aristotle introduced it in the course of a chapter
on the ideal tragic figure. Here, in Bywater's translation, is the interpretation of the tragic act which stood in my way:

There remains, then, the intermediate kind of personage, a man not
pre-eminently virtuous and just, whose misfortune, however, is brought
upon him not by vice and depravity but by some error of judgement, of
the number of those in the enjoyment of great reputation and pros-
perity; e.g. Oedipus, Thyestes, and the men of note of similar families.
The perfect Plot, accordingly, must have a single, and not (as some tell
us) a double issue; the change in the hero's fortunes must not be from
misery to happiness, but on the contrary from happiness to misery; and
the cause of it must lie not in any depravity, but in some great error on
his part . . .[1]

It might sound ungenerous to describe this translation as a stumbling
block, since it makes a salutary correction of the version provided by
S. H. Butcher in his book, *Aristotle's Theory of Poetry and Fine Art*,
1895: 'The change of fortune should be not from bad to good, but,

---

[1] Ingram Bywater, *Aristotle on the Art of Poetry*, 1909, pp. 35–7.

reversely, from good to bad. It should come about as the result not of vice, but of some great error *or frailty* . . .' (my italics) (p. 43). S. H. Butcher was too honest to claim that Aristotle actually mentioned *frailty*, but, as it were, he wished Aristotle had, for Butcher thought:

> Modern literature, and above all the Shakespearian drama, while proving that the formula of Aristotle is too rigid, have also revealed new meanings in the idea of the tragic *hamartia*. Its dramatic possibilities have been enlarged and deepened. In Hamlet, Othello, Lear, Macbeth, Coriolanus, we have the ruin of noble natures through some defect of character. In infinitely various ways it has been shown that the most dramatic of motives is the process by which a frailty, or flaw of nature, grows and expands till it culminates in tragic disaster. (p. 309.)

I take it that those Victorian critics who were anxious to make the tragic act plausible, both morally and psychologically, were glad to have Tennyson's support, when he wrote:

> It is the little rift within the lute,
> That by and by will make the music mute,
> And ever widening slowly silence all.

> The little rift within the lover's lute,
> Or little pitted speck in garner'd fruit,
> That rotting inward slowly moulders all . . .[2]

The honest Victorian, who wished to defend Aristotle's view of *hamartia*, found it very hard to find a place for Macbeth as a tragic hero. Butcher had no doubt that we should have to 'enlarge the meaning' if we were going to be able to bring him in:

> Macbeth does not start with criminal purpose. In its original quality his nature was not devoid of nobility. But with him the *hamartia*, the primal defect, is the taint of ambition, which under the promptings of a stronger character than his own and a more vivid imagination works in him as a subtle poison. In a case such as this, tragic fear is heightened into awe, as we trace the growth of a mastering passion, which beginning in a fault or frailty enlarges itself in its successive stages, till the first false step has issued in crime, and crime has engendered fresh crime. It is of the essence of a great tragedy to bring together the beginning and the end; to show the one implicit in the other. The intervening process disappears; the causal chain so unites the whole that the first *hamartia* bears the weight of the tragic result. (p. 300.)

---

[2] Alfred Tennyson, *Idylls of the King*, 1859 'Vivien' ll. 240–6, pp. 113–14.

On the other hand, to confine the tragic act to the description 'error of judgement' seems to exclude almost all the great figures save the Oedipus of Sophocles' first play. For it makes it hard to find room for the sense in which the tragic deed is a *guilty* act, and it eliminates our feeling of sympathy for the falling hero. Textual fidelity to Aristotle might therefore lead us to abandon the Greeks altogether and to search elsewhere for the law governing the tragic act. And if we did so, we could find that the classical commentators are among the first to point out that the ancient Greeks seem to be totally disqualified for finding this law simply because they never developed the necessary vocabulary for talking about any tragic act. For want of the now simple-seeming distinctions in ethical discourse which we owe to Immanuel Kant, the Greeks in their tragedies found themselves at one and the same time about one single act proclaiming the doer of the deed both innocent and guilty, irresponsible and yet responsible. M. Vernant has put this difficulty of the Greeks' vocabulary into a striking phrase. His special topic was:

Il faut d'autre part rappeler le caractère foncièrement intellectualiste de tout le vocabulaire grec de l'action, qu'il s'agisse de l'acte accompli de plein gré ou de celui qui est exécuté malgré soi, de l'action imputable ou non imputable au sujet, répréhensible ou excusable. (pp. 54–5.)

On the other hand we must bear in mind the fundamentally intellectualist bias in all the Greek expressions concerning tragic action, which is just as apparent when the act is done with the agent's full consent as in actions performed unwillingly, when they attribute credit to or blame the agent, when the act was one for which the agent was as for one for which he was not accountable.

He sums up for all these cases with a fine phrase: 'Là où un moderne s'attend à trouver une expression du vouloir, il rencontre un vocabulaire de savoir.' (p. 55.) ('Where we would expect to be confronted with "willing" and the like, we find only words implying "knowing".') He rightly refers us to an excellent book by A. W. H. Adkins, *Merit and Responsibility* (1960), which makes clear how deficient for ethical discussion the Greek vocabulary is in the tragedies at the points where we need expositions of the nature of duty, the conditions for responsible action, and any terms for starting a discussion of the 'will'.

Nevertheless for all this intellectualist cast of vocabulary the Greek tragedians have revealed to us in their best plays the real mechanism of the tragic act. It is Aristotle who is at fault, not the tragedies he

comments on. It is plain that Aristotle does not present us with anything corresponding to the portrait I drew in my last two chapters of
the tragic soul as a sensitive plant in tender response to a spiritual
climate. All too often he appears to think of the agent in a tragedy as
more like the non-tragic soul I sketched. For reasons of a not dissimilar
sort M. Vernant is inclined to write Aristotle off as a critic of Greek
tragedy. The following sentence is not an isolated remark:

La tragédie surgit en Grèce à la fin du VIe siècle. Avant même que ne
se soient écoulés cent ans, la veine tragique déjà est tarie, et lorsque,
au IVe siècle, Aristote entreprend dans la *Poétique* d'en établir la
théorie, il ne comprend plus ce qu'est l'homme tragique, qui lui est
devenu pour ainsi dire étranger. (p. 21).

Barely a hundred years span the course of tragedy. The spring dried up
before the fourth century BC. So when Aristotle sat down to compose
his *Poetics*, and give a theoretical account of tragedy, he found himself
unable to picture what a tragic figure was like. Such a creature, we
might almost say, had become alien to his imagination.

One of M. Vernant's strongest supports for this line of attack is his conviction that Greek tragedy was the product of a set of conditions,
social, religious, political, which came and went in a short period. His
second assumption is that the notions underlying the tragic act were
left behind as the Greeks learned to clarify their thought. Consequently,
Aristotle arrived too late:

Quand Aristote écrit la *Poétique*, dans le public et chez les auteurs de
théâtre, le ressort tragique déjà est brisé. On ne sent plus la nécessité
d'un débat avec le passé 'héroïque', d'une confrontation entre l'ancien
et le nouveau. Aristote, qui élabore une théorie rationnelle de l'action
en s'efforçant de distinguer plus clairement les degrés d'engagement
de l'agent dans ses actes, ne sait plus ce que sont la conscience ni
l'homme tragiques: ils appartiennent à une époque pour lui révolue.
(p. 80.)

By the time Aristotle came to compose his *Poetics* the inner spring
animating tragedy was broken. Neither the poets nor their audiences
understood that tragedy required them to engage in a confrontation
between new and old values, and in a debate with their 'heroic' past.
By attempting to work out a rational account of the tragic act and to
distinguish more clearly the extent to which the hero was responsible
for his act, Aristotle showed that he did not know what constituted
the tragic figure or tragic feeling. They both belonged, as far as he was
concerned, to a time that was gone for ever.

That is too sweeping for me. I find something to be retained from his *Poetics*. Aristotle at the very least reminds me that Greek tragedy does not permit the implied either/or of my two portraits. He also reminds me that Greek tragedies move on several planes. He rightly insists that the chief personages spend a lot of their time on what I have called the 'daylight' plane. And on any other day in their lives except the fatal day when tragedy descends, we must imagine these personages as very shrewd men of business, capable of assessing the true situation they find themselves in, weighing up correctly the near and remote possibilities, and taking rational decisions of impeccable justness. There can be no tragic surprise without this cool 'iambic' background of decent rationality. For the incommensurable to erupt with tragic intensity there must pre-exist a peaceful mode of life in which the hero was managing quite nicely, thank you.

A reader might well take offence at this borrowing from Kafka about the 'irruption of the incommensurable' into human affairs. Yet it has always seemed to me a happy shorthand for such an event as the emergence of a sea monster, which frightened the horses and so led to the horrible death of the hero, Hippolytus. But the wonder of Greek tragedy is that what interrupts the even tenor of life is not a monster or a miracle but quite simply, the real. The figures in these tragedies who thought they were managing quite nicely, thank you, suddenly find that they have been living in a dream and that the horrible calamity is just that, a taste of the waking reality. So, in my simple picture language, what the man in the spheroid thought was a mistake or a miscalculation in direction, producing a bump, turns into a total transformation. He is suddenly tumbled out into the void, and even if *he* never finds out what has hit him, *we* learn before the play is over that the real has reasserted itself, and that man cannot barricade himself or close the port-holes of the soul or take off for any purely egoistic 'trip'.

In what follows I shall stick to *Macbeth* as the natural centre for a discussion of this essential constituent of all tragedy. But before continuing, I should like to read into the record two remarkable passages from M. Vernant, which seem to me packed with suggestive thought, and are even more pregnant and powerful when put back into their contexts in his book. The first is a somewhat rhetorical flourish defining the ambiguous nature of the tragic hero:

. . . quel est cet être que la tragédie qualifie de *deinós*, monstre incompréhensible et déroutant, à la fois agent et agi, coupable et innocent, lucide et aveugle, maîtrisant toute la nature par son esprit industrieux et incapable de se gouverner lui-même? (p. 24).

How shall we speak of this creature, who in Greek tragedies is called *deinos*, terrible, frightful, awe-inspiring, an incomprehensible and disconcerting prodigy, at one and the same time the active agent and the passive sufferer, in one and the same moment both innocent and guilty, clear-sighted and blind, mastering nature with his active intelligence, yet incapable of bringing himself under control?

It is the second passage which gives me great confidence that the confluence of our thought on the *dual* nature of the tragic act and that of, for instance, Albin Lesky and one or two other leading critics is the result of hitting on, at the very lowest, *part* of the truth:

Dans la perspective tragique, agir comporte donc un double caractère: c'est d'un côté tenir conseil en soi-même, peser le pour et le contre, prévoir au mieux l'ordre des moyens et des fins; c'est de l'autre, miser sur l'inconnu et l'incompréhensible, s'aventurer sur un terrain qui vous demeure impénétrable, entrer dans le jeu de forces surnaturelles dont on ne sait si elles préparent, en collaborant avec vous, votre succès ou votre perte. Chez l'homme le plus prévoyant, l'action la plus réfléchie garde le caractère d'un appel hasardeux lancé vers les dieux, et dont on apprendra seulement par leur réponse, le plus souvent à ses dépens, ce qu'il valait et voulait dire au juste. C'est au terme du drame que les actes prennent leur vraie signification et que les agents découvrent, à travers ce qu'ils ont réellement accompli sans le savoir, leur vrai visage. Tant que tout n'est pas encore consommé, les affaires humaines restent des énigmes d'autant plus obscures que les acteurs se croient plus assurés de ce qu'ils font et de ce qu'ils sont. (pp. 37–8.)

The tragic act has two aspects. On the one hand, it is the work of an agent shrewdly taking thought and weighing the pros and cons and doing his best to fit means to ends. On the other hand, he is playing a blind game of chance with the unknown and the unknowable. He is venturing out into a Tom Tiddler's ground where he will never be able to make headway, however long he tries. He is submitting to the play of supernatural powers about which there is no knowing whether they are joining with you to help you or to ruin you. For be he never so far-sighted, still the tragic agent in his most deeply-considered act will always be at best drawing a bow at a venture, making a desperate random shot aimed heavenwards in the hope of a reply, and only when the answer comes will he know, often to his cost, the import and true meaning of his act. It is only at the end of the play that this truth about the act emerges. Its real face is then revealed to the actors, who then, and only then, learn what they have unwittingly brought about by their acts. Until the last word is spoken, the tragic act remains a mystery, a mystery which is deepest and darkest for those who are most confident that they know what they are and what they are doing.

Although I was willing in a preceding chapter to pay a public debt to Leavis and Lawrence when I was sketching the tragic soul, the attentive reader may have noticed how closely every detail applied to the soul of Macbeth. Shakespeare seems to have introduced all the stage conventions at his disposal to make us aware of the *porosity* of that soul and of the consequent confusion which occurs in that soul when what we take to be an 'I', a person or an individual speaking, turns out to be a god or a devil who has momentarily taken possession of it. And when I first came upon the passage of M. Vernant I have just quoted, I could not help exclaiming, 'Why, that's exactly the use Shakespeare was putting the conventional picture of the witches to! He has transformed them into a vehicle for presenting the inexplicable mystery of the tragic act in all its aspects, at one time putting all the responsibility on the "daylight" Macbeth, at another suggesting that Macbeth committed his crime in a heavy Scotch mist!'

Nevertheless, paradoxical as it may sound, although I regard *Macbeth* as by far the profoundest treatment of the tragic act I know, it has the great drawback of being *too* mysterious. We are therefore driven to speak of the *absence* of a motive rather than the presence of an effective moving power. The Greek vocabulary, it can now be said, is far more adequate to the tragic facts than any other when it comes to presenting ultimate mysteries. This is because of the very indeterminacy of their vocabulary for numinous entities who hover on the borderline between mere forces and mere persons. They have all the sinister suggestions of Shakespeare's 'Spirits' or 'Ministers' but with the great advantage of not being fabricated by the poets but inherited from times long before any literature had been produced. I do not say that Shakespeare could not have passed a stiff examination on the following lines, spoken by Lady Macbeth in *Scena Quinta* of the First Act:

> Come you Spirits,
> That tend on mortall thoughts, vnsex me here,
> And fill me from the Crowne to the Toe, top-full
> Of direst Crueltie: make thick my blood,
> Stop vp th'accesse and passage to Remorse,
> That no compunctious visitings of Nature
> Shake my fell purpose, nor keepe peace betweene

Th'effect, and hit. Come to my Womans Brests,
And take my Milke for Gall, you murth'ring Ministers,
Where-euer, in your sightlesse substances,
You wait on Natures Mischiefe. Come thick Night . . .

but everybody notices how the powers tend to merge into Night and Nature, and we do not get the strong impression that *they themselves* enter into the woman's veins.

The great advantage possessed by the Greek poets was that they had Homer, and a successful embodiment of the motive power for the tragic act at the heart of the *Iliad*. It is characteristic of Homer that he first opens the *Iliad* with a dramatic presentation of this motive power, and defers to the Nineteenth Book an analytical explanation of what in fact had caused Agamemnon to alienate Achilles and so ruin his chances of winning the war. This passage, where, as Pope would say, Homer 'opens the Moral' of his poem, was naturally a prime text for Albin Lesky, and in a moment I shall be drawing once again on his essay. But the reader without Greek or German could benefit from certain pages in a book by E. R. Dodds, entitled *The Greeks and the Irrational* (1951), where he discusses the moment in this Nineteenth Book when Agamemnon openly admits that he had done wrong, or allows it to be clearly implied by offering to make a material compensation. But before he in this way accepts responsibility for his misdeed, he says, as Dodds puts it: 'Not I was the cause of this act, but Zeus and my portion and the Erinys who walks in darkness: they it was who in the assembly put wild *ātē* in my understanding, on that day when I arbitrarily took Achilles' prize from him. So what could I do? Deity will always have its way.' (p. 3.) I have not attempted to make this translation more intelligible because I do not think that Homer could have given a lecture on all the operative terms. If all a man had to go on if he wished to build up a systematic account of the spiritual forces in the universe was this single passage from the *Iliad*, he would have a lot to do! The most mysterious agent among them is the shapeless figure Dodds quite properly leaves in Greek, and yet doesn't quite have the guts to give her a capital letter. The status of *ātē* is as indeterminate as that of *moira*, which Dodds here translates as 'my portion'. These words are often used in the tragedies as agents or persons, and yet don't quite acquire the amount of personality that one of the forces of the universe has when called by an Olympian name, such as Aphrodite. I mention *her* because I think that Racine was employing the same double account of the motive power in the tragic act in Phèdre's description of her possessed soul:

> Ce n'est plus une ardeur dans mes veines cachée;
> C'est Vénus toute entière à sa proie attachée.

> It is more than a hidden flame running through my veins,
> Venus has fastened her whole body on her desired quarry.

Although I heartily agree with Albin Lesky when he protests against Dodds's word for this double motivation, *overdetermination,* I should like first to consider Dodds's general account:

The Homeric poets were without the refinements of language which would have been needed to 'put across' adequately a purely psychological miracle. What more natural than that they should first supplement, and later replace, an old unexciting threadbare formula like μένος ἔμβαλε θυμῷ (the god cast courage into his heart) by making the god appear as a physical presence and exhort his favourite with the spoken word? (p. 14.)

Dodds's 'natural' strikes me as both glib and trivial. Let me take one of his examples, from the First Book of the *Iliad,* at the point where Achilles has half-drawn his sword to dispatch the King of Men, and is arrested by Athene tugging at his back hair:

> Just as in Anguish of Suspence he stay'd,
> While half unsheath'd appear'd the glitt'ring Blade,
> *Minerva* swift descended from above,
> Sent by the Sister and the Wife of *Jove;*
> (For both the Princes claim'd her equal Care)
> Behind she stood, and by the Golden Hair
> *Achilles* seiz'd; to him alone confest;
> A sable Cloud conceal'd her from the rest.[3]

Because nobody but Achilles saw her, Dodds blandly concludes: 'That is a plain hint that she is the projection, the pictorial expression, of an inward monition.' (p. 14.) I have elsewhere[4] given my reasons for considering this a poor way of interpreting the incident.

Once again, therefore, I think that M. Vernant bears away the bell. His great merit, to my mind, is that he never tries to systematize a notion which appears in the tragedies in many different and distinct

---

[3] Alexander Pope, *The Iliad of Homer,* 1715, p. 14.
[4] *To Homer through Pope,* p. 28.

forms. Although I would confine the *tragic* appearance of *ātē* to the one she makes when uncalled for, and dooms the hero for no apparent fault, there are instances where she is *sent*, and sent to punish the guilty. But her *action* in all cases is the same. M. Vernant well describes the doom of Eteocles in the play by Aeschylus we call *The Seven against Thebes:*

La folie meurtrière qui va désormais définir son *êthos* n'est pas seulement un sentiment humain, c'est une puissance démonique qui dépasse Etéocle de toute part. Elle l'enveloppe dans le nuage obscur de l'*átē*, elle le pénètre à la façon d'un dieu prenant du dedans possession de celui dont il a décidé la perte, sous forme d'une *mania*, d'une *lússa*, d'un délire engendrant des actes criminels d'*húbris*. (p. 28.)

The murderous rage which from now on will dominate his moral being is more than a purely human feeling. It is a demonic power, which completely envelops the hero. He is now wrapped in the black cloud of *ātē*, who passes into him and through and through. It is as if a god were encamped inside him and totally possessed him to destroy him by driving him mad, and forcing him in his wild fury to commit guilty acts of *hubris*.

The beauty of this passage lies in the manner in which a package of Greek concepts and Greek words is held in suspense together in such a way that any arbitrarily weighted interpretation is defeated. The moral seems to be that if we wish to find the truly tragic we should give up our modern categories altogether. We should cease in particular from trying out and trying on the greatest tragedies words such as 'free will' and 'determinism'. We must neither reduce the forces in the universe to merely physical entities or psychical entities compelling obedience nor exalt them into persons with personal malignancy. In a way, all these thoughts are present in the package, but none is trying to get out and rule the roost.

To close this first stage in my argument I offer M. Vernant's excellent summary, where all the ambiguities which make tragedy possible are admirably preserved:

L'hamartia est une maladie mentale, le criminel la proie d'un délire, un homme qui a perdu le sens, un *demens, hamartínoos*. Cette folie de la faute ou, pour lui donner ses noms grecs, cette *átē*, cette *Erinús*, investit l'individu du dedans; elle le pénètre comme une force religieuse maléfique. Mais tout en s'identifiant en quelque façon avec lui, elle lui reste en même temps extérieure et le dépasse. (p. 55.)

The word Aristotle uses to describe tragic error, *hamartia*, is a disease of the mind. The guilty man becomes the prey of an invading madness, and loses his sanity. This guilty blindness, which the Greeks described as *ātē* or *Erinys*, enters and possesses the individual. He is penetrated through and through as by a malignant religious power. Eventually the victim and his madness in a sense become one, yet the invading power comes from the outside and is always larger than the individual attacked.

All this, however admirable as a summary account of the main meaning of the word *hamartia* in Greek tragedy, is irrelevant if the Greeks were not divining one of the deepest truths about human action and human responsibility for actions which could be described as blameworthy, creditable, or merely excusable. We are looking for a touchstone with which to try all the great tragedies in the world. We must therefore now take leave of the historical. But before doing so, there is one reflection which might speed us on the way. It is quite possible that the Greek tragic poets themselves sensed the need to plunge back into their religious past in the very act of confronting the dismaying facts of a present-day society undergoing the great change from a tribe to a collection of individuals. People who have followed out the evolution of Greek thought from the so-called 'primitive' times down to the 'philosophical' times of Aristotle and his successors have noted that if this evolution could be expressed by a curve on a graph, the short moment of Greek tragedy would not fall on the evolutionary line.

The question for us, therefore, is whether we can transpose the historical into the permanent, whether in fact the ambiguity at the heart of the tragic act in Greek plays has to be recognized as an essential feature of all tragedy. We clearly do not have to retain every aspect of the Greek notion of, for instance, a taint or a religious stain blighting a whole family throughout the generations. But we must, for example, keep to a sense in which the guilt of many can be felt as the guilt of one, and to a sense in which guilt can be incurred without deliberate intention. At the same time we must embrace the most enlightened modern feeling for personal commitment. M. Vernant puts the difficulty like this:

Pour un esprit moderne ces deux conceptions paraissent radicalement s'exclure. Mais la tragédie, tout en les opposant, les assemble en des équilibres divers d'où la tension n'est jamais entièrement absente, aucun des termes de cette antinomie ne disparaissant tout à fait. Jouant à un double niveau, décision et responsabilité revêtent, dans la tragédie, un caractère ambigu, énigmatique; elles se présentent comme des questions qui demeurent sans cesse ouvertes faute de comporter une réponse fixe et univoque. (p. 72.)

These two views of culpability present a radical contradiction to the modern mind. Tragedy, however, plays them off against each other, and brings them together in different ways but never without a degree of awkward tension. The inherent antinomy, however, is never entirely removed. In tragedy decision and responsibility remain mysterious and ambiguous entities. They raise questions to which no clear answers can be given which would settle the problems once and for all.

One method by which I have occasionally been able in the course of 'supervisions' to bring people across the bridge from the Greek past to the Cambridge present may sound incredible at first hearing if I inform the reader that I originally came across it in a Cambridge students' magazine. However bright university students are, when they rush into print while still *in statu pupillari* they more often present themselves as clever-silly than intelligent. *Experto credite*. I have assisted at the birth and even contributed to several undergraduate periodicals, all of which were, I now see, open to this criticism. But there was one little magazine which appeared in Cambridge during my Oxford undergraduate years which impressed me favourably then and still impresses me. The Spring 1931 number of *Experiment* contains an article by William Empson, as he then was, which I thought very helpful at the time, and has turned out to be even more useful in a context like the present where an attempt is being made to define the tragic act.

In 1931, I must confess, I admired the article as a rare example of mental generosity. In those days there still was a valuable difference between the Universities of Oxford and Cambridge. It was felt on both sides that this was a difference to be kept alive. Now that 'unisex' has arrived, there seems to be little to mark one place off from the other. But in 1931 for an undergraduate at Oxford the great literary event had been the meteoric passing across the sky of the poet, W. H. Auden, who had edited two remarkable numbers of the Blackwell annual, *Oxford Poetry*. When he brought out a deceptively-entitled play called *Charade*, many at Oxford vaguely hoped that this was the harbinger of a serious attempt to bring tragedy back to the English theatre whither it appeared destined never to return. But I never expected to find a far better critic than any I had met at Oxford during those years in the shape of a rival contemporary poet at 'the other place'. Empson's

'Note' is characteristic of Cambridge at its best. After perusing the part of it printed here, the fair-minded reader will, I think, understand why I called the writing of it a generous act.

A NOTE ON W. H. AUDEN'S 'PAID ON BOTH SIDES'

I must first try to outline the plot, as it is not obvious on one's first reading. There is a blood-feud, apparently in the North of England, between two mill-owning families who are tribal leaders of their workmen; it is at the present day, but there are no class distinctions and no police. John, the hero of the play, is born prematurely from shock, after the death by ambush of his father; so as to be peculiarly a child of the feud. As a young man he carries it on, though he encourages a brother who loses faith in it to emigrate. Then he falls in love with a daughter (apparently the heiress) of the enemy house; to marry her would involve ending the feud, spoiling the plans of his friends, breaking away from the world his mother takes for granted, and hurting her by refusing to revenge his father. Just before he decides about it, a spy, son of the enemy house (but apparently only her half-brother) is captured; it is the crisis of the play; he orders him to be taken out and shot. He then marries Anne; she tries to make him emigrate, but he insists on accepting his responsibility and trying to stop the feud; and is shot on the wedding day, at another mother's instigation, by a brother of the spy.

This much, though very compressed, and sometimes in obscure verse, is a straightforward play. But at the crisis, when John has just ordered the spy to be shot, a sort of surrealist technique is used to convey his motives. They could only, I think, have been conveyed in this way, and only when you have accepted them can the play be recognised as a sensible and properly motivated tragedy.

The reason for plunging below the rational world at this point is precisely that the decision to end the feud is a fundamental one; it involves so much foreknowledge of what he will feel under circumstances not yet realisable that it has to be carried through on motives (or by choosing to give himself strength from apparent motives) which do not belong to what is then the sensible world he lives in. For the point of the tragedy is that he could not know his own mind till too late, because it was just that process of making contact with reality, necessary to him before he could know his own mind, which in the event destroyed him. So that the play is 'about' the antinomies of the will, about the problems involved in the attempt to change radically a working system.

Empson then went into details of the plot which do not concern us here, but returned at the close of his article to the decisive act:

Hence we sink down, in this crucial and solvent instant of decision, into a childish scheme of judgment, centring round desire for, and fear of, the mother; jealousy of, and identity with, the brother, who is also the spy; away from the immediate situation, so that younger incidental reminiscences of the author become relevant; below the distinction between murderer and victim, so that the hero escapes from feeling his responsibility; below intelligible sexuality; and in the speech of the Man-Woman (a 'prisoner of war behind barbed wire, in the snow') we are plunged into a general exposition of the self-contempt of indecision. Then the spy is shot, and we return, with circus farce like the panting of recovery, into the real world of the play; from then on he knows his own mind, and is fated to destruction.

One reason the scheme is so impressive is that it puts psycho-analysis and surrealism and all that, all the irrationalist tendencies which are so essential a part of the machinery of present-day thought, into their proper place; they are made part of the normal and rational tragic form, and indeed what constitutes the tragic situation. One feels as if at the crisis of many, perhaps better, tragedies, it is just this machinery which has been covertly employed. Within its scale (twenty-seven pages) there is the gamut of all the ways we have of thinking about the matter; it has the sort of completeness that makes a work seem to define the attitude of a generation.

The biblical quotation with which I began this chapter is now due for a final reappearance to promote from the dust-heap *The Women of Trachis*, the one play by Sophocles which, until Ezra Pound resurrected it, was generally neglected. I have printed elsewhere[5] a list of disparaging remarks on its failure, culled from our most respected pundits, commentators, and critics. Let me here add to that list one last Frenchman, who, like the others, shall remain anonymous:

Les opinions les plus divergentes ont été émises sur les *Trachiniennes* . . . . Pour les uns, c'est une oeuvre de la maturité du poète . . . . Pour d'autres enfin l'auteur était vieux quand il l'a composé et sur son déclin. On a même prétendu que les *Trachiniennes* n'étaient pas de Sophocle. Après toutes ces contradictions ... on semble revenu aujourd'hui à une idée plus raisonnable: la pièce est bien de notre poète, mais elle est un peu indécise, disons le mot, imparfaite.

People seem to differ widely in their estimate of *The Women of Trachis*. Some critics suppose it is an early work, others think that Sophocles

---

[5] *Arion*, vol. 2, 1963, *The Cambridge Quarterly*, vol. 4, 1969, *Ezra Pound* ed. J. P. Sullivan, 1970, pp. 279–310.

composed it while at the height of his powers. But there are some who regard it as the product of old age when the poet's genius had begun to leave him. There are even one or two who refuse to believe that Sophocles had a hand in it. In the light of this conflicting series of verdicts the most sensible conclusion appears to be that while we cannot reject it from the Sophoclean canon, the play must be judged to lack firm outlines and to have gone without the artist's finishing touches.

My reason for selecting this play to go with *Macbeth* is not only that I think it the best Greek illustration of the double attitude to *hamartia* which gives us the complex of guilt-in-innocence which in turn makes the hero a tragic figure, but that I have been made to go through a revolution in my attitude to the play as a direct result of the arguments presented in this chapter. If I had been called upon to give my views on the tragic act at any time in the last few years I should have been prevented from pressing the distinction between the psychological level and that which I am now attempting to define as a distinct tragic plane because of one powerful negative instance: for the distinction could not be shown to occur in the one Greek play which has, as it were, taken the defining of *hamartia* as its central topic. I am therefore obliged now to come out with the confession that I have totally changed the view to be found in my essays on the play, in which I maintained that Deianeira's tragic act, which resulted in the death of Heracles, was done after a clear and minutely-worked-out decision presented exclusively in *psychological* terms. I have not altered a jot in my admiration for Sophocles' art in presenting the steps by which Deianeira came to deal out an extremely painful death to her unfaithful husband, but I have given up my original conviction that this psychological account was the point of the tragedy. It is still as clear as ever to me that the play exists in great part to go into the whole gamut of feelings we have about the tragic act, but I am no longer so sure that the act is to be seen as occurring so exclusively on the human plane.

The play opens with a key-word (*ekmathein*) which instantly tells us that we are in for a series of surprise discoveries, and that not until the two principal figures are dead shall we be able to make up our minds about them. Sophocles moves with marvellous assurance and speed to bring about a confrontation between the heroine, Deianeira, the wife of Heracles, and Heracles' latest mistress, the principal female captive, Iole. Sophocles goes out of his way to assure us that the wife is a woman of good sense with all the humanity we could wish. When against all expectations this long-suffering wife learns that her missing husband is alive and well, her joy is instantly restrained by the sight of the captives sent back to swell the slave population. Deianeira appears to enter into the feelings of the striking young princess, but Iole goes to the slave quarters along with the others without uttering a word. (The full meaning of this surprise silence will dawn later after other revelations have been made.)

The next surprise is the revised account of the massacre at Iole's home-town, Oechalia. The message is succinct. Only one god was able to conquer Heracles with his magic charms. This was *Erōs*, the god of love, who so completely subjugated Heracles that the hero literally stopped at nothing to obtain possession of the girl. We must imagine his state as if his mind were enveloped in flames.[6] Worse than this, he apparently has determined to instal Iole in the palace not as a slave but as *maîtresse en titre*. When Deianeira hears this, she sees the whole action repeated in different colours. Now the extreme beauty of Iole has a new message. Deianeira now passes her own life in review, for she herself came on the scene in very similar circumstances. She was the young beauty Heracles won after defeating a bestial rival, a god-spirit-man, a shape-shifter, the never-static power of a great river. Some modern critics have felt shocked by the directness of Deianeira's summary of her new feelings: 'So now there are going to be two of us under the same blanket waiting to be gathered up in the man's embrace. I could bear the thought of his loving another woman, but who could stand sharing a husband?' She foresees the inevitable day when her charms will have faded and all she will have left will be the legal title of wife while Iole enjoys the position.

But even under this pressure she keeps her head. At least, she thinks she is using her head. Here we learn a strange story of how she had acquired a love-charm having all the powers Othello attributed to the handkerchief his mother had obtained from an Egyptian, who

>   told her, while she kept it,
> 'T would make her Amiable, and subdue my Father
> Intirely to her loue . . .

[6] Dante used the same image when placing 'Alcides' in the Ninth Canto of his *Paradiso*:

> Alcide
> quando Iole nel core ebbe rinchiusa.

The Provençal love-poet confesses that in his youth he had *flamed* more than Dido or the Hercules who locked up Iole in his heart.

We have to cast back to a time when Deianeira was still not much more than a girl, but is now married to Heracles. Both had to cross a river. For some reason Heracles was not able to carry her over himself and entrusted this task to a professional transporter, a man-horse, of the race of passionate and angry Centaurs. Nessus craftily waited until he was in mid-stream before making a sexual attempt on the girl, but he could not stifle her shout, and, just like that, an arrow from Heracles was in his lungs. He might have survived this blow, but the arrow was dipped in a deadly poison Heracles had extracted from an earlier conquest of the Hydra of Lerna. When Nessus knew that his ordinary chances of revenge were over, he made one last desperate bid. He persuaded Deianeira that if she took the arrow out of his lungs, the mixture left on the tip would act as an infallible love-charm on Heracles. The long-suffering woman had never been desperate before, but this time she decided to use it. So, although in her conscious mind she is innocent, she has unwittingly paid her husband out by giving him a death of exquisite torture, since the charm was a deadly poison.

The third surprise is a triumph of particularization. No stage representation could ever have made credible the actual affliction which killed Heracles when he put on the ceremonial sacrificial robes made for him by his loyal wife. Sophocles was inspired in showing us *multum in paruo* by telling us how one little portion of cotton wool used to 'dope' the robes was totally consumed when the sun warmed it. When Deianeira sees this, she understands in a flash that, although she had meant well, she had done for her husband. And, to reinforce the point, in comes her son fresh from the scene of horror with the brutal message: 'To-day as ever is, know that you have killed your husband and my father.' He curses her for killing the best of men, and wishes her a bad death like her husband's.

The next surprise is that the heroine refuses to say a word in her own defence and walks straight into the palace and out of this world. But now comes a further surprise. When the son learns the facts of her suicide, he is heart-broken, he bends over his mother's body, presses his body to hers, and lies howling in remorse for accusing her wrongfully. This remains his conviction, but Heracles is made of harder stuff. The same news of the death provokes only this remark:

> What a shame! She should have died hereafter.
> Then I could have seen to it that she got the death she deserves.

But Sophocles insists through the son on the favourable verdict:

ἅπαν τὸ χρῆμ᾽ ἥμαρτε χρηστὰ μωμένη. (p. 1136.)

She certainly committed *hamartia*, but her intentions were pure.

I do not conclude from this that we have the right to suppose even that the heroine's unconscious took over and forced her into the tragic act. On the other hand, as she herself told herself too late, what reason was there to suppose that the Centaur was her friend? Nevertheless it long seemed to me that the tragic error was purely psychological, the product of 'day-light' reflection, such as might have formed the basis of a modern novel. So strong was my conviction that the tragedy occurred on this plane, that I rejected out of hand the suggestion that in the final moments of the play the palace gates opened, and Iole was revealed, once again in silence, as she contemplated Heracles being carried off the stage to die. It was not until I re-read a remark by the Chorus Leader that I was prepared to consider Iole in a new light. This remark was made immediately on learning that the heroine had killed herself. Then we hear these words said about Iole:

ἔτεκ᾽ ἔτεκε μεγάλαν ἁ
νέορτος ἅδε νύμφα
δόμοισι τοῖσδ᾽ Ἐρινύν. (893-5.)

The young thing has hardly been bedded yet she has already produced a child. Yes, she has given birth to the utter ruin of this family.

The word for *ruin* in the Greek is *Erinys*. At once two of the passages I have used in this chapter rushed into my mind. First, there was Agamemnon in the *Iliad* trying to account for his 'great mistake' when he alienated Achilles by taking away from him the beautiful Briseis: 'Not I was the cause of this act, but Zeus and my portion and the Erinys who walks in darkness: they it was who in the assembly put wild *ātē* in my understanding, on that day when I arbitrarily took Achilles' prize from him . . .' Then there was M. Vernant's excellent summary:

The word Aristotle used to describe tragic error, *hamartia*, is a disease of the mind. The guilty man becomes the prey of an invading madness, and loses his sanity. This guilty blindness, which the Greeks described as *ātē* or *Erinys*, enters and possesses the individual. He is penetrated through and through as by a malignant religious power. Eventually the victim and his madness in a sense become one, yet the invading power comes from the outside and is always larger than the individual attacked.

And I then remembered the words of the son cursing the mother:

> τοιαῦτα, μῆτερ, πατρὶ βουλεύσασ᾽ ἐμῷ
> καὶ δρῶσ᾽ ἐλήφθης, ὧν σε ποίνιμος Δίκη
> τείσαιτ᾽ ᾽Ερινῦς τ᾽, εἰ θέμις γ᾽, ἐπεύχομαι. (807-9.)

If it is right to wish such a terrible thing on you, Mother, for plotting such a death as you found for Father, I pray that you may be justly punished, and that the Erinys may pay you out.

Once we let in *Ātē* and the Erinys as causal agents, the tragic plane is clear. The change is like that in the confusion during the sack of Troy in the Second Book of Virgil's *Aeneid*, when the soldiers clambered down from the famous horse, and Venus appeared to her son, Aeneas, and showed him that what he thought was a mortal fight was really a destruction carried out by the gods:

> aspice (namque omnem, quae nunc obducta tuenti
> mortalis hebetat uisus tibi et umida circum
> caligat, nubem eripiam; tu ne qua parentis
> iussa time neu praeceptis parere recusa):
> hic, ubi disiectas moles auulsaque saxis
> saxa uides, mixtoque undantem puluere fumum,
> Neptunus muros magnoque emota tridenti
> fundamenta quatit totamque a sedibus urbem
> eruit. hic Iuno Scaeas saeuissima portas
> prima tenet sociumque furens a nauibus agmen
> ferro accincta uocat.
> iam summas arces Tritonia, respice, Pallas
> insedit nimbo effulgens et Gorgone saeua.
> ipse pater Danais animos uirisque secundas
> sufficit, ipse deos in Dardana suscitat arma. (604-18)

> Now cast your Eyes around; while I dissolve
> The Mists and Films that mortal Eyes involve:
> Purge from your sight the Dross, and make you see
> The Shape of each avenging Deity.
> Enlighten'd thus, my just Commands fulfill;
> Nor fear Obedience to your Mother's Will.
> Where yon disorder'd heap of Ruin lies,
> Stones rent from Stones, where Clouds of dust arise,
> Amid that smother, *Neptune* holds his place: ⎫
> Below the Wall's foundation drives his Mace: ⎬
> And heaves the Building from the solid Base. ⎭

Look, where, in Arms, Imperial *Juno* stands,
Full in the *Scaean* Gate, with loud Commands;
Urging on Shore the tardy *Grecian* Bands.
See, *Pallas*, of her snaky Buckler proud,
Bestrides the Tow'r, refulgent through the Cloud:
See, *Jove* new Courage to the Foe supplies,
And arms against the Town, the partial Deities.[7]

Nobody pretends to know what Sophocles meant by the last lines of the play:

You see how little compassion the Gods have shown in all that's happened; they who are called our fathers, who begot us, can look upon such suffering. No one can foresee what is to come. What is here now is pitiful for us and shameful for the Gods; but of all men it is hardest for him who is the victim of this disaster. Maiden, come from the house with us. You have seen a terrible death and agonies, many and strange, and there is nothing here which is not Zeus.[8]

But I think that we are meant to understand that the play is primarily concerned with an action carried out by the gods, and principally by the Cyprian, Aphrodite. If it is *Zeus praktōr* who reigns, it is *Kupris praktōr* who governs. I therefore feel with greater conviction that I was right to regard as the central pillar of the play lines 860-1: 'There was no need for the goddess of love to open her mouth. She obviously is the power in charge who has brought about everything that has happened', and to use this remark to direct us to the right perspective on the play as a whole. The goddess appears in all her majesty as the one who subjugates all the gods and Zeus more than the others. She presides over every aspect where love has a part to play. Beauty brings fatality on all alike. Consequently, the lines 457-8 in the chorus:

The goddess of love wins every war:
there is no resisting her might . . .

apply as much to the infatuation which subjugated the hero — in the play it is called a disease — as to the desire for him — in Greek it is called *pothos* — felt by the wife. Could there be a more satisfactory example of guilt-in-innocence, innocence-in-guilt, of a doer who is at the same time a victim, as this splendid woman, Deianeira, faced with

[7] John Dryden, *Virgil's Aeneis,* 1697, Book II, ll. 819-36.
[8] *The Women of Trachis*, trans. Michael Jameson, p. 119.

the beautiful, silent girl, Iole, who certainly could not have *wanted* to act the part of a divine *ātē* or an avenging *Erinys*?

Could we now make one broad claim about all tragedy by comparing *Macbeth* and *The Women of Trachis*, that, just as we find Shakespeare's play tragic when we come to see that the hero's 'horrible imaginings' are not a solipsistic phenomenon but the result of an intermingling of one man's thought and universal powers, so we call the situation in Sophocles' play tragic when we can say more than 'the heroine's admirable balance and poise were shattered when she was suddenly confronted with Iole' and see two invisible forces at work in her soul, forces which in the play go by the names Aphrodite and Erinys but are clearly not local discoveries of a small Aegean community but plausible figures in a timeless universe?

5
THE TRAGIC END

If my linked treatment of the tragic figure, the tragic bond, and the tragic act has served any useful purpose, it will have incidentally reinforced some of the propositions thrown out as hypotheses in my first chapter, and one, in particular, that ambiguity is an essential constituent of tragedy. In these chapters we have been constantly forced to maintain as true two propositions which are logically contradictory. The very type of such contradictions seems to me the impossibility of distinguishing the guilt from the innocence of the tragic hero. Deianeira, we saw, was both cleared and condemned. If she was cleared of the charges made against her by her husband, she was condemned outright by her own decision to kill herself. Now, while this plainly seems to be where Sophocles wishes to leave us, he never systematizes, or philosophizes on, the precarious balance he has by the time he brings his play to an end so painfully and beautifully erected. Negatively, we may say, he has abandoned those underlying thoughts of *just punishment* which some people regard as fundamental to the surviving plays of Aeschylus, but he does not seem to ally himself with a thought that some people have found fundamental to the *Hippolytus* of Euripides, that injustice or anarchy is the law of his universe. In fact, I am inclined to purloin, as better suited to Sophocles, a phrase F. R. Leavis once used about Blake: 'His awareness of terrible complexities, and of problems for which he has no solutions, doesn't entail any protest against the essential conditions of life.'[1]

In my introductory chapter my general aim was to make various hints seem more probable, first, by floating them as mere hypotheses, and then, in later chapters, as crucial instances were assembled, to assist their progress as they filter their way down to the serious depths of the mind. In this chapter I should like to hasten on their downward path two of the greatest paradoxes which I touched upon at the beginning of

---

[1] F. R. Leavis, *Lectures in America* 1969, p. 77, 'Yeats: the Problem and the Challenge'.

this enquiry. The first concerns the contradictory claim that Tragedy is a form of fiction, presents a fictional world, and the claim that it leaves us finally with a truth. The second is that Tragedy, as a branch of literary art, must contradict life in the interests of an order which imposes itself on us as more 'real' than the 'real' itself. These paradoxes are not confined to Tragedy, but when we turn to the tragic *end*, we find that they are essential constituents of Tragedy as distinct from other forms of literature. Since there is not the slightest probability of my settling the problem of the relation of 'life' to literature and of fiction to 'reality', I make no apology for resorting to the traditional way of introducing ultimate realities that will remain mysterious, that is, of dealing in *parables*.

These two parables have for me one thing in common. They both played a part in arresting me during a phase of literary enthusiasm, and in forcing me to entertain a grain of doubt whether my enthusiasm contained an element of that self-delusion which led Byron to coin the word 'enthusy-musy'. There was a time in the years 1936–56 when in the eyes of poetry-lovers W. B. Yeats could do no wrong, when no doubt could be tolerated of his status as a major poet, a modern classic. During those years his masterpiece was thought to be a poem composed in 1927, entitled 'Sailing to Byzantium'. The grain of doubt was planted in the course of one of the many occasions when I heard F. R. Leavis reading out this poem and making a telling comparison with the poem entitled plain 'Byzantium'. I regret that the tape-recorder was not present on one of those occasions, for my memory tells me that for touch and intensity some of the earlier debates on the major status of Yeats's poems were finer than the ripe, almost valedictory, lecture by Leavis from which I have already taken one sentence.

The phrase in Yeats's poem which pulled me up occurs in this stanza:

> O sages standing in God's holy fire
> As in the gold mosaic of a wall,
> Come from the holy fire, perne in a gyre,
> And be the singing masters of my soul.
> Consume my heart away; sick with desire
> And fastened to a dying animal
> It knows not what it is; and gather me
> Into the artifice of eternity.

In the course of one of those debates I suddenly found myself regarding that last phrase as a mere conceit, in which the two elements, 'artifice' and 'eternity', failed to coalesce to form a strange, new entity, but touched lightly only to fly apart, and whereas 'eternity' went on booming into the infinite, 'artifice' dropped away as a piece of ineffectual irony. I will not say that it is because I myself am come to the sixty years and more of Yeats's age at the time he wrote this poem that the two terms now seem to define the kind of finality great tragedy may achieve, for, I ask myself, if so, why didn't Leavis in 1966, the date of his essay, give Yeats credit for having achieved a tragic paradox?

My second parable is an anecdote from a book of reminiscences made by Edith Wharton, a life-long admirer of Henry James, and to some extent his pupil in the art of writing fiction.

I was naturally much interested in James's technical theories and experiments, though I thought, and still think, that he tended to sacrifice to them that spontaneity which is the life of fiction. Everything, in the latest novels, had to be fitted into a predestined design, and design, in his strict geometrical sense, is to me one of the least important things in fiction. Therefore, though I greatly admired some of the principles he had formulated, such as that of always letting the tale, as it unfolded, be seen through the mind most capable of reaching to its periphery, I thought it was paying too dear even for such a principle to subordinate to it the irregular and irrelevant movements of life. And one result of the application of his theories puzzled and troubled me. His latest novels, for all their profound moral beauty, seemed to me more and more lacking in atmosphere, more and more severed from that thick nourishing human air in which we all live and move. The characters in 'The Wings of the Dove' and 'The Golden Bowl' seem isolated in a Crookes tube for our inspection:

(The felicity of this analogy is lost unless we recall the exploits of the great physicist, Sir William Crookes (1832–1919), who produced a radiant effect in a vacuum glass tube in which the exhaustion had been carried to a high degree. It appears that what impressed contemporaries about his tube was the extremely tenuous condition of the residual gas or gases.)

his stage was cleared like that of the Théâtre Français in the good old days when no chair or table was introduced that was not *relevant to the action* (a good rule for the stage, but an unnecessary embarrassment to fiction). Preoccupied by this, I one day said to him: 'What was your idea in suspending the four principal characters in 'The Golden Bowl' in the void? What sort of life did they lead when they were not watching each other, and fencing with each other? Why have you stripped them of all the *human fringes* we necessarily trail after us through life?'

He looked at me in surprise, and I saw at once that the surprise was painful, and wished I had not spoken. I had assumed that his system was a deliberate one, carefully thought out, and had been genuinely anxious to hear his reasons. But after a pause of reflection he answered in a disturbed voice: 'My dear – I didn't know I had!' and I saw that my question, instead of starting one of our absorbing literary discussions, had only turned his startled attention on a peculiarity of which he had been completely unconscious.[2]

Edith Wharton made her point in terms of the novel, as the form was understood in the first years of this century. To convert the anecdote into a parable for Tragedy, I must beg leave to generalize, and ask what her little story is putting to us about the general proposition that 'art imitates nature or life'. How far then could we continue to maintain with her that art should faithfully follow life in all life's 'irregular and irrelevant movements'? And is it reasonable to ask that a great work of literary art should take account of 'all the *human fringes* we necessarily trail after us through life'? To move into an area where Tragedy would naturally come to the fore, I should now like to link this extract from Edith Wharton to one from Samuel Johnson's account of Shakespeare's plays:

Shakespeare's plays are not in the rigorous or critical sense either tragedies or comedies, but compositions of a distinct kind; exhibiting the real state of sublunary nature, which partakes of good and evil, joy and sorrow, mingled with endless variety of proportion and innumerable modes of combination; and expressing the course of the world, in which the loss of one is the gain of another; in which, at the same time, the reveller is hasting to his wine, and the mourner burying his friend; in which the malignity of one is sometimes defeated by the frolick of another; and many mischiefs and many benefits are done and hindered without design.[3]

My argument will be that if we allow this to be a true account of life, then great tragic art must be described as its *antithesis*.

But a prior question might be, 'is this a fair account of *any* of Shakespeare's extant tragedies?' Let us take his *Macbeth*. Macbeth

[2] Edith Wharton, *A Backward Glance*, 1934, pp. 190–1.
[3] Samuel Johnson, *Preface*, 1765, p. xiii.

himself at a certain point in his story had good reason to think of the succession of events in his life as literally without sense or design:

> a Tale
> Told by an Ideot . . .
> Signifying nothing.

It is Shakespeare's art which has imposed the plan and the design on the higgledy-piggledy chronicle. All art is artifice, a deliberate opposition to what Johnson called 'the course of the world'. The tragedy of *Macbeth* was concocted by Shakespeare, who tampered with the events of Macbeth's life as he found them in the chronicles. If we multiply the clear examples showing artists altering the facts of life to make up a design, we are bound to stop and ask where the paradox is leading us. Are we driven into an admission that art 'imitates' life by *contradicting* it?

I have let in this somewhat artificial expression 'imitates' to recall the masterly exposition of this paradox in Aristotle's *Poetics*. I have never received so much critical light from so few sentences as from Aristotle's account of the three constituents of the main action of a tragedy, the beginning, the middle, and the end. Nevertheless I have to admit that what Aristotle said is a paradox in that he combines two propositions which in fact are incompatible. He wants to have it both ways, art both imitates life and contradicts it. On the one hand, we find him saying: 'Tragedy is essentially an imitation not of human beings but of life and actions, of things which bring about joy or sorrow.' (1450^a 16-17.) The context makes it clear that for Aristotle Tragedy is not essentially bound up with psychology or ethics, character or morals, but with acts such as occur 'in the course of the world'.

But what a change we find when he passes from the actions which make up life to the action which makes up a tragedy! Here is Aristotle's definition:

Now it is an agreed proposition that Tragedy is an imitation of an action that is complete in itself, a whole of some magnitude — I throw this in because there are actions which are wholes but of no extension to speak of. When I say an action is 'whole', I mean it has a beginning, a middle, and an end. The beginning is that which is not a necessary consequence of something else. On the contrary, a beginning is that which is naturally followed by a consequence, inherent in it, or developing from it. The end is the opposite of this. It is that which follows something logically either by a necessary consequence or a regular consequence in nature, but is followed by nothing else. A middle is that which follows the beginning and is followed by the end.

[Presumably, follows necessarily or naturally, but Aristotle doesn't say so.]

A well-constructed action must obey these laws. The poet is not free to begin where he likes or to end where he chooses. (1450^b 23-34.)

To discover the meaning of this last, rather cryptic, sentence, we have to turn to his criticism of bad poets (though we might think that, if he were alive to-day, he would apply his remarks to some novels which have carried to excess the principles implicit in Edith Wharton's remark to Henry James): 'What is wrong with these writers [Aristotle appears to be saying, the text is disputed] is that instead of choosing one single action with the structure I have described, that is to say, a natural development from beginning to middle to end, they choose one segment of time in which anything may happen with no design and no inner connection between the incidents.' (1459^a 21-4.) And to reinforce his point, he contrasts these poets with Homer, who confined the action of the *Iliad* to one event, with a clear beginning, middle, and end.

   La mer à boire! A vast and difficult debate threatens, since so much truth is to be found on each of the opposing sides. My intention, however, in this chapter is to concentrate attention on the tragic *end*, since here the contradictions are most obvious and acute. For nobody thinks that *life* presents us with an end. After every catastrophe, no matter how great, life picks up and carries on. *Tragic finality* must therefore be something other than the lesson of life. The paradox to be discussed emerges if we nevertheless claim that, if tragedy ever deals with the real, it is just at this point where we say everything *ends*, and ends *inevitably*. In keeping with the principle laid down in my first chapter, that we rest our case on our deep response to tragedies, I propose to examine some actual ends of tragedies to discover what appears to make us regard them as satisfactory as ends and as truly tragic.

> − Is this the promis'd end?
> − Or image of that horror.
> − Fall and cease.

These are the three remarks which greet the appearance of Lear with the dead Cordelia in his arms. I choose this moment first, because for me as for many others it has proved at once the most disturbing and the most satisfactory ending of a tragedy. It is an ending which, just because of this, forces us to think hard about both the disturbance and the satisfaction. The deepest thoughts I have come across in my reading are those forced out of A. C. Bradley by the disturbance, distress, and discomfort he suffered at this close of a play which he had up to that point been taking without inner resistance. The page in *Shakespearean Tragedy* is not easy to grasp at one reading, but my experience tells me that its power increases the more often it is read. The account Bradley gives of his feeling has a further advantage for us because for him it is a

feeling not confined to *King Lear*, but present at the close of other tragedies; and that the reason why it has an exceptional tone or force at the close of *King Lear*, lies in that very peculiarity of the close which also — at least for the moment — excites bewilderment, dismay, or protest. The feeling I mean is the impression that the heroic being, though in one sense and outwardly he has failed, is yet in another sense superior to the world in which he appears; is, in some way which we do not seek to define, untouched by the doom that overtakes him; and is rather set free from life than deprived of it. Some such feeling as this — some feeling which, from this description of it, may be recognised as their own even by those who would dissent from the description — we surely have in various degrees at the deaths of Hamlet and Othello and Lear, and of Antony and Cleopatra and Coriolanus. It accompanies the more prominent and specific tragic impressions, and it itself can hardly be called tragic. For it seems to imply (though we are probably quite unconscious of the implication) an idea which, if developed, would transform the tragic view of things. It implies that the tragic world, if taken as it is presented, with all its error, guilt, failure, woe and waste, is no final reality, but only a part of reality taken for the whole, and, when so taken, illusive; and that if we could see the whole, and the tragic facts in their true place in it, we should find them, not abolished, of course, but so transmuted that they had ceased to be strictly tragic . . . (p. 324.)

This is not the only page in *Shakespearean Tragedy* which makes me look smaller in my own eyes, and tells me what a large, comprehensive soul wrote that book. For in so confessing to a human weakness I fancy that Bradley is speaking for a noble chorus of all those who have been in, really in, at the death of the hero, and been tempted to wish for some mitigation of his fate. The reader may recall that in my first chapter I raised the thought that this chorus might include Shakespeare himself! When we see the end of a tragedy coming on us with an inevitable rush, many of us cannot help in our small way producing our equivalent of that feeling of reluctance before the moment of death which is so memorably recorded in the Gospels: 'Abba, father, all thinges are possible vnto thee, take away this cup from me.'[4]

Nevertheless the call of Tragedy is to overcome this reluctance. What Tragedy demands of us is to believe with Aristotle that the end is the end, and at the same time believe that at this crisis the fictional has become in the fullest sense the *real*. In the page I quoted, Bradley is telling us indirectly what is one essential constituent of Tragedy at the point when the hero dies. *He must die indeed, and there can be no hereafter for him or us.* Bradley himself makes the telling contrast with the close of Shakespeare's *The Tempest*. Although there is much talk of forgiveness and reconciliation in the winding up of that play, everybody notices that there is no hint of permanent change. Once back in Europe, things will take their old course: evil remain potent, human weakness perennial. Tragedy flies away when we hear this speech:

> Our Reuels now are ended: These our actors,
> (As I foretold you) were all Spirits, and
> Are melted into Ayre, into thin Ayre,
> And like the baselesse fabricke of this vision
> The Clowd-capt Towres, the gorgeous Pallaces,
> The solemne Temples, the great Globe it selfe,
> Yea, all which it inherit, shall dissolue,
> And like this insubstantiall Pageant faded,
> Leaue not a racke behinde; we are such stuffe
> As dreames are made on; and our little life
> Is rounded with a sleepe . . .

We can form some impression of the importance to be attached to the sense that the death of the hero must be both *real* and *final*, if we consult actors and producers of plays and those for whom the supreme experiences of Tragedy have occurred on the stage. They all tell us that this moment at the end of a tragedy puts the greatest strain on our power of believing in the reality of what is presented on the stage. Although I think we are all capable for moments during the course of a play of forgetting that the actors are only actors, I believe that when the hero dies, before our eyes, we are inevitably reminded of the contrast between real and make-believe. There never has been an audience who rushed on the stage to rescue the heroine from death

---

[4] William Tyndale, *The Gospell of S. Marke*. The . xiiii. Chapter.

or a fate worse than death. This moment of tension between the desire for belief and the impossibility of believing is greatest in tragedies written by and for actors, tragedies such as some of Shakespeare's. It is always a sad falling-off in his plays when we have a double consciousness that now the chief actor is about to make his last, impressive, exit, and now the hero is going to meet his death. In such cases there is an inevitable impurity in our response.

This is clearly another instance where one should say more or say less. If the reader or spectator has not been troubled in Shakespeare's best plays by the sense every now and then that an actor is being provided with a 'fat' part, and that this actor is occasionally 'spouting' rather than addressing himself seriously to what was clearly his 'business', then it could be said that if there were no other reason for including Greek plays in a study of Tragedy, the consequent sharpening of this sense that Shakespeare was an actor, interested in acting, as well as a great poet would be ample justification. In the course of this chapter I shall be relying on the reader's verdict that, if he considers the last speech made by Othello in Shakespeare's play and the last long speech by Heracles in *The Women of Trachis*, he feels the difference between a pure and an impure response, and the difference between a histrionic and a dramatic close, and learns something of what must go into the definition of a truly tragic ending.

I have often been laughed at for wanting a different end to Shakespeare's *Othello*, an ending more like that in Cinthio's tale, where Othello is killed by Desdemona's kinsmen, and I have had to live with the complaint, 'only a man with a grudge against actors and acting could think like that.' I must therefore not seek to belittle the impact on the audience made by a good actor delivering Othello's last words. The word 'impure' is only in place if there is a distinction between a theatrical close and a dramatic close. The word 'impure' would not be fairly used of the end of *Othello* if we were persuaded by F. R. Leavis. In an essay first printed in the December 1937 number of *Scrutiny*, after quoting Othello's speech ending: 'And smote him, thus. [*Stabs himself*]' Leavis remarked:

It is a superb *coup de théâtre*.

As, with that double force, a *coup de théâtre*, it is a peculiarly right ending to the tragedy of Othello. The theme of the tragedy is concentrated in it — in the final speech and action as it could not have been had Othello 'learnt through suffering'. That he should die acting his ideal part is all in the part: the part is manifested here in its rightness and solidity, and the actor as inseparably the man of action. The final blow is as real as the blow it re-enacts, and the histrionic intent symbolically affirms the reality: Othello dies belonging to the world of action in which his true part lay.[5]

But even if we believe that the theatrical and the dramatic coincide in this close, we still ought to be able to distinguish the two things. Although I happen not to believe they are ever identical, I can see that they have one important resemblance. With my eye now on Aristotle's insistence that the end is the end, I would say that both may have the necessary finality. But whereas the theatrical effect merely brings down the curtain satisfactorily and sends us home happy, the dramatic effect lasts as long as we possess the whole play, and possess it as a whole.

So far I have been tacitly assuming that Othello's speech is a *coup de théâtre*. Bradley claimed that it was never that, but a fully dramatic and indeed triumphantly tragic close:

And pity itself vanishes, and love and admiration alone remain, in the majestic dignity and sovereign ascendancy of the close. Chaos has come and gone; and the Othello of the Council-chamber and the quay of Cyprus has returned, or a greater and nobler Othello still. As he speaks those final words in which all the glory and agony of his life — long ago in India and Arabia and Aleppo, and afterwards in Venice, and now in Cyprus — seem to pass before us, like the pictures that flash before the eyes of a drowning man, a triumphant scorn for the fetters of the flesh and the littleness of all the lives that must survive him sweeps our grief away, and when he dies upon a kiss the most painful of all tragedies leaves us for the moment free from pain, and exulting in the power of 'love and man's unconquerable mind.'[6]

If I find that I leave the theatre unsatisfied, it was because there was more for me in the play than a noble Moor, more, too, than an enigmatic Iago; my mind goes on working on what seem to be larger considerations, which this trick ending cuts short. In a word, for me the curtain falling on the histrionic triumph of a leading actor does not end the play but interrupts it. I must therefore continue to seek to find what constitutes the tragic end, and pursue the paradox, how can we believe in the reality of an end which nothing can follow, when we know that life never produces an end? How can we come to take for truth an artifice which suspends creation and brings time to a stop?

[5] Reprinted in *The Common Pursuit*, 1952, p. 152.
[6] A. C. Bradley, *Shakespearean Tragedy*, p. 198.

Although I shall almost certainly fail to work out the full implications of this paradox, there are some attendant features of it on
which we might instantly agree. If I were to venture to refer again to
the death of the great hero of the Christian religion, it would be
because I was supposing that everybody regards that death as heroic but
not tragic. Of course, we could not even use the word 'heroic' if we
thought of the figure on the Cross as a 'super-man'. Heroes are by
definition *human*, whatever becomes of them when they die. We lose
the *tragic* hero when we say out the Creed to the end:

And in Jesus Christ his only Son our Lord,
Who was conceived by the Holy Ghost,
Born of the Virgin Mary,
Suffered under Pontius Pilate,
Was crucified, dead, and buried,
He descended into Hell;
The third day he rose again from the dead,
He ascended into heaven,
And sitteth on the right hand of God the Father Almighty;
From thence he shall come to judge the quick and the dead . . .

Merely to recite this creed serves to remind us that the glory of man is
that he is not a figure in a fairy story with armour that no enemy can
pierce, whose triumph is assured before his birth. The tragic end must
among other things assert the dignity of a creature born in weakness
and living in radical uncertainty, who yet, in some such way as Bradley
suggested, emerges in triumph, and, like Dante's friend, runs his last
race as a *winner*:

e parue di costoro
quelli che uince, non colui che perde.[7]

and of them he was seen as the winner, not the loser.

Nevertheless the grandeur of the last moment of Christ on earth has
so filled the minds of many reluctant atheists or agnostics during the
last 150 years that they have projected their feelings on to what they
regarded as a similar moment, namely, the last hour on earth of
Heracles in Sophocles' play, *The Women of Trachis*. In their view the
hero rises to his full height — or in some variants ceases for a moment
to be the villain of the piece — when the oracles are revealed and

---

[7] *La Diuina Commedia, Inferno*, Canto Decimoquinto, ll. 123–4.

Heracles sees and understands what in fact has brought about his ruin and is bringing about his death. May I once again present the moment in the words of Ezra Pound?

> My father told me long ago
> that no living man should kill me,
> but that someone from hell would, and
> that brute of a Centaur has done it.
> The dead beast kills the living me.
> And that fits another odd forecast
> breathed out at the Selloi's oak —
> those fellows rough it, sleep on the ground, up in the hills there —
> I heard it and wrote it down under my Father's tree.
> Time lives, and it's going on now.
> I am released from trouble.
> I thought it meant life in comfort.
> It doesn't. It means that I die.
> For amid the dead there is no work in service.
> Come at it that way, my boy, what
> SPLENDOUR,
>   IT ALL COHERES.[8]

Pound printed this last phrase in capitals, and added this note: 'This is the key phrase, for which the play exists.' His stage direction follows: '[He turns his face from the audience, then sits erect, facing them without the mask of agony; the revealed make-up is that of solar serenity. The hair golden and as electrified as possible.]'

Although Pound doesn't tell us explicitly, he does not seem to quarrel with the view held by some scholars that Heracles' passage is from service on earth to freedom in heaven, that he puts off mortality and puts on immortality, and that the fire in which his body is consumed is merely, as it were, a *rite de passage*, a glorious consummation. The scholars who hold this view have two undeniable facts on their side. Heracles behaves in a quite different manner after taking in the relevant information. Second, the play stresses consistently the mythological fact that the hero is the Beloved Son of his Father, Zeus. True, he is chastened by that Father for his misdeeds, but there is a strong suggestion that the whole play is designed to expound God's plan. The play ends, as Pound puts it, with the words: 'And all of this is from Zeus'. The scholars therefore think of Heracles submitting to

---

[8] Ezra Pound, *Sophocles: The Women of Trachis*, 1956, pp. 49–50.

the Father in the words of *Christ*: 'O my father, yf this cuppe can not passe away from me, but that I drinke of it, thy wyll be fulfylled.[9] For them, Heracles dies in the full assurance that in a few seconds he will be with his Father in the Olympian paradise. The scholars conclude that the end of the play, so far from being final, is a prelude to a joyful sequel, which was designed to comfort both the hero and the audience.

Such an ending would for me be empty of tragedy. The dignity of the hero depends on his dying a painful death in total uncertainty of the future. This is, to my mind, what Sophocles has provided. What makes me regard this ending as an example of true tragedy is a passage which is obscured in Pound's translation. Yet it was Pound who put me on the track when he made Heracles say: '. . . my mother was a notable woman and my father in heaven, Zeus, mid the stars. *That's what they say*.' [My italics.] This translation is supported by a Dutch scholar, J. C. Kamerbeek, who thought that the hero's language at this point suggested how estranged Heracles felt from his sonship to Zeus. Emboldened by this, I find the height of the tragedy occurring where Heracles abruptly stops feeling sorry for himself, recognizes that the end has come, but dies as the son of *Alcmene*, his mother, his human mother. I therefore take up Pound but continue with my own version of Heracles' words:

> I understand perfectly well
> where things have got to. Son,
> your father is done for. Go and
> collect the whole family, all your
> brothers and sisters, all those who
> have been fathered by me. And call
> my poor dear mother, Alcmene.
> What good did it do her to have
> Zeus for a husband?

I need to stress this point because my chief conclusion is that the proper state of mind for the spectator at the end resembles what I supposed was the actual frame of mind in which Sophocles composed the whole play. May I remind the reader of the phrase I stole from F. R. Leavis? 'His awareness of terrible complexities, and of problems for which he has no solutions, doesn't entail any protest against the essential conditions of life.' But I should just as much wish to recall my

---

[9] William Tyndale: *The Newe Testament* 1534, The Gospell of S. Mathew, Chap. xxvi.

earlier remark that Sophocles, when he reaches the point where he leaves us, never systematizes or philosophizes on, the precarious balance he has so painfully and beautifully erected.

When looking round for authorities to support this view of the end, I found a strange ally in Maurice Bowra, strange to me, that is, because his *Sophoclean Tragedy* in all other points failed to command my respect. But in the following lines I find much illumination:

... in the *Women of Trachis* no word is said of apotheosis or life on Olympus or marriage to Hebe, no word of amends for suffering or reward for labours. The tragic events take place in a human world; nothing is said of the hereafter. The plot is rigidly restricted to the mortal existence of Heracles which ends in a tragic calamity. The future glory is treated as if it had nothing to do with the play. Indeed, so painful and effective is the play, so strong the will of the gods revealed in it, that we hardly look outside it.[10]

I should like to erect that last remark into a law of tragedy, that in the effective possession of the end of a tragedy we are totally enclosed in a moment. It is like coming to the edge of the universe. There is nowhere to go for further enlightenment or explanation. The fine point of the close is paradoxically the revelation of a whole universe of discourse, it is *all* we know and all we need to know.

Although I would willingly continue with further examples contrasting non-tragic endings and those that seem to call for the epithet 'tragic', I must hasten on to record a radical change of view implied in these reflections on Bowra. So far I have been dwelling chiefly on 'finality' as the mark of the tragic end, and have been insisting on the fact that the tragic end is really the end. I should now like to change, and view the end of a play as seen from the beginning, and to examine some of the thoughts supporting the claim that the end becomes tragic because the final event seems to have been *inevitable*. My reason for this change of perspective is that it may cause us to adopt a hitherto unmentioned view of what is essentially tragic in tragedies.

Once again, though, I should like to ease my progress by dealing first with a clearly inferior view of that inevitability which gives tragedy its peculiar stamp. I associate this view with the French, and, in particular, with the Cocteau who wrote *La Machine Infernale*. Put simply, and, I am afraid, crudely, in this play the tragic end is likened to a mine which is exploded *mechanically* by putting a light to a fuse. Interest in the end

[10] M. Bowra, *Sophoclean Tragedy*, 1944, p. 159.

as an end is thereby lost, and tragedy attaches itself to this mechanical inevitability, the doom which is set in motion in the opening of the play, and moves inexorably to an explosion at the close. To counter the dangers of over-simplification, let me offer an extract from Anouilh's *Antigone* which deals explicitly with this view. The author clears the stage before the guards bring the captured girl before Creon, and the 'Chorus' utters this monologue:

Et voilà. Maintenant le ressort est bandé.[11] Cela n'a plus qu'à se dérouler tout seul. C'est cela qui est commode dans la tragédie. On donne le petit coup de pouce pour que cela démarre, rien, un regard pendant une seconde à une fille qui passe et lève les bras dans la rue, une envie d'honneur un beau matin, au réveil, comme de quelque chose qui se mange, une question de trop qu'on se pose un soir . . . . C'est tout. Après, on n'a plus qu'à laisser faire. On est tranquille. Cela roule tout seul. C'est minutieux, bien huilé depuis toujours. La mort, la trahison, le désespoir sont là, tout prêts, et les éclats, et les orages, et les silences, tous les silences: le silence quand le bras du bourreau se lève à la fin, le silence au commencement quand les deux amants sont nus l'un en face de l'autre pour la première fois, sans oser bouger tout de suite, dans la chambre sombre, le silence quand les cris de la foule éclatent autour du vainqueur — et on dirait un film dont le son s'est enrayé, toutes ces bouches ouvertes dont il ne sort rien, toute cette clameur qui n'est qu'une image, et le vainquer, déjà vaincu, seul au milieu de son silence . . .

C'est propre, la tragédie. C'est reposant, c'est sûr . . . . Dans le drame, avec ces traîtres, avec ces méchants acharnés, cette innocence persécutée, ces vengeurs, ces terre-neuve, ces lueurs d'espoir, cela devient épouvantable de mourir, comme un accident. On aurait peut-être pu se sauver, le bon jeune homme aurait peut-être pu arriver à temps avec les gendarmes. Dans la tragédie on est tranquille. D'abord, on est entre soi. On est tous innocents en somme! Ce n'est pas parce qu'il y en a un qui tue et l'autre qui est tué. C'est une question de distribution. Et puis, surtout, c'est reposant, la tragédie, parce qu'on sait qu'il n'y a plus d'espoir, le sale espoir; qu'on est pris, qu'on est enfin pris comme un rat, avec tout le ciel sur son dos, et qu'on n'a plus qu'à crier, — pas à gémir, non, pas à se plaindre, — à gueuler à pleine voix ce qu'on avait à dire, qu'on n'avait jamais dit et qu'on ne savait peut-être même pas

---

[11] Cf. Jean Cocteau *La Machine Infernale*, 1934: 'Regarde, spectateur, remontée à bloc, de telle sorte que le ressort se déroule avec lenteur tout le long d'une vie humaine, une des plus parfaites machines construites par les dieux infernaux pour l'anéantissement mathématique d'un mortel.' (Spoken by 'La Voix' at the opening of the play.)

encore. Et pour rien: pour se le dire à soi, pour l'apprendre, soi. Dans le
drame, on se débat, parce qu'on espère en sortir. C'est ignoble, c'est
utilitaire. Là, c'est gratuit. C'est pour les rois. Et il n'y a plus rien à
tenter, enfin!

A fairly loose translation will save the need for a commentary in the
places where the text is obscure:

There you are then. The spring is now coiled tight. It will be able to
uncoil without further assistance. That is what is so convenient about
Tragedy, the slightest shove and the boat moves out. All it needs is a
swift glance at a girl raising her arms as you pass by her in the street.
Or you wake up one fine morning with an itch for an honour you long
to possess as if it were a desirable morsel of food, or, of an evening, you
ask one question too many. That's enough to set Tragedy in motion.
No worry at all. It runs by itself. It works with the smooth precision of
a machine which has never been allowed to rust since time began.
Death, treachery, despair, they're all there waiting for you with the
attendant storms, crescendos, diminuendos and silences, all the forms
of silence. The silence of the headsman raising his axe to put an end to
his victim. The silence of the first few seconds in the darkened room
where two naked lovers stand face to face for the first time in their lives
and dare not make a move. The silence which falls on the crowd
cheering the victor. It's like a talkie with the sound cut off − all those
open mouths merely a picture with no shout to be heard, leaving the
victor to become a victim isolated in the surrounding silence.
   There's nothing messy about Tragedy. Restful, too, and reliable.
Ordinary commercial plays or melodramas are another kettle of fish.
In that sort of drama you find regular villains, desperate ne'er-do-wells
with innocent creatures for their perpetual prey, and heroes who come
to their rescue, St Bernard dogs, gleams of hope; death is terrible when
it comes as an accident. And there was always the possibility that death
might have been avoided, a handsome young man turn up with a posse
of the Mounties. Tragedy is free of such disturbing possibilities. We are
all cosily at home together. The long and the short of it is that there are
no villains in tragedies, we are all innocent. We should not think of ourselves as murderers and victims, we are all cast for parts we receive
without choosing. But, as I said, Tragedy is, above all else, restful,
restful because there is nothing left to hope for. Hope is filthy. We are
all caught, trapped like rats, the skies have fallen; all you can do is
shout − shout, mark you, not groan or lament or complain − no, all
we can do about it is to bawl out what we had to say, what we never
found ourselves able to say before, things we perhaps never knew we
had it in us to say. And all this is done without ulterior motive, it's all

for nothing. Just to let ourselves know what we really are. In the other kinds of plays people struggle in an effort to get out of their misery. That's unspeakably low. They do things because they hope to gain by them. In tragedy we believe in what André Gide used to call the 'motiveless act'. We are spiritual aristocrats, we do not condescend to fight misery. And in any case, there is nothing we could do about it.

What chiefly offends me in this at bottom sentimental attitude is that it would be more appropriate if said about a Hell like Dante's, which would have the same warning over the gate as in Dante's poem:

LASCIATE OGNE SPERANZA, VOI CH'INTRATE.

(Notice to entrants to this area: hope must be dropped for ever.) But to appreciate the speech in Anouilh's play, we must imagine a rider attached to this notice to the effect that for the rest of eternity prison conditions have been liberalized to remove all pain and discomfort, and consequently the motto to be worn by the damned must henceforward run:

Viuemo sanza speme e sanza disio.

(We live without hope and without desire.) It forces me to protest that, for tragedy, hell is *on earth*. Perhaps only a Frenchman could make the distinction between Tragedy and other plays that Anouilh draws. I would argue that it is in Tragedy above all that men combat and struggle against misery, even when there are no rational grounds for hope. Anouilh has some truth on his side, of course, but we need to match his 'Quietism' with the opposite view, well expressed by D. H. Lawrence (whose conviction is perhaps caricatured in the phrase which has become something of a by-word, 'a great big kick at misery') when he wrote in the preface he composed for the printed version of *Touch and Go* (1919):

In tragedy the man is more than his part. Hamlet is more than Prince of Denmark, Macbeth is more than murderer of Duncan. The man is caught in the wheels of his part, his fate, he may be torn asunder. He may be killed, but the resistant, integral soul in him is not destroyed. He comes through, though he dies. He goes through with his fate, though death swallows him. And it is in this facing of fate, this going right through with it, that tragedy lies. Tragedy is not disaster. It is a disaster when a cart-wheel goes over a frog, but it is not a tragedy. Tragedy is the working out of some immediate passional problem within the soul of man. If this passional problem and this working out be absent, then no disaster is a tragedy, not the hugest: not the death of ten million men. It is only a cart-wheel going over a frog. There must be a supreme *struggle*.[12]

I was glad to be able to bring in Anouilh because it enables me to say something kind about Aristotle's view of inevitability before rejecting the claim that it is an adequate account of what makes the end tragic. The view I attribute to Aristotle is that 'the end is satisfactory when, on looking back on what, in terms of the play, is shown to have happened, the spectator feels both that it *did* happen and that it *had* to happen just like that'. I have no quarrel with this claim; my objection is that it does not apply specifically to Tragedy. This is how we should praise a good detective story or what in the nineteenth century was known as a 'well-made play'. My difficulty arises if we substitute *tragic* for *satisfactory* in my formulation of Aristotle's law. In none of the great tragedies does it seem to me that the specifically tragic was brought about by a well-constructed plot with a beginning, and a middle leading to a probable, plausible, or necessary end.

Aristotle, if we may believe the commentators, rested his sense of inevitability on the extent to which the spectator was bounced into believing that each event followed necessarily on its predecessor. But he clearly relied on a point which powerfully disposes the spectator to believe; that no event is merely a particular happening. We are bound to see this particular as standing for the general. Samuel Johnson brought this out well when writing of Shakespeare:

Shakespeare has no heroes; his scenes are occupied only by men, who act and speak as the reader thinks that he should himself have spoken or acted on the same occasion: Even where the agency is supernatural the dialogue is level with life. Other writers disguise the most natural passions and most frequent incidents; so that he who contemplates them in the book will not know them in the world: *Shakespeare* approximates the remote, and familiarizes the wonderful; the event which he represents will not happen, but if it were possible, its effects would be probably such as he has assigned; and it may be said, that he has not only shewn human nature as it acts in real exigences, but as it would be found in trials, to which it cannot be exposed.

This therefore is the praise of *Shakespeare*, that his drama is the mirrour of life; that he who has mazed his imagination, in following the phantoms which other writers raise up before him, may here be cured of his delirious extasies, by reading human sentiments in human

---

[12] *Touch and Go*, A Play in Three Acts by D. H. Lawrence, 1920, pp. 8-9.

language; by scenes from which a hermit may estimate the transactions of the world, and a confessor predict the progress of the passions.[13]

This is a far more acceptable account of the relation of great literature to life. It rests, as Johnson makes clear in his critical writings, on a doctrine of General Nature. Ours is an age of insane worship of the particular and an insane mistrust of the general. I must therefore, before giving a telling instance of the particular, insist on the indispensability of this doctrine of General Nature. If there is no ideal norm of nature to justify the word 'human', then the basic words in our language have no reference. We may know a hundred forms which 'hate' has taken in the civilizations open to our inspection and study, but if we cannot relate them to an ideal 'hate', no particular presentation of hate in a great poem can fill us with the conviction that we enter fully into the greatness of the poem. I wish we could use Aristotle's word 'catholic' for this valuable quality which 'universalizes' the particular endings we admire in tragedy. I wish it would be generally helpful to call to mind the train of thought which made the phrase 'securus iudicat orbis terrarum' a turning-point in Newman's conversion to what we call the Roman church but he thought the universal, catholic church.

I can see, however, that I am not going to get beyond the point I made in the first chapter when discussing the impression of truth, and the sense we have that a great tragedy is true to all experience. As then, however, so now I feel the need to say that, whereas we must feel that the particular locality of the tragedy sends us to a *quod ubique*, the particular hero to a *quod ab omnibus*, and the particular time to a *quod semper*, that, in short, the tragic end must hold good of an everywhere, everybody and all time, yet I still feel that, while universality is an indispensable condition for all Tragedy, it is not that which marks Tragedy off from other forms of great literature.

But I can now make one new point: though Tragedy issues into universality and embraces the whole of experience, that is to say, ends in the general, it does not *start* from a large general truth, but that truth emerges from particulars. This point will come to the fore whenever we are discussing French practice in the seventeenth century. The French claimed Aristotle's authority in his seventeenth chapter for the view that the tragic poet begins his work by thinking up a general situation with universal probability and naturally connected, and then looks round for a story in the stock of legends, and fits the proper names of mythology to the universal ideas. That Aristotle did not claim that the poet begins with a philosophical idea and later finds particulars to suit is admirably expounded by S. H. Butcher in his commentary on the *Poetics*. He aptly draws on a conversation Goethe had with Eckermann, in which he complains about the peculiar predilection his German contemporaries had for discovering 'ideas' in literary works, 'Why, they even asked me what idea I had tried to embody in my *Faust*! As if I knew or could tell them!' And he summed up his thought in these words:

Generally speaking it was never my way as a poet to try to embody anything *abstract*. I had a lively imagination which presented manifold delightful and varied sense impressions to my inner self. My activity as a poet consisted exclusively in giving artistic shape to these views and impressions, and my aim was to present them in such a way that my readers could share the same impressions I had received.[14]

But it is clear that Bowra, for instance, thought that Sophocles began the *Women of Trachis* with a general idea — the relation of the sexes in marriage — and adapted some of the details of the Heracles legend to illustrate the main aspects of that relation. Here are some quotations:

The subject of the play is the simple, shared destiny of a man and a woman.

The main theme . . . is a woman's tragic love for her husband.

The two chief characters . . . are man and woman, husband and wife. They might be typical of any married pair [but Sophocles' play] is of universal interest because he makes his woman extremely womanly and his man extremely manly . . . the conflict between man and wife . . . is . . . the kind of conflict that may arise when a dependent highly feminine woman is deeply in love with an independent highly masculine man.

For Bowra, Deianeira is a member of a large class of women, those whose husbands are away for long periods. It is implied that the tragic effect arises when we see this membership of a class so vividly that we forget Deianeira's bizarre mythological self, lose it in our sense of the large class of abandoned wives. (The French confess that for a great

---

[14] S. H. Butcher *Aristotle's Theory of Poetry and Fine Art*, pp. 180–4. Goethe's conversation took place on Sunday 6 May 1827.

many adulterous males this play is known as 'La Seconde'.) I ought to say in passing that I am using the *Women of Trachis* because the play has been before our minds. I could equally well have taken Shakespeare's *King Lear*. Many people write of that play as if Shakespeare had started from a similar domestic problem, that of the relation between fathers and children, and fitted it very clumsily into a never-focused Ancient Britain and an unreal set of political circumstances.

An advantage of *The Women of Trachis* for this argument is that it faces us with a clear either/or: either Sophocles was a fool, an incompetent practitioner, or we have been looking for Tragedy in the wrong place. For if Sophocles had been primarily interested in general nature, what could have induced him to give his perfect wife so many odd, particular, accoutrements? The prominence of the story of the battle over her waged by Heracles and the River-God is a pure embarrassment. Aristotle permitted some absurdities on the grounds that what has appeared in some popular legends has thereby for the spectator of the tragedy some probability. But what could have been pushing Sophocles into offering us so much *detail*? I have elsewhere made fun of Gilbert Murray's version. Here is a reminder:

> All was a thud of fists, a deadly whirr
> Of arrows, clash of wild-beast horn on horn,
> Grapples of writhing trunks, brows battle-torn
> And one o'ermastering groan . . .[15]

Before coming out with the radical departure from Aristotle which was forced upon me, I must complete the grounds for expressing my sense of debt to that part of the *Poetics* which insists on the interconnection of the parts of a tragedy to form a *whole*. One of the reasons for looking to the end of a play to discover the essentially tragic is undoubtedly the experience we all have that by the end we are fully aware that a play has been bound together specifically in order to make that end the moment of fullest revelation. The great impression Aristotle made on me was due to an addition I have deliberately reserved for this point of the argument, the implications of his use of the Greek word for a living thing, ζῷον, *zōion*. He uses this word when tacking on two further features of the well-made plot, that it must be beautiful and like a living thing. The commentators suppose that the analogy postulated here is taken from something which sounds similar

[15] *Arion*, vol. ii, No. 1, Spring 1963, pp. 69–72.

in Plato's dialogue, *Phaedrus*.[16] When Ingram Bywater came to the part where Aristotle lays down the laws for narrative poetry, and points out the resemblance to those for tragedy, he translated as follows: 'The construction of its stories should clearly be like that in a drama; they should be based on a single action, one that is a complete whole in itself, with a beginning, middle, and end, so as to enable the work to produce its own proper pleasure *with all the organic unity of a living creature.*[17]

The question is, are the words I have put into italics a genuine translation of the original:

$$\overline{\omega}\sigma\pi\epsilon\rho \; \zeta\tilde{\omega}ov \; \tilde{\epsilon}v \; \tilde{\delta}\lambda ov$$

or is the introduction of 'organism' one further instance of the nineteenth-century infatuation with Darwin combined with remnants of Romantic theory about the genesis of a work of art? If this was a delusion, it is one which I shared. The formulation which attracted me most came in S. H. Butcher's commentary:

A unity is composed of a plurality of parts which cohere together and fall under a common idea, but are not necessarily combined in a definite order. The notion of a whole implies something more. The parts which constitute it must be inwardly connected, arranged in a certain order, structurally related, and combined into a system. A whole is not a mere mass or sum of external parts which may be transposed at will, any one of which may be omitted without perceptibly affecting the rest. It is a unity which is unfolded and expanded according to the law of its own nature, an organism which develops from within. By the rule, again, of beauty, which is a first requirement of art, a poetic creation must exhibit at once unity and plurality. If it is too small the whole is perceived but not the parts; if too large the parts are perceived but not the whole. The idea of an organism evidently underlies all Aristotle's rules about unity;[18]

I loyally adhered to this view, and saluted further contributions to it, particularly in the work of G. Wilson Knight, until I came upon an unfinished Ph.D. thesis by a German killed in the first World War. Although I put down *Die dramatische Technik des Sophokles*, 1917, by Tycho von Wilamowitz-Moellendorff as decisive for my change of view, he is not to be thought of as actually putting forward the change I now

[16] *Phaedrus* 264 C.
[17] Ingram Bywater, *Aristotle on the Art of Poetry*, 1909, pp. 71-3.
[18] S. H. Butcher *Aristotle's Theory of Poetry and Fine Art*, 1895, pp. 175-6.

advocate. What he chiefly did for me was to destroy the supposition that the essentially tragic runs through a play like the central core of Brighton rock. His main task was to wean his contemporaries from their longings for tragedies to be tragedies of *character*, and to demonstrate on the part of Sophocles a willingness to sacrifice consistency of plot and psychological probability for the sake of intense dramatic power in isolated spots. He destroyed for me the possibility of continuing to treat tragedies as *organisms*. Here is a characteristic judgement:

Es ist also der Sophokleischen Kunst gegenüber eine von vornherein unrichtige Forderung, so elementar sie den modernen Ansprüchen scheinen mag, daß sich aus allem, was innerhalb eines Stückes geschieht, und gar noch aus allem, was nur als geschehen vorausgesetzt wird, ein einheitlicher und bis ins einzelne konsequent und verständlich motivierter Hergang müßte konstruieren lassen; denn Sophokles hat dies gar nicht als einen an das Drama gestellten Anspruch empfunden, und Derartiges zu erreichen also niemals auch nur die Absicht gehabt. Bei einem Dramatiker, der noch als den einzigen Zweck seiner Stücke die Aufführung auf der Bühne im Auge haben mußte, ist es im Grunde nur natürlich, daß ihm die dramatische Wirkung der einzelnen Szene, der einzelnen Situation höher stand als Einheitlichkeit und Zusammenhang des Ganzen, daß er also nicht nach einem organischen und überall klaren Aufbau strebte, sondern wirklich, nach Goethes Ausdruck, einzelne Purpurstreifen zusammennähte, ohne sich davor zu scheuen, daß die Naht auch einmal sichtbar blieb.[19]

(Although it is nowadays regarded as a fundamental principle of dramatic art, it is altogether improper to ask that in the tragedies of Sophocles it should be possible to piece together from all the separate actions which occur in the play (to say nothing of all that must be assumed to have happened) a single, unified course of action, logically connected and plausibly motivated in every link. Since Sophocles never recognized this as a legitimate claim on him as a playwright, he never even attempted to introduce any such principle into his work. The sole aim of his dramatic production being to make a satisfactory impression on the stage, it is only natural that he should have cared more about the dramatic effectiveness of the single scene or situation than about the unity and coherence of the play as a whole. He therefore never aimed at bringing about a clearly-grasped organic structure, but, as Goethe put it, he sewed together purple patches without worrying too much whether here and there a seam should be visible to a spectator's eye.)

[19] Tycho von Wilamowitz-Moellendorff, *Die dramatische Technik des Sophokles*, 1917, pp. 39–40.

The final push was given to me when I began to put the name of Shakespeare in the place occupied by Sophocles in these formulations. I then came to see how mistaken I had been in the implied basic theory of my *Shakespeare's Tragedies of Love*. This in turn brought up in an acute form what I suppose everybody feels in a mild form, that the ending of *Macbeth* is *not* the place where we feel that the play is most tragic. It then came over me that the end of a tragedy is not the most tragic place in a tragedy just because it is the end but in virtue of another power which may not always be present at the end. I was then driven to contrast two things which happen to us in experiencing a tragedy. We may run through the whole length of a play, gaining a sense that all the conditions are right for a tragedy to occur. Some of these conditions are those I have been describing as essential constituents, that the people, the situation, the intellectual field of reference, the critical decisions taken by the hero, as well as all those conditions which form the basis of Aristotle's demands, are all such as to induce in us the conviction that our most serious self is being appealed to, and that if we let ourselves go we shall be taken up to a height we could not otherwise hope to ascend to. But Tragedy is not there until the sudden elevation occurs.

So long as we are attempting to define Tragedy by the response in the audience, we are bound to use some such phrase as 'sudden elevation' to describe the specific mark of the tragic. Unfortunately, we cannot say that on every occasion when we are lifted out of our seats the cause is discernibly the same. But, negatively, it can be firmly said that the sudden visitation by a sense of the tragic is not the inevitable result of the way the main action has been slowly constructed. This intense moment is not, strictly speaking, a *dramatic* event, although it will always be the one moment the play is remembered by. So rather than think of a range of mountain peaks, and call the moment of sudden tragic elevation a sort of Everest, we should think of it rather as the breath of a *supervenient spirit* coming unexpectedly down on the dramatic events. It will sound helplessly vague to use the language of the Bible: 'The wynde bloweth where he listeth, and thou hearest his sounde; but canst not tell whence he cometh and whether he goeth.'[20] But if we look at places in tragedies where it is generally agreed that the impression which tells us that 'here suddenly the tragic has come upon us' is forcibly felt, it might be possible to

---

[20]   William Tyndale, *The Gospell of S. John*, The iii. Chapter.

argue that the specifically tragic is different from a highly dramatic spot.

Different, but almost always coincidental with a moment of high drama. In fact, so difficult are the two aspects to separate in our impressions that it may sound artificial to split off a tragic side of a massive stage effect. A small example occurs when we come upon Lady Macbeth sleepwalking. Everybody feels the dramatic arrest and the close fit of the event with what has gone before and what we suspect will shortly be happening on the stage. But do we not also feel that by letting in news of what was going on in the unconscious mind we have entered a new dimension? But in this play this dimension has already been established in the 'visions' or 'hallucinations' undergone by Macbeth. The sleep-walking scene is a Snowdon rather than an Everest.

A more striking case occurs in the *Agamemnon* of Aeschylus, when *Cassandra* opens her mouth and on the dramatic plane forces us to think vividly of what is happening off-stage as Clytemnestra captures her husband, Agamemnon, in a net. I often used to wonder, when told by successive 'generations' of undergraduates how this moment seemed to them to dominate the whole play, whether they were responding to more than the powerful dramatic effect of this scene. But it is only recently that it has come over me that here we may detect the essence of the tragic. It will not convince readers that this is a verdict we are bound to accept unless we are equally convinced that the *Agamemnon* is more obviously a drama than a tragedy. We need not go so far as to call it a melodrama, but we notice how *broad* some of the dramatic moments are felt to be. The sight of Agamemnon stepping on to the red carpet is only one instance of an obviously melodramatic stroke. A proper balance must, however, be struck. The play contains more than this melodramatic core, and if we say that when Cassandra begins to reveal herself we feel we are in a new dimension, this is not the first time in the play that we have had such a hint. For although the play is strong on the *human* plane, it has been moving simultaneously, if obscurely, on a *religious* plane.

Nevertheless, if hard put to it to illustrate an earlier phrase 'the irruption on the scene of the incommensurable', I could point to the *difference* between Cassandra and all the other characters. Aeschylus, however, is just as anxious to show us a suffering *girl* with all the human anxieties and dreads. But the tragic aspect, I maintain, is there. I notice that the learned commentators do not want us to see her as divine in the remark by the Chorus:

μένει τὸ θεῖον δουλίᾳ περ ἐνφρενί (1084.)

and chide us into accepting that the phrase refers merely to the gift of prophecy. But Aeschylus goes out of his way to stress the powerful physical struggle between Cassandra and Apollo in which the god transmitted his gift of prophecy to the girl as a sort of wedding present, but later cursed the gift when the girl jilted him.

My suggestion would be that we separate the scene out into the 'prophecy' which concerns *us*, the audience, who know that she is not having a vision of the future but a hallucination of the present, and the awe and horror felt by the Chorus when they hear how the inspired girl, who is a complete stranger, yet detects the smell of blood which has been lingering about the place since the dreadful meal prepared by Atreus for Thyestes.

– τί δ' ἐστὶ χρῆμα; τίς σ' ἀποστρέφει φόβος;
– φεῦ φεῦ.
– τί τοῦτ' ἔφευξας; εἴ τι μὴ φρενῶν στύγος.
– φόνον δόμοι πνέουσιν αἱματοσταγῆ.
– καὶ πῶς; τόδ' ὄςει θυμάτων ἐφεστίων.
– ὅμοιος ἀτμὸς ὥσπερ ἐκ τάφου πρέπει. (1306–11.)

– What's wrong with you? Are you frightened? Why do you turn away?
– Horror! Horror!
– There's no cause for alarm, unless, that is, there lurks a feeling of loathing in your mind.
– The house breathes murder, a smell of dripping blood.
– Impossible! That is the usual smell of victims slaughtered in the sacrifice on the altar in the palace.
– I smell the stench from a charnel-house.

It is this divine apprehension of the blood crimes which down the centuries have defiled the families that lifts us above the dramatic plane.

Since we may not be able to enter sufficiently intimately into the sense that a god is speaking through Cassandra, I tentatively propose an event in Christian times which might be used as a helpful analogy. For it is comparatively easy for us to become shepherds in seventeenth-century England and inhabitants of the little town of Lichfield, and through their eyes witness the spectacle of the crazy Quaker, George Fox, walking barefoot through the streets. I cannot do better than give the Quaker's own account of the incident:

And as I was walking along, with several *Friends*, I lifted up my Head, and saw *Three Steeple-house-Spires*; and they struck at my *Life*. And I asked *Friends*, What Place that was? and they said, *Lichfield*. Immediately the *Word* of the *Lord* came to me, that I must *go thither*. So being come to the House, we were going to, I wish'd *Friends*, that were with me, to walk into the House; saying nothing to them, whither I was to go. And as soon as they were gone, I stept away, and went by my Eye over Hedge and Ditch, till I came within a *Mile* of *Lichfield*; where, in a great Field, there were *Shepherds* keeping their *Sheep*. Then was I commanded by the Lord to *pull off my Shoos*. And I stood still (for it was *Winter*:) And the *Word* of the *Lord* was like a *Fire* in me. So I *put off my Shoos*, and left them with the *Shepherds*; and the poor *Shepherds trembled*, and were astonished. Then I walked on about a *Mile*, till I came into the *City*; and as soon as I was got within the *City*, the *Word* of the *Lord* came to me again, saying; *Cry, Wo unto the bloody City of Lichfield*! So I went up and down the Streets, Crying with a loud Voice, *WO TO THE BLOODY CITY OF LICHFIELD!* And it being *Market-Day*, I went into the *Market-Place*, and to and fro in the several Parts of it, and made stands, Crying as before, *WO TO THE BLOODY CITY OF LICHFIELD!* And no one laid Hands on me. But as I went thus Crying through the Streets, there seemed to me to be a *Channel* of *Blood* running down the *Streets*, and the *Market-Place* appeared like a *Pool* of *Blood*. Now, when I had declared, what was upon me, and felt my self Clear, I went out of the Town in Peace; and returning to the *Shepherds*, gave them some Money, and took my *Shoos* of them again. But the *Fire* of the *Lord* was so in my *Feet*, and all over me, that I did not matter to put on my *Shoos* any more; and was at a stand, whether I should or no; till I felt freedom from the *Lord* so to do: and then, after I had washed my Feet, I put on my *Shoos* again. After this, a deep Consideration came upon me, Why, or for what reason, I should be sent to *Cry against that City*, and call it *THE BLOODY CITY*? For though the *Parliament* had the *Minister* one while, and the *King* another while, and much *Blood* had been shed in the *Town,* during the *Wars* between them; yet that was no more, than had befallen many other Places. But afterwards I came to understand, that in the Emperor *Diocletian*'s Time a *Thousand Christians* were *Martyred* in *Lichfield*. So I was to go, without my *Shoos*, through the *Channel* of their *Blood*; and into the *Pool* of their *Blood* in the *Market-Place*, that I might *Raise up the Memorial of the Blood of those Martyrs*, which had been shed above a *Thousand Years* before, and lay *Cold* in their *Streets.* So the Sense of this *Blood* was upon me, and I obeyed the *Word* of the *Lord*. *Ancient Records* testify, how many of the *Christian Britains* suffered there. And much I could write of the

Sense I had of the *Blood* of the *Martyrs*, that hath been shed in this
Nation for the *Name* of *Christ*, both under the *Ten Persecutions*, and
since; but I leave it to the *Lord*, and to his *Book*, out of which all shall
be Judged: For his *Book* is a most certain, true *Record*, and his *Spirit*
a true *Recorder*.[21]

Returning to the *Agamemnon*, it seems to me a reasonable claim
that we see further into the human condition as a result of getting
through Cassandra truths otherwise inaccessible to mortals. It is because
Cassandra makes the divine agents, *Ātē* and Erinys, concrete, as in this
passage (see pp. 1186–93):

I tell you that this house is for ever haunted by a company of drunken
singers making hideous melody of their unison. Human blood has made
them bold. They refuse to leave the palace, they keep up their ghastly
parties there. These squatters noone dare evict are the Erinyes who are
looking to avenge their dead connections in this family. What they sing
in their blood-tipsy songs as they occupy all the best rooms is the story
of the *Ātē* who blinded and infatuated the first in the line of defile-
ment. Each Erinys spits in turn on each brother's bed with hatred of
the men who defiled them . . .

that we are carried up to the tragic plane. (I shall return to this theme
when discussing the figure of Cassandra in Euripides' play, *The Trojan
Women*.)

Much as I could wish to promote this suggestion, I must guard
against two possible misconceptions. Although I am likening the
essence of Tragedy to a visiting spirit, a wandering voice like that of
Ariel to the human beings on the island in Shakespeare's *The Tempest*,
I do not think we find it in pregnant *sentences*. I have elsewhere
deprecated the use made of *Ripeness is all* as in some way expressing
the essence of Tragedy. I feel equally strongly about a similar misuse of
the line in Dante:

> E'n la sua uoluntade è nostra pace.
>
> And in his will is our peace.

Another misconception could arise if the definition of the spirit of
Tragedy were used to elevate cryptic fragments, such as *Woyzeck*,

[21] George Fox *his Journal*, 1694, pp. 53–4. This version was prepared by
Thomas Ellwood. It has, for my purpose, the advantage over the text based on
Fox's MSS, published by the CUP in 1952, of adding little touches telling us how
the story struck a contemporary.

into great tragedies. This abuse forces me to declare that there must be something pretty extensive already there in the dramatic way for the spirit to supervene upon.

The upshot of this long discussion has been to present us with the greatest possible paradox, that we enter a vast universe of infinite depth in what might take in the theatre less than a minute, that all time is present in a moment which does not occur in a sequence of time. But how can we speak of such moments? They seem as difficult to pin down as the moment described in Eliot's *The Dry Salvages*:

> But to apprehend
> The point of intersection of the timeless
> With time, is an occupation for the saint —
> No occupation either, but something given
> And taken, in a lifetime's death in love,
> Ardour and selflessness and self-surrender.
> For most of us, there is only the unattended
> Moment, the moment in and out of time,
> The distraction fit, lost in a shaft of sunlight,
> The wild thyme unseen, or the winter lightning
> Or the waterfall, or music heard so deeply
> That it is not heard at all, but you are the music
> While the music lasts.

They certainly cannot be lifted out of their contexts in the plays and then placed side by side. Which has the unfortunate consequence that further exploration cannot be pursued in these pages, for justification of my claims for these supreme moments could only emerge out of a running commentary on a whole play, such as I hope to present in a separate volume dealing with the plays by Euripides, Seneca, and Racine on the theme of Phaedra and Hippolytus.

Yet even when allowed the necessary space in a full commentary on a whole play, I should still find it difficult to say much about the apprehension of the supervenient tragic spirit. Although great offence can be given if the sudden elevation undergone by a man wholly attending to the tragic moment with his whole being is likened to the ecstasy of the mystic, there does seem to be something of the same order going on, at least so far as we can judge by the literary remains of people who had such a visitation to report. Although nobody, I take it, would care to define what St Paul was referring to when he told the Corinthians that he was once snatched up as far as the 'third heaven', we can sympathize with his phrase εἴτε ἐν σώματι οὐκ οἶδα, εἴτε ἐκτὸς τοῦ σώματος οὐκ οἶδα, ὁ θεὸς οἶδεν (was I in the body or out of it? God knows.) And when S. Juan de la Cruz in his *Cántico Espiritual* has his female figure say:

> Apártalos, Amado,
> Que voy de vuelo.

> Take them away from me, Beloved, for I fly away.

we can travel some way across the frail bridge constructed by his later commentary, where the saint described the visitations of God to the desiring Soul. We may seem to be following him when he goes on:

Y como ahora el alma con tantas ansias había deseado estos divinos ojos, que en la canción pasada acaba de decir, descubrióle el Amado algunos rayos de su grandeza y divinidad, según ella deseaba; los cuales fueron de tanta alteza y con tanta fuerza comunicados, que la hizo salir por arrobamiento y éxstasi . . .

The soul was in such rapture and ecstasy that she flew out of the body when she felt the full majesty and violence of the lights from the eyes of the Beloved (as mentioned in the preceding lines of the poem), those divine eyes which she had been wishing for with such passionate longing . . .

But perhaps this is merely another instance of *obscurum per obscurius*?

6

PATHOS (I): THE DEATH OF PRIAM

Some of the most interesting problems concerning Tragedy are also the most intractable. Here, the only policy for the would-be elucidator is 'by indirections find directions out'. One such problem, for me, is that of Form, and, in particular, the question, why does tragedy seem to require such tight restriction? It is a great fallacy to suppose that one Big Question calls for one Big Answer. Ducking that Temptation, I propose in this chapter to start from a single thought, that Tragedy is a way of making the unbearable bearable, that is to say, I shall try to keep to the *feelings* involved in tragedies both on the stage and among the audience. Although in the nature of things the feelings which crop up most frequently are those aroused by pain and suffering, the enquiry is general, and includes joy and ecstasy. I am asking myself why people seem to require tight restriction in the expression of such feelings both on the stage and among the audience. In this attempt to discover the laws of true and false pathos as they affect Tragedy, and the emotional quality of the proper response to Tragedy, I shall ignore the possible case of feeling failing to reach the tragic volume and intensity. My question will always presuppose that the tragic situations are such that the poet rightly tells us, 'If you haue teares, prepare to shed them now', and that therefore any restrictions to be imposed on Tragedy are restrictions on a full or overflowing flood of emotion.

In any European country but England the parenthesis I am about to enter on would sound ridiculous. It might not be so urgently called for in other English universities as it is in Cambridge. But if all those in English universities who are professionally engaged in discussing poems and plays with undergraduates could assemble to compare notes, they might remove my suspicion that Cambridge is the only place where the leader in a discussion finds himself surrounded with Men (and Women) of No Feeling, who pride themselves on their possession of Bacon's *siccum lumen* (dry light). But all my experience confirms a general note which I. A. Richards included in his *Practical Criticism*:

The man who, in reaction to the commoner naïve forms of sentimentality, prides himself upon his hard-headedness and hard-heartedness, his hard-boiledness generally, and seeks out or invents aspects with a bitter or squalid character, for no better reason than this, is only displaying a more sophisticated form of sentimentality. Fashion, of course, is responsible for many of these secondary twists. Indeed the control of Society over our sentiments, over our publicly avowable sentiments, is remarkably efficient. Compare, for example, the attitudes to tears (especially to masculine tears) approved by the eighteenth and twentieth centuries. Very little reflection and inquiry will show conclusively that the eighteenth century in regarding a profuse discharge of the lachrymal glands as a proper and almost necessary accompaniment of tender and sorrowful emotion was much more representative of humanity in all ages than are our contemporary wooden-eyed stoics. . . .

A widespread general inhibition of all the simpler expansive developments of emotion (not only of its expression) has to be recognised among our educated population. It is a new condition not easily paralleled in history, and though it is propagated through social convention its deeper causes are not easy to divine.[1]

Fifty years do not seem to have brought about any difference. Richards cited as a poem his undergraduates could not take seriously Wordsworth's *We Are Seven*. It is still too much (or too little) for undergraduates today. And has the reader never come across a budding literary critic who has found Miranda gushing, when she saw the shipwreck and exclaimed:

> Oh! I haue suffered
> With those that I saw suffer . . .?

Be that as it may, whatever our little local difficulties with the expression of our English feelings, there is no doubt that it has always and everywhere been difficult to distinguish true and false pathos in actual experience, and even more difficult to find the laws or principles involved. To illustrate the point, that here critics are bound to disagree, and that we may find it hard to choose between them, I take an eminent example from Homer's *Odyssey*, which forces us to say whether we believe or repudiate the claim that the restriction on the expression of feeling imposed by the poet and projected on to the heroine was made with a proper regard for the difference between true and false pathos.

The passage I have chosen concerns the silent interview between

---

[1] I. A. Richards, *Practical Criticism*, 1929, pp. 268–9.

Penelope and Odysseus in the Twenty-Third Book. It qualifies as a good test case because Homer expressly tells us that as Penelope came downstairs to meet her husband, who, after killing the suitors and tidying up the mess, was sitting against a pillar awaiting his wife,

$$\pi o\lambda\lambda\grave{\alpha} \ \delta\acute{\epsilon} \ o\acute{\iota} \ \kappa\tilde{\eta}\rho$$

ὅρμαιν',

(her heart was in tumult,)

and her first impulse was to embrace her husband. Instead, as Madame Dacier wrote:

En finissant ces mots elle commence à descendre, & en descendant elle délibéroit en son cœur si elle parleroit à son mari sans l'approcher, ou si elle l'aborderoit pour le saluer & l'embrasser. Quand elle fut arrivée dans la salle, elle s'assit près de la muraille vis-à-vis d'Ulysse, qu'elle vit à la clarté du feu, & qui assis près d'une colomne, les yeux baissez depuis qu'il l'eut apperceue, attendoit ce que lui diroit cette verteuse épouse. Mais elle gardoit le silence, le cœur serré de crainte & d'étonnement. Tantôt elle jettoit les yeux sur lui & sembloit le reconnoître, & tantôt elle les détournoit and le méconnoissoit, trompée par les haillons dont il était couvert.[2]

It is not because I wish my view to predominate that I have offered the scene in dry French prose. But I must admit that in this garb the passage affects me more than in the version by Robert Fitzgerald:

> She turned then to descend the stair, her heart
> in tumult. Had she better keep her distance
> and question him, her husband? Should she run
> up to him, take his hands, kiss him now?
> Crossing the door-sill she sat down at once
> in firelight, against the nearest wall,
> across the room from the lord Odysseus.
>   There
> leaning against a pillar, sat the man
> and never lifted up his eyes, but only waited
> for what his wife would say when she had seen him.
> And she, for a long time, sat deathly still
> in wonderment — for sometimes as she gazed
> she found him — yes, clearly — like her husband,
> but sometimes blood and rags were all she saw.[3]

---

[2] Madame Dacier *L'Odyssée d'Homere* (1717), Livre XXIII pp. 269–70.
[3] Robert Fitzgerald, *Homer: The Odyssey*, 1962, p. 388.

But what makes this an eminent test case for me is that I find I am obliged to differ from both of the views expressed by two eminent critics, René Rapin and Alexander Pope. The latter sets out his difference with the former very fairly in the note on this passage in his translation:

This book contains the Discovery of *Ulysses* to *Penelope*. Monsieur *Rapin* is very severe upon some parts of it; whose objections I shall here recite.

The discovery of *Ulysses* to his Queen was the most favourable occasion imaginable for the Poet to give us some of the nicest touches of his art; but as he has manag'd it, it has nothing but faint and weak surprizes, cold and languishing astonishments, and very little of that delicacy and exquisiteness which ought to express a conjugal tenderness: He leaves his wife too long in doubt and distrust, and she is too cautious and circumspect; the formalities she observes in being fully assur'd, and her care to act with security, are set down in number and measure, lest she should fall into any mistake; and this particularity makes the story dull, in a place that so much requires briskness and liveliness. Ought not the secret instinct of her love to have inspir'd her with other sentiments? and should not her heart have told her, what her eyes could not? Love is penetrating, and whispers more to us than the senses can convey; but *Homer* understood not this Philosophy: *Virgil*, who makes *Dido* foresee that *Aeneas* designs to leave her, would have made better advantage of this favourable opportunity.

The strength of this objection consists chiefly in the long incredulity of *Penelope*, and the slowness she uses to make an undeniable discovery: This *Rapin* judges to be contrary to the passion of love, and consequently that the Poet writes unnaturally.

There is somewhat of the *Frenchman* in this Criticism: *Homer* in his opinion wants vivacity; and if *Rapin* had been to have drawn *Ulysses*, we had seen him all transport and ecstasy. But where there is most fancy, there is often the least judgment. *Penelope* thought *Ulysses* to be dead; he had been absent twenty years; and thro' absence and his present disguise, he was another person from that *Ulysses* whom she knew, when he sail'd to Troy; so that he was become an absolute stranger. From this observation we may appeal to the Reader's judgment, if *Penelope*, without full conviction, ought to be persuaded that this person was the real *Ulysses*? And how could she be convinc'd, but by asking many questions, and descending to particularities, which must necessarily occasion delay in the discovery? If indeed *Ulysses* and *Penelope* had met after a shorter absence, when one view would have assured her that he was her real husband, then too much transport could not have been express'd by the Poet; but this is not the case, she is first to know her husband, before she could or ought express her fondness for his return, otherwise she might be in danger of misplacing it upon an impostor: But she is no sooner convinced that *Ulysses* is actually returned, but she receives him with as much fondness as can be expressed, or as *Rapin* could require.

> While yet he speaks, her pow'rs of life decay,
> She sickens, trembles, falls, and faints away:
> At length recov'ring, to his arms she flew,
> And strain'd him close, as to his breast she grew.

'Till this moment the discovery was not evidently made, and her passion would have been unseasonable; but this is no sooner done, but she falls into an agony of affection. If she had here appear'd cool and indifferent, there had been weight in *Rapin*'s objections.[4]

Nobody can deny that Penelope is constantly being presented to us in this poem as a canny creature, peculiarly given to shrewd calculations. Nevertheless I find myself unsatisfied with the view that she appears at this moment solely in this character. I cannot help wondering whether the pleasure I get from the tautness of this interview, where the eyes are active but the heart is silent, does not come from a sense that both figures are behaving in this restrained way from an inward greatness, a feeling governed by the critical moment, and the tension over so many years of waiting and absence, knowing, as it were, it is about to snap. To me, at this moment, both figures fill out and assume their heroic proportions. We learn what it is to be a man and a woman.

If this is true of Homer, it is certainly true of Shakespeare at the point in *Macbeth* when news is brought to Macduff that:

> Your Castle is surpriz'd: your Wife, and Babes
> Sauagely slaughter'd: To relate the manner
> Were on the Quarry of these murther'd Deere
> To adde the death of you . . .

and he is unable to say anything, while Malcolm expostulates:

> What, man, ne're pull your hat vpon your browes:
> Giue sorrow words . . .

But Macduff cannot take in the full enormity of the deed, and gasps out the details. And when Malcolm challenges him with:

---

[4] Alexander Pope *The Odyssey of Homer* Vol. V. (1726), 'Observations on the Twenty-Third Book', pp. 193–5. The reader who wishes to attribute these remarks to *Broome* is asked to pardon my wish to father them on Pope.

          Dispute it like a man

he replies:

                    I shall do so:
          But I must also feele it as a man . . . .

The critical moment comes when he decides to let reality invade him,
but to convert his feeling *into action:*

                         let griefe
               Conuert to anger: blunt not the heart, enrage it.
             — O I could play the woman with mine eyes,
               And Braggart with my tongue. But gentle Heauens
               Cut short all intermission: Front to Front,
               Bring thou this Fiend of Scotland, and my selfe,
               Within my Swords length set him, if he scape
               Heauen forgiue him too.
             — This tune goes manly.

   It will take me some time to develop the full significance of this
response. In the meantime let me say that the general law to be derived
from these two examples is easy to draw out because we can arrive at it
by so many different routes. If 'restraint' is to be considered a literary
virtue, it must be free of the suspicion voiced by Roy Campbell in his
poem *On Some South African Novelists:*

               You praise the firm restraint with which they write —
               I'm with you there, of course:
               They use the snaffle and the curb all right,
               But where's the bloody horse?[5]

Restraint is to be valued only where there was something powerful to
restrain. A severe form is valued in proportion to the tension created
between the expanding and the retaining forces. (Is that what Blake
meant by his 'wiry bounding line'?)[6] In the realm of pathos we are not
touched unless we feel that the suffering figures on the stage were
feeling the pain keenly. It would be utterly frigid if they struck us as
trained Stoics or hardened Red Indians.
   A similar contrast of 'manly' and 'womanly' will be found in a

---

   [5] Roy Campbell, *Adamastor*, 1930, p. 104.
   [6] No doubt he had much more than this in mind when he wrote in his
Descriptive Catalogue of 1809, 'The great and golden rule of art, as well as of life,
is this: That the more distinct, sharp and wiry the bounding line, the more
perfect the work of art. . . .'

passage of the Tenth Book of Plato's *Republic*: 'When a private afflic-tion visits us, you know how we pride ourselves on our ability to keep calm and bear it to the end, because that is what we think a man ought to do, and anything else would be what we should expect from a woman.' (605 E.) But behind this merely sociological observation there lies a deeper thought, that in supreme tragedy the hero fights against his misery and finds a spirit inside him which triumphs even when the hero himself is killed. Plato holds that there is a conflict inside a man who has lost somebody dear to him. He has to fight back and use all his strength to moderate his grief. Plato uses his tripartite 'scheme' of the soul to define the two internal contestants. On the one hand, we have the noble faculty which is equipped to obey reason and law, and, on the other, a passionate desire to give grief the long rein and abandon the whole soul to expressing it. Plato accuses tragic poets of working up and gratifying this insatiable appetite for tears and lamentation. Plato undoubtedly strikes home when he speaks of the pleasure we obtain from 'giving way' to such feelings and allowing these feelings to swell with the increase of gratification. He is surely right in saying that the audience, too, loves such moments. (It is possible that Dickens's popularity rested more on the provision of such emotional outings than on his presentation of general nature.) At any rate the following passage will set out the main argument of this chapter:

I should like the best among you to listen to what I have to say. For you know what happens to us whenever we hear Homer or one of the great tragic poets presenting a hero who in his affliction and suffering reels off a long tirade, abandons the tone of ordinary iambic verse, and takes to lyric and dithyrambic modes, and accompanies his rant with beating of his breast and tearing of his hair. You all know how keenly we follow him in every step of his suffering and abandon our whole souls to him. We take in everything with the utmost seriousness, and the more the hero makes us share in his sufferings, the greater we think the poet who created him. (605 C–D.)

Although this passage from the *Republic* will serve as a *Leitmotiv* throughout my consideration of pathetic *tirades*, and although it confirms the first point I have been making, that one mark of true pathos is a certain *restraint*, yet we cannot expect to remain any longer with Plato for the simple reason that he is not only averse to false pathos but to *all* expressions of powerful feelings which require the whole soul to become involved. For Plato, *all* tirades are out. My task must be to discriminate. Given that this is a field where opinions are usually divided, in order to open the argument in a way which might command attention, I need to hit on an easy and obvious distinction between a true and a false form of pathos. But even with the crassest examples, difficulties, and difficulties that are not easily to be removed, arise to cast a mist on the mirror, as will be immediately apparent when the reader discovers that my first try to increase clarity is supposed to emerge from contrasting two narratives concerning an event in the Trojan War in which the Greeks finally triumph and the Trojan King, *Priam*, is brutally murdered by the son of Achilles. For the sake of economy and in the hope of getting much done in the space of two chapters, I shall confine myself to examples of pathos which arise as a direct consequence of this war.

Several advantages accrue from this strategy. Not the least is the exemplary treatment this war received from both Homer and Virgil, who make it easy for us to consider all wars, past, present, and future, as alike subjects for pathos. Second, and as a result of this huge background, we break out of the narrow consideration of the conflict inside the individual. I have not lost sight of the distinction D. H. Lawrence was drawing between huge but meaningless disasters and true tragedies, but I hope I can take for granted that when the topic is the fall of a *precious civilization* rather than a casualty list running into millions, and when the loss of a father merges into the sense that an empire falls with him, the grief to be expressed by the survivors demands an enormous space in our imaginative response.

There is, however, a special disadvantage for a reader to whom my chosen examples are not very familiar. All decisions about true and false pathos are determined by the *context* in which they occur. For in all tragedies we attend most keenly and critically to the actual speaker who is venting his feelings. We do not therefore neglect our estimate of the general situation to which the speaker is responding, but everything depends on our *fellow-feeling* with the speaker. (I shall incidentally be demonstrating the truth of this remark in shifting attention in the course of these two chapters from Priam to *Hecuba*, and then from Hecuba to *Cassandra*, in order to bring out the different demands we make when these figures come up separately for consideration.) But we must have some prior feeling about this war in which all three are victims. We must know what right we have to call the fall of Troy the death of a precious civilization, and, although we need not imitate our ancestors in thinking that it was a *historical* catastrophe, and that the

Romans, the French and the English, are actually the remnants of Troy, we must be able to feel that the fiction is large enough to embrace all the civilizations of Western Europe, including, of course, that of classical Greece.

My first example requires us to appreciate the situation of two men reacting to the same fact of a dear father murdered, but the call for action in each case is very different, and we are therefore going to bring different criteria to bear on our verdict on their pathetic tirades. *Aeneas*, the hero of Virgil's *Aeneid*, has been presented by the author as doing all that a fighter like Macbeth could be expected to do. It is not his fault that the Greeks proved the stronger and Priam fell a victim to a brutal assault. Readers of Virgil know how often when left to himself the Trojan hero was liable to hysterical outbursts of grief, and needed severe divine admonition to turn away from prostrate grief to effective evasive action. All the time Aeneas is a *reluctant* hero, and more attached to all that made Troy a precious homeland than to vague promises of a larger empire in the West. He is still reluctant to return to these events when Dido presses him to retell the tale of the fall of Troy. He is no loose-mouthed whore enjoying an opportunity to 'let himself go' in a gorgeous wallow of grief. We must place weight on his first word:

Infandum, regina, iubes renouare dolorem.

Your majesty is asking me to feel afresh a pain I cannot express in words.

There is a religious overtone to *infandum*, a suggestion of things *tabu*, things religion requires us to keep silent about. Nevertheless if you open the Second Book of the *Aeneid*, you know what Dante was alluding to when he expressed his awed admiration of the poet who had come to save him from damnation:

Or se' tu quel Virgilio e quella fonte
che spandi di parlar sì largo fiume?

I take it that you are the famous poet who pours out such a stream of words from your abundant spring.

The contrast with the situation of Shakespeare's Hamlet when he met the Players may appear at first sight to be so great as to be crushing. Hamlet is not the leader of a nation, he has not yet been able to convince himself that he could outshine a Fortinbras. But he had a real father murdered, and that father a King. On the other hand, we might come to think that he still had a field for action, that his grief had a proper vent in avenging the murder and taking over the kingdom of Denmark. There is one great advantage for us, however, in that Shakespeare was very much in our position as regards this moment in the *Aeneid*. He rightly saw the death of Priam as an occasion for tears. My comparison of Virgil and Shakespeare requires it to be taken as a fact that when Aeneas asked:

> quis talia fando
> temperet a lacrimis?

who could tell such a tale without bursting into tears?

the *orbis terrarum* has replied *nem. con.* 'nobody'. Since my argument fails without this universal chorus, I will mention another poet who, like Shakespeare, could not refrain from tears, – Tennyson. In case we recall him only as the man who was always giving way to 'female' outbursts such as

> Always I long to creep
> To some still cavern deep
> And to weep and weep and weep
>   My whole soul out to thee . . .

we need to retain the impeccable witness of FitzGerald, who twice recorded that in a long and intimate friendship he only twice saw a tear glisten in the poet's eye – thus confirming how powerful nineteenth-century society was in restraining manly tears – and one of the occasions was on rereading this part of Virgil's *Aeneid*.

Has the chain Dante-Shakespeare-Tennyson snapped for us in this century? Do we find the passage on the death of Priam in Virgil *too abundant* a stream of words? Are we all nowadays more like Polonius than Hamlet? Or even if we are still capable of tears and prepared to shed them, do we find them springing from the perusal of Latin hexameters? To enable us to appreciate Hamlet's situation more keenly, I have chosen to accompany the original Latin with *Dryden*'s version because of the remarkable fact that, although from his Westminster days a fanatical devotee of Virgil's Latin, when in his old age he undertook to translate this author, the very passage of *Hamlet* I am about to use for my comparison came into Dryden's mind, and, what is more, came *between* him and Virgil. For this reason alone we cannot regard Shakespeare's passage as a failure to create pathos.

Vestibulum ante ipsum primoque in limine Pyrrhus
exsultat telis et luce coruscus aëna:
qualis ubi in lucem coluber mala gramina pastus,
frigida sub terra tumidum quem bruma tegebat,
nunc, positis nouus exuuiis nitidusque iuuenta,
lubrica conuoluit sublato pectore terga
arduus ad solem, et linguis micat ore trisulcis.
una ingens Periphas et equorum agitator Achillis,
armiger Automedon, una omnis Scyria pubes
succedunt tecto et flammas ad culmina iactant.
ipse inter primos correpta dura bipenni
limina perrumpit postisque a cardine uellit
aeratos; iamque excisa trabe firma cauauit
robora et ingentem lato dedit ore fenestram.
apparet domus intus et atria longa patescunt;
apparent Priami et ueterum penetralia regum,
armatosque uident stantis in limine primo.
at domus interior gemitu miseroque tumultu
miscetur, penitusque cauae plangoribus aedes
femineis ululant; ferit aurea sidera clamor.
tum pauidae tectis matres ingentibus errant
amplexaeque tenent postis atque oscula figunt.
instat ui patria Pyrrhus; nec claustra nec ipsi
custodes sufferre ualent; labat ariete crebro
ianua, et emoti procumbunt cardine postes.
fit uia ui; rumpunt aditus primosque trucidant
immissi Danai et late loca milite complent.
non sic, aggeribus ruptis cum spumeus amnis
exiit oppositasque euicit gurgite moles,
fertur in arua furens cumulo camposque per omnis
cum stabulis armenta trahit. uidi ipse furentem
caede Neoptolemum geminosque in limine Atridas,
uidi Hecubam centumque nurus Priamumque per aras
sanguine foedantem quos ipse sacrauerat ignis.
quinquaginta illi thalami, spes tanta nepotum,
barbarico postes auro spoliisque superbi
procubuere; tenent Danai qua deficit ignis.
    Forsitan et Priami fuerint quae fata requiras.
urbis uti captae casum conuulsaque uidit
limina tectorum et medium in penetralibus hostem,
arma diu senior desueta trementibus aeuo
circumdat nequiquam umeris et inutile ferrum
cingitur, ac densos fertur moriturus in hostis.

aedibus in mediis nudoque sub aetheris axe
ingens ara fuit iuxtaque ueterrima laurus
incumbens arae atque umbra complexa penatis.
hic Hecuba et natae nequiquam altaria circum,
praecipites atra ceu tempestate columbae,
condensae et diuum amplexae simulacra sedebant.
ipsum autem sumptis Priamum iuuenalibus armis
ut uidit, 'quae mens tam dira, miserrime coniunx,
impulit his cingi telis? aut quo ruis?' inquit.
'non tali auxilio nec defensoribus istis
tempus eget; non, si ipse meus nunc adforet Hector.
huc tandem concede; haec ara tuebitur omnis,
aut moriere simul.' sic ore effata recepit
ad sese et sacra longaeuum in sede locauit.
    Ecce autem elapsus Pyrrhi de caede Polites,
unus natorum Priami, per tela, per hostis
porticibus longis fugit et uacua atria lustrat
saucius, illum ardens infesto uulnere Pyrrhus
insequitur, iam iamque manu tenet et premit hasta.
ut tandem ante oculos euasit et ora parentum,
concidit ac multo uitam cum sanguine fudit.
hic Priamus, quamquam in media iam morte tenetur,
non tamen abstinuit nec uoci iraeque pepercit:
'at tibi pro scelere,' exclamat, 'pro talibus ausis
di, si qua est caelo pietas quae talia curet,
persoluant grates dignas et praemia reddant
debita, qui nati coram me cernere letum
fecisti et patrios foedasti funere uultus.
at non ille, satum quo te mentiris, Achilles
talis in hoste fuit Priamo; sed iura fidemque
supplicis erubuit corpusque exsangue sepulcro
reddidit Hectoreum meque in mea regna remisit.'
sic fatus senior telumque imbelle sine ictu
coniecit, rauco quod protinus aere repulsum,
et summo clipei nequiquam umbone pependit.
cui Pyrrhus: 'referes ergo haec et nuntius ibis
Pelidae genitori. illi mea tristia facta
degeneremque Neoptolemum narrare memento.
nunc morere.' hoc dicens altaria ad ipsa trementem
traxit et in multo lapsantem sanguine nati,
implicuitque comam laeua, dextraque coruscum
extulit ac lateri capulo tenus abdidit ensem.
haec finis Priami fatorum, hic exitus illum

sorte tulit Troiam incensam et prolapsa uidentem
Pergama, tot quondam populis terrisque superbum
regnatorem Asiae. iacet ingens litore truncus,
auulsumque umeris caput et sine nomine corpus.[7]

    Before the Gate stood *Pyrrhus*, threat'ning loud,
With glitt'ring Arms conspicuous in the Crowd.
So shines, renew'd in Youth, the crested Snake,
Who slept the Winter in a thorny Brake:
And casting off his Slough, when Spring returns,
Now looks aloft, and with new Glory burns:
Restor'd with pois'nous Herbs, his ardent sides
Reflect the Sun, and rais'd on Spires he rides:
High o're the Grass, hissing he rowls along,
And brandishes by fits his forky Tongue.
Proud *Periphas*, and fierce *Automedon*,
His Father's Charioteer, together run
To force the Gate: The *Scyrian* Infantry
Rush on in Crowds, and the barr'd Passage free.
Ent'ring the Court, with Shouts the Skies they rend,
And flaming Firebrands to the Roofs ascend.
Himself, among the foremost, deals his Blows,
And with his Axe repeated Stroaks bestows
On the strong Doors: then all their Shoulders ply,
'Till from the Posts the brazen Hinges fly.
He hews apace, the double Bars at length
Yield to his Ax, and unresisted Strength.
A mighty Breach is made; the Rooms conceal'd
Appear, and all the Palace is reveal'd.
The Halls of Audience, and of publick State,
And where the lonely Queen in secret sate.
Arm'd Souldiers now by trembling Maids are seen,
With not a Door, and scarce a Space between.
The House is fill'd with loud Laments and Cries,
And Shrieks of Women rend the vaulted Skies.
The fearful Matrons run from place to place,
And kiss the Thresholds, and the Posts embrace.
The fatal work inhuman *Pyrrhus* plies,
And all his Father sparkles in his Eyes.
Nor Bars, nor fighting Guards his force sustain;
The Bars are broken, and the Guards are slain.
In rush the *Greeks*, and all the Apartments fill;

    [7] P. Vergili Maronis, *Aeneidos*, Liber II, 469–558.

Those few Defendants whom they find, they kill.
Not with so fierce a Rage, the foaming Flood
Roars, when he finds his rapid Course withstood:
Bears down the Dams with unresisted sway,
And sweeps the Cattle and the Cots away.
These Eyes beheld him, when he march'd between
The Brother-Kings: I saw th' unhappy Queen,
The hundred Wives, and where old *Priam* stood,
To stain his hallow'd Altar with his Blood.
The fifty Nuptial Beds: (such Hopes had he,
So large a Promise of a Progeny.)
The Posts of plated Gold, and hung with Spoils,
Fell the Reward of the proud Victor's Toils.
Where e're the raging Fire had left a space,
The *Grecians* enter, and possess the Place.
  Perhaps you may of *Priam*'s Fate enquire.
He, when he saw his Regal Town on fire,
His ruin'd Palace, and his ent'ring Foes,
On ev'ry side inevitable woes;
In Arms, disus'd, invests his Limbs decay'd
Like them, with Age; a late and useless aid.
His feeble shoulders scarce the weight sustain:
Loaded, not arm'd, he creeps along, with pain;
Despairing of Success; ambitious to be slain!
Uncover'd but by Heav'n, there stood in view
An Altar; near the hearth a Lawrel grew;
Dodder'd with Age, whose Boughs encompass round
The Households Gods, and shade the holy Ground.
Here *Hecuba*, with all her helpless Train
Of Dames, for shelter sought, but sought in vain.
Driv'n like a Flock of Doves along the skie,
Their Images they hugg, and to their Altars fly.
The Queen, when she beheld her trembling Lord,
And hanging by his side a heavy Sword,
What Rage, she cry'd, has seiz'd my Husband's mind;
What Arms are these, and to what use design'd?
These times want other aids: were *Hector* here,
Ev'n *Hector* now in vain, like *Priam* wou'd appear.
With us, one common shelter thou shalt find,
Or in one common Fate with us be join'd.
She said, and with a last Salute embrac'd
The poor old Man, and by the Lawrel plac'd.
Behold *Polites*, one of *Priam*'s Sons,

Pursu'd by *Pyrrhus*, there for safety runs.
Thro Swords, and Foes, amaz'd and hurt, he flies
Through empty Courts, and open Galleries:
Him *Pyrrhus*, urging with his Lance, pursues;
And often reaches, and his thrusts renews.
The Youth transfix'd, with lamentable Cries
Expires, before his wretched Parent's Eyes.
Whom, gasping at his feet, when *Priam* saw,
The Fear of Death gave place to Nature's Law.
And shaking more with Anger, than with Age,
The Gods, said He, requite thy brutal Rage:
As sure they will, Barbarian, sure they must,
If there be Gods in Heav'n, and Gods be just:
Who tak'st in Wrongs an insolent delight;
With a Son's death t' infect a Father's sight.
Not He, whom thou and lying Fame conspire
To call thee his; Not He, thy vaunted Sire,
Thus us'd my wretched Age: The Gods he fear'd,
The Laws of Nature and of Nations heard.
He chear'd my Sorrows, and for Sums of Gold
The bloodless Carcass of my *Hector* sold,
Pity'd the Woes a Parent underwent,
And sent me back in safety from his Tent.

This said, his feeble hand a Javelin threw,
Which flutt'ring, seem'd to loiter as it flew:
Just, and but barely, to the Mark it held,
And faintly tinckl'd on the Brazen Shield.

Then *Pyrrhus* thus: go thou from me to Fate;
And to my Father my foul deeds relate.
Now dye: with that he dragg'd the trembling Sire,
Slidd'ring through clotter'd Blood, and holy Mire,
(The mingl'd Paste his murder'd Son had made,)
Haul'd from beneath the violated Shade;
And on the Second Pile, the Royal Victim laid.
His right Hand held his bloody Fauchion bare;
His left he twisted in his hoary Hair:
Then, with a speeding Thrust, his Heart he found:
The lukewarm Blood came rushing through the wound,
And sanguine Streams distain'd the sacred Ground.
Thus *Priam* fell: and shar'd one common Fate
With *Troy* in Ashes, and his ruin'd State:
He, who the Scepter of all *Asia* sway'd,
Whom Monarchs like domestick Slaves obey'd.

On the bleak Shoar now lies th' abandon'd King,
A headless Carcass, and a nameless thing.[8]

Although making out the contrast between the Virgil and the
Player's own tirade will present no difficulties, it is quite another
matter to account for its presence in the play. In fact I have yet to read
a satisfactory explanation. Indeed for many critics who discuss the
whole play this episode has to be simply ignored. And we can see why.
Hamlet appears to be gratifying a mere whim, a sudden thought, in
asking for the speech. On the other hand, when we hear what Hamlet
apparently spouts with relish, and we see how Hamlet behaves during
the tirade, and, above all, what he says as soon as he is alone, it is
tempting to think that the tirade was nearer to both Shakespeare's and
to Hamlet's heart than either seems willing to make explicit. (For my
argument, however, it is not a fatal drawback that we cannot be sure
whether the tirade is entirely Shakespeare's own work.)

Enter the Players.

Ham. You are welcome maisters, welcome all, I am glad to see thee
  well, welcome good friends, oh old friend, why thy face is valanct
  since I saw thee last, com'st thou to beard me in Denmark? what my
  young Lady and mistris, by'r lady your Ladishippe is nerer to heauen,
  then when I saw you last by the altitude of a chopine, pray God
  your voyce like a peece of vncurrant gold, bee not crackt within the
  ring: maisters you are all welcome, weele ento't like French
  Falkners, fly at any thing we see, weele haue a speech straite, come
  giue vs a tast of your quality, come a passionate speech.
Player. What speech my good Lord?
Ham. I heard thee speake me a speech once, but it was neuer acted,
  or if it was, not aboue once, for the play I remember pleasd not
  the million, t'was cauiary to the generall, but it was as I receaued
  it and others, whose judgements in such matters cried in the top of
  mine, an excellent play, well digested in the scenes, set downe with
  as much modestie as cunning. I remember one sayd there were no
  sallets in the lines, to make the matter sauory, nor no matter in the
  phrase that might indite the author of affection, but cald it an
  honest method, as wholesome as sweete, and by very much, more
  handsome then fine: one speech in't I chiefely loued, Twas *Aeneas*
  talke to *Dido*, and there about of it especially when he speakes of
  Priams slaughter, if it liue in your memory begin at this line, let me

[8] John Dryden *The Second Book of the Aeneis*, 1697, 639–763. Dryden
acknowledged that he had taken the whole last line from Sir John Denham.

see, let me see, the rugged *Pirhus* like Th'ircanian beast, tis not so, it
beginnes with *Pirrhus,* the rugged *Pirhus*, he whose sable Armes,
Black as his purpose did the night resemble,
When he lay couched in th'omynous horse,
Hath now this dread and black complection smeard,
With heraldy more dismall head to foote,
Now is he totall Gules horridly trickt
With blood of fathers, mothers, daughters, sonnes,
Bak'd and empasted with the parching streetes
That lend a tirranus and a damned light
To their Lords murther, rosted in wrath and fire,
And thus ore-cised with coagulate gore,
With eyes like Carbunkles, the hellish *Pirrhus*
Old grandsire *Priam* seekes; so proceede you.
    Pol. Foregod my Lord well spoken, with good accent and good
    Play. Anon he finds him,   (discretion.
Striking too short at Greekes, his anticke sword
Rebellious to his arme, lies where it fals,
Repugnant to commaund; vnequall matcht,
Pirrhus at *Priam* driues, in rage strikes wide,
But with the whiffe and winde of his fell sword,
Th'vnnerued father fals: Then senselesse Illium,
Seeming to feele this blowe, with flaming top
Stoopes to his base; and with a hiddious crash
Takes prisoner *Pirrhus* eare, for loe his sword
Which was declining on the milkie head
Of reuerent *Priam*, seem'd i'th ayre to stick,
So as a painted tirant *Pirrhus* stood
Like a newtrall to his will and matter,
Did nothing:
But as we often see against some storme,
A silence in the heauens, the racke stand still,
The bold winds speechlesse, and the orbe belowe
As hush as death, anon the dreadfull thunder
Doth rend the region, so after *Pirrhus* pause,
Arowsed vengeance sets him new a worke,
And neuer did the Cyclops hammers fall,
On *Marses* Armor forg'd for proofe eterne,
With lesse remorse then *Pirrhus* bleeding sword
Now falls on *Priam*.
Out, out, thou strumpet Fortune, all you gods,
In generall sinod take away her power,
Breake all the spokes, and fellies from her wheele,

And boule the round naue downe the hill of heauen
As lowe as to the fiends.

    Pol. This is too long.

    Ham. It shall to the barbers with your beard; prethee say on,
he's for a Iigge, or a tale of bawdry, or he sleepes, say on, come to
Hecuba.

    Play. But who, a woe, had seene the mobled Queene,

    Ham. The mobled Queene.

    Pol. That's good: mobled Queene is good.

    Play. Runne barefoote vp and downe, threatning the flames
With *Bison* rheume, a clout vppon that head
Where late the Diadem stood, and for a robe,
About her lanck and all ore-teamed loynes,
A blancket in the alarme of feare caught vp,
Who this had seene, with tongue in venom steept,
Gainst fortunes state would treason haue pronounst;
But if the gods themselues did see her then,
When she saw *Pirrhus* make malicious sport
In mincing with his sword her husbands limmes,
The instant burst of clamor that she made,
Vnlesse things mortall mooue them not at all,
Would haue made milch the burning eyes of heauen
And passion in the gods.

    Pol. Looke where he has not turnd his cullour, and has teares
in's eyes, prethee no more.

    Ham. Tis well, Ile haue thee speake out the rest of this soone,
Good my Lord will you see the players well bestowed; doe you
heare, let them be well vsed, for they are the abstract and breefe
Chronicles of the time; after your death you were better haue a
bad Epitaph then their ill report while you liue.

    Pol. My Lord, I will vse them according to their desert.

    Ham. Gods bodkin man, much better, vse euery man after his
desert, and who shall scape whipping, vse rhem after your owne
honor and dignity, the lesse they deserue the more merrit is in your
bounty. Take them in.

    Pol. Come sirs.

    Ham. Follow him friends, weele heare a play to morrowe; dost
thou heare me old friend, can you play the murther of *Gonzago?*

    Play. I my Lord.

    Ham. Weele ha't to morrowe night, you could for a neede study
a speech of some dosen or sixteene lines, which I would set
downe and insert in't, could you not?

    Play. I my Lord.

    Ham. Very well, followe that Lord, and looke you mock him

not. My good friends, Ile leaue you tell night, you are welcome
to *Elsinoure.* *Exeunt Pol. and Players*
  Rof. Good my Lord. *Exeunt.*
  Ham. I so God buy to you, now I am alone,
O what a rogue and pesant slaue am I.
Is it not monstrous that this player heere
But in a fixion, in a dreame of passion
Could force his soule so to his owne conceit
That from her working all his visage wand,
Teares in his eyes, distraction in his aspect,
A broken voyce, an his whole function suting
With formes to his conceit; and all for nothing,
For *Hecuba*.
What's *Hecuba* to him, or he to her,
That he should weepe for her? what would he doe
Had he the motiue, and the cue for passion
That I haue: he would drowne the stage with teares,
And cleaue the generall eare with horrid speech,
Make mad the guilty, and appale the free,
Confound the ignorant, and amaze indeede
The very faculties of eyes and eares; yet I,
A dull and muddy metteld raskall peake,
Like Iohn-a-dreames, vnpregnant of my cause,
And can say nothing; no not for a King,
Vpon whose property and most deare life,
A damn'd defeate was made: am I a coward,
Who cals me villaine, breakes my pate a crosse,
Pluckes off my beard, and blowes it in my face,
Twekes me by the nose, giues me the lie i'th throate
As deepe as to the lunges, who does me this,
Hah, s'wounds I should take it: for it cannot be
But I am pidgion liuerd, and lack gall
To make oppression bitter, or ere this
I should a fatted all the region kytes
With this slaues offall, bloody, baudy villaine,
Remorslesse, trecherous, lecherous, kindlesse villaine.
Why what an Asse am I, this is most braue,
That I the sonne of a deere Father murthered,
Prompted to my reuenge by heauen and hell,
Must like a whore vnpacke my hart with words,
And fall a cursing like a very drabbe; a stallyon, fie vppont, foh.

One of the puzzles of this passage is the conflict between what
Hamlet says of the tirade and what almost everybody has thought.

In particular, the praise 'set downe with as much modestie as cunning' jars with the general impression that the tirade is guilty of the vice known to the French as *forcer la note*. French comes to mind because the law which is violated here was stated with classic power by Boileau in 1686 or thereabouts, when he found himself offended by the pompous inscriptions placed under the paintings of Le Brun, which were designed to portray the martial triumphs of Louis XIV, and in particular what was considered by contemporaries as his greatest exploit, the crossing of the Rhine in 1672. The law Boileau lays down for such inscriptions seems to me to fit our demand for modesty in an avowedly pathetic tirade which causes us to wipe away a tear: 'La pompe, ni la multitude des paroles n'y valent rien, et ne sont point propres au stile grave, qui est le vray stile des Inscriptions . . . .' and he points out the absurdity of trying to gild the lily by exaggerating the facts. It is his example which for me clinches the law: 'Il suffit d'énoncer simplement les choses pour les faire admirer. *Le passage du Rhin* dit beaucoup plus, que *le merveilleux passage du Rhin*.'[9]

What 'merveilleux' does to ruin the inscription is done, in my judgement, for Hamlet's part of the tirade by 'totall Gules'. Virgil makes it clear that beside being an offence to Heaven the sight of Priam's slaughter is an offence to the eyes. There is in fact blood all over the place. Dryden, too, missed the proper restraint, and therefore the powerful note of true pathos, in translating:

> hoc dicens altaria ad ipsa trementem
> traxit et in multo lapsantem sanguine nati

by:

> with that he dragg'd the trembling Sire,
> Slidd'ring through clotter'd Blood, and holy Mire,
> (The mingl'd Paste his murder'd Son had made,) . . .

But what are we to think of Hamlet's presentation of Pyrrhus?

> The rugged *Pirrhus*, he whose sable Armes,
> Black as his purpose, did the night resemble,
> When he lay couched in th'omynous horse,
> Hath now this dread and black complection smeard,
> With heraldry more dismall: head to foote,
> Now is he totall Gules, horridly trickt

---

[9] *Discours sur le Style des Inscriptions* (1684-6)

> With blood of fathers, mothers, daughters, sonnes,
> Bak'd and empasted with the parching streetes
> That lend a tirranous and a damned light
> To their Lords murther. . . .

By protesting too much, by 'forcing the note', Hamlet makes his Pyrrhus the kind of devil to frighten children but not one who might enter the region of our religious apprehension.

We notice that everything in the Player's narrative is designed to lead up to the following explosion:

> Out, out, thou strumpet Fortune, all you gods,
> In generall sinod take away her power,
> Breake all the spokes, and fellies from her wheele,
> And boule the round naue downe the hill of heauen
> As lowe as to the fiends.

This is the false, hysterical note which divides the restrained pathos of Virgil's narrative from Hamlet's and the Player's empty and consequently ridiculous conceits, which are forcible-feeble efforts to exaggerate each pathetic incident.

Some of these conceits are so silly and wide of the mark, that critics have been driven to conclude that Shakespeare must have seen this, too, and that Hamlet, Shakespeare's double here, must have been holding the tirade up to ridicule. This strikes me as desperate, and I will consider one example, the claim that Shakespeare was writing a *witty parody* of Marlowe when he composed this tasteless quip:

> *Pirrhus* at *Priam* driues, in rage strikes wide,
> But with the whiffe and winde of his fell sword,
> Th'vnnerued father fals . . .

It is true that in Marlowe's *Dido Queene of Carthage* our only text has *wound* for *wind*, but I expect that any reader of the passage would consider that Fredson Bowers was justified in printing Shakespeare's *wind*, as first suggested by Collier:

> *Aeneas.* At which the franticke Queene leapt on his face,
> And in his eyelids hanging by the nayles,
> A little while prolong'd her husbands life:
> At last the souldiers puld her by the heeles,
> And swong her howling in the emptie ayre,
> Which sent an eccho to the wounded King:
> Whereat he lifted up his bedred lims,

> And would have grappeld with *Achilles* sonne,
> Forgetting both his want of strength and hands,
> Which he disdaining whiskt his sword about,
> And with the wind thereof the King fell downe:[10]

It was only then, according to Marlowe, that the brutal murderer (who had already 'strooke off' Priam's hands) proceeded to give him the death-blow with his sword. What deters me from this speculation is the strong impression that the passages are too similar, that if Shakespeare had Marlowe before him, he was *imitating* rather than writing a parody. But the deepest puzzle for me is still the impossibility of deciding where Shakespeare stood in relation to his hero. Did he at this point regard Hamlet as wholly *compos mentis* and capable of detached irony at the Player's devotion to bathetic art, or did he wish us, his audience, to see Hamlet as a sick soul besotted with fantasies about playing a heroic part? Or, worse still, was Shakespeare, the actor and the actor-manager, so much uppermost that he uncritically approved of the tirade, and for this reason allowed Hamlet to admire it?

At any rate, the text suggests that Hamlet the Prince is in more than one respect identical with the actor who spouts this tirade on the death of Priam. Let us for the moment dismiss the self-reproach of cowardice, and ponder the self-betraying phrase, 'the Cue for passion'. Was not, we may think, Hamlet here exemplifying every word of Plato's complaint about poets, when we find Hamlet concluding that his response to his father's murder should take *this* form?

> Why, what an Asse am I, this is most braue,
> That I, the sonne of a deere Father murthered,
> Prompted to my reuenge by heauen and hell,
> Must like a whore vnpacke my hart with words,
> And fall a cursing like a very drabbe ...

The resemblance of Hamlet and the Player is best seen here:

> What's *Hecuba* to him, or he to her,
> That he should weepe for her? What would he doe,
> Had he the motiue and the Cue for passion
> That I haue? He would drowne the Stage with teares,
> And cleaue the generall eare with horrid speech:
> Make mad the guilty, and apale the free,

[10] *The Complete Works of Christopher Marlowe*, ed. Fredson Bowers, 2nd Ed., 1981, Vol. I, pp. 22–3.

Confound the ignorant, and amaze indeede
The very faculties of Eyes and Eares.

That, surely, is how we expect a complacent 'ham' actor to describe
the effect aimed at in his tirades.

7
PATHOS (II): HECUBA AND CASSANDRA

But who, a woe, had seene the mobled Queene . . .

The strongest impression on a reader who passes rapidly from the long speech in Virgil to the Player's tirade is of the almost diametrical opposition of scope. Virgil opens the eyes of the imagination on all the horrors of war, past, present, and to come. The Player focuses our minds on a distracted mother and wife. Virgil, however, gives the pacifist in us a jolt by showing us that the horror felt by the pacifist is not tragic. This is a hard saying, and must sound both heartless and graceless to those who cannot forget dear ones killed in the fighting. I am not one who can read Wilfred Owen's *Strange Meeting* without succumbing to the feeling of pity there evoked:

The pity of war, the pity war distilled.

But I must stand by the conviction that what arouses *tragic* pity is not the fate of the fighters in wars but the fate of those who are war's helpless victims. (And it is possible to believe that this is what Owen's combatants had become.) Consequently I am bound to pass the judgement that there was something a shade wrong (caused, perhaps, at least in part, by the guilty conscience of those of us who were non-combatants) in the proportion of our grief over the 'victims', as we called the soldiers and sailors of the First World War, and that we were ready to feel for the vaster numbers of the real victims of that war and its immediate aftermath. No young person to-day can have missed seeing at least one 'Cenotaph' in his native region. But I doubt whether he has given a thought to the scale of suffering in Europe endured by non-combatant women and children, who died as a direct or indirect consequence of the fighting.

To be a subject of Tragedy, war must come in, not as fighting, but as a type of those conditions which produce helpless victims. We see the right rule for pathos in Tragedy best when we concentrate on Hecuba rather than on Priam. Perhaps I should say 'several right rules', for she answers the need for our largest vistas over all that we cannot manage in our lives, and also for our concentrated sympathy as we are made to dwell on the particulars of her predicament. Hecuba could not figure in a successful tragedy if we thought she had a chance of escaping from her captors. But merely to *understand* that she is a helpless victim is not enough, we must *feel* it with her, in her own words. Yet she must somehow feel for everybody while feeling for herself. Hecuba would not be tragic if she did not feel her condition as Woman, as all humanity personified in the channels of a woman's body and mind. An immense outpouring is therefore required of her to bring about such a powerful effect. The golden rule is that expressed by Horace in his *Art of Poetry*: 'ut ridentibus arrident, ita flentibus adflent humani uultus. si uis me flere, dolendum est primum ipsi tibi . . .'[1] ('Just as we smile at those who smile, we weep with those who weep. If you want tears from me, you must first show me your own . . .') who explicitly applied the rule to two famous pathetic figures in Tragedy. *Hecuba must howl.* She must be felt to be suffering the unbearable in order that we may suffer bearably as we listen to her.

This view has excited formidable opposition, so formidable indeed that it would be suspicious behaviour to turn a blind eye on all that has been said against allowing *passive suffering* to be included among the heights of Tragedy. We certainly admire a dash of Quixotry in our heroes. We like to see them refusing to bow to what they know to be superior odds.

> What though the field be lost?
> All is not lost; the unconquerable Will,
> And study of revenge, immortal hate,
> And courage never to submit or yield:
> And what is else not to be overcome?[2]

This reference to Milton's Satan forces us to draw a necessary distinction between the heroic and the tragic. Not all heroes are tragic heroes. In fact we might say that supreme tragedy exists to bring heroes into situations which cannot be carried off by heroic behaviour. In the deepest tragedies the deepest moment sometimes comes when the hero knows that it would be romantic to act as if pride and the will to

---

[1] *Q. Horati Flacci qui uulgo uocatur liber De Arte Poetica*, 101-3. *Adsunt* is the reading of almost all the manuscripts. *Adflent* is an emendation strongly supported by Bentley.

[2] Milton, *Paradise Lost*, Book One, ll. 105-9.

struggle would carry him through. The triumph of the tragic hero lies on the other side of defeat and humiliation.

Nevertheless further progress in my argument cannot be made until the strength of the opposition has been tested. In the context of war, the pity of war, and the poetry written to express this pity, one instance could hardly be passed over. In 1935 W. B. Yeats was invited to collect poems for a volume to be called the *Oxford Book of Modern Verse*. He faced a chorus of reviewers, who objected in particular to the exclusion of 'War Poems', or rather to the omission of Wilfred Owen[3] and the inclusion of Herbert Read, and also to Yeats's defence of his anthology in his own Introduction:

I have a distaste for certain poems written in the midst of the great war; they are in all anthologies, but I have substituted Herbert Read's *End of a War* written long after. The writers of these poems were invariably officers of exceptional courage and capacity, one a man constantly selected for dangerous work, all, I think, had the Military Cross; their letters are vivid and humorous, they were not without joy — for all skill is joyful — but felt bound, in the words of the best known, to plead the suffering of their men. In poems that had for a time considerable fame, written in the first person, they made that suffering their own. I have rejected these poems for the same reason that made Arnold withdraw his *Empedocles on Etna* from circulation; passive suffering is not a theme for poetry. In all the great tragedies, tragedy is a joy to the man who dies; in Greece the tragic chorus danced. When man has withdrawn into the quicksilver at the back of the mirror no great event becomes luminous in his mind; it is no longer possible to write *The Persians, Agincourt, Chevy Chase*: some blunderer has driven his car on to the wrong side of the road — that is all.[4]

Yeats had every right to appeal to *Matthew Arnold*, for in the Preface to the first edition of his *Poems* (1853) Arnold based the exclusion of his poem on Empedocles on a remark he attributed to

---

[3] Yeats was impenitent. In a letter dated December 1936, he wrote: 'My Anthology continues to sell and the critics get more and more angry. When I excluded Wilfred Owen, whom I consider unworthy of the poets' corner of a country newspaper, I did not know I was excluding a revered sandwich-board Man of the revolution and that some body has put his worst and most famous poem in a glass-case in the British Museum — however if I had known it I would have excluded him just the same. He is all blood, dirt and sucked sugar stick (look at the selection in Faber's Anthology — he calls poets "bards", a girl a "maid" and talks about "Titanic wars"). There is every excuse for him but none for those who like him.' *Letters on Poetry from W. B. Yeats to Dorothy Wellesley*, 1940, p. 124.

[4] *The Oxford Book of Modern Verse 1892-1935*, 1936, p. xxxiv.

Schiller: 'The right Art is that alone, which creates the highest enjoyment.' The following passage from Arnold's Preface applies almost literally to our plays:

In presence of the most tragic circumstances, represented in a work of Art, the feeling of enjoyment, as is well known, may still subsist: the representation of the most utter calamity, of the liveliest anguish, is not sufficient to destroy it: the more tragic the situation, the deeper becomes the enjoyment; and the situation is more tragic in proportion as it becomes more terrible.

What then are the situations, from the representation of which, though accurate, no poetical enjoyment can be derived? They are those in which the suffering finds no vent in action; in which a continuous state of mental distress is prolonged, unrelieved by incident, hope, or resistance; in which there is everything to be endured, nothing to be done. In such situations there is inevitably something morbid, in the description of them something monotonous. When they occur in actual life, they are painful, not tragic; the representation of them in poetry is painful also.

Not the least of my difficulties in attempting to refute this case is that on some points we appear to agree! I am hoping, however, that Hecuba will see me through, but no longer the Hecuba of Shakespeare's play or the suffering queen of Virgil's epic, but the Hecuba who is the leading figure of a play by Euripides entitled *The Trojan Women*. Through her it should be possible to see more clearly both the similarity and the difference in the two positions. I would concede almost everything to Arnold where the tragic situation is such as to allow something, however little, to be done by the hero. Shakespeare seems in this to have been consistent: he regularly distinguished admirable from despicable conduct under the blows of Fortune very much as has been argued so far in attempting to distinguish true from false pathos. The hero bears the blows and fights back: he is praised for behaving like Cordelia, who, if she had not to suffer for and with her father, boldly declared:

> My selfe could else outfrowne false Fortunes frowne.

In this she resembles Jocasta in Seneca's *Oedipus:*

> haud est uirile terga Fortunae dare.

A man does not run away when attacked by Fortune.

But how are we to phrase the law when no vent is possible? This point becomes sharper where the cue *is* for passion, where the play demands that we push to the limit of the bearable our participation in the plight of a helpless victim. My method here as throughout this chapter is to work by comparison and contrast. But before showing Hecuba in a questionable light, let me state what I hope will be found two acceptable principles. What do we require in a *tirade* to avoid Arnold's charges, 'morbid', 'monotonous', 'painful, not tragic'? We must readily admit that these are the common verdicts of the trapped spectator. My answer runs, the focus must never be on the grief expressed. The mind must never be forced to rest and dwell on the painful particulars. In the very act of suffering with those we see suffer, we must be aware of *being moved on*. And the movement must be away from the particular to the general. We love to find the sufferers' feelings merging and being eventually lost in larger feelings. I hope that the two examples I am about to offer will give substance to these principles. But in the meantime I could present them as the formula in Hopkins's poem beginning:

> Margaret, are you grieving
> Over Goldengrove unleaving?

and ending:

> It is the blight man was born for,
> It is Margaret you mourn for.

Once Europe awoke in the years 1916–18 from its century-old dreams of military glory, and began to face the facts of modern war (the same facts, of course, which confronted Homer, but numbers and technical advances made a difference), *The Trojan Women* acquired a new stage notoriety. For people saw in the play a wider understanding than that of the pathetic condition of the defeated after the Trojan War. If that great popularity lapsed a little in the disillusioned aftermath of the last World War, it was in part revived by an excellent adaptation made in 1965 by Jean-Paul Sartre. His version stresses the main 'lesson' of the play,[5] that in war there is no victory but only disaster, as much for the victors as for the conquered, a lesson expressed by Poseidon as he leaves the stage in the opening 'scene':

[5] Léon Parmentier, in his edition of the play (1959) comments: 'Les trois derniers vers que prononce Poseidon (95 sqq.) expriment toute la pensée morale de la pièce.' (*Notice*, p. 10.)

μῶρος δὲ θνητῶν ὅστις ἐκπορθεῖ πόλεις,
ναούς τε τύμβους θ᾽, ἱερὰ τῶν κεκμηκότων,
ἐρημίᾳ δοὺς αὐτὸς ὤλεθ᾽ ὕστερον. (95-7.)

A mere mortal is a fool to raze cities to the ground. If he empties the temples of the gods and deprives tombs of the holy rites that are due to those laid to sleep in them, he himself will pay for it with his own life.

Sartre makes sure that we do not miss the message by making the following the *last* words of his adaptation:

> Faites la guerre, mortels imbéciles,
> ravagez les champs et les villes,
> violez les temples, les tombes,
> et torturez les vaincus.
> Vous en crèverez.
> Tous.

(Where the mere Englishman must recall the difference between *crever* and *mourir*.)

It may sound ungracious to pick on a speech in Euripides' play where the pathos seems to me to defeat or prevent the spirit of Tragedy supervening. I notice that Sartre has dropped it from his adaptation. In what follows I have slightly exaggerated the note which ruins the pathos, but I do not think I have been false to the spirit. Hecuba is addressing the Chorus: 'Well now, girls, let me compose myself to make a set speech or tirade, as they say in the theatre, for which iambics are the most appropriate metre. My first and introductory remark is that there is a certain pleasure in keening over good fortune when it is gone for ever. It also increases the pity by-standers feel when they witness my present misfortunes.'[6] (When I hear this I am irresistibly reminded of the women in Shakespeare's play, *The Tragedy of Richard the Third*. I see Queen Margaret rushing in with her hair about her ears exclaiming:

> Ah! who shall hinder me to waile and weepe,
> To chide my Fortune, and torment my Selfe?
> Ile ioyne with blacke dispaire against my Soule,
> And to my selfe, become an enemie.

There is a scene in the Fourth Act which I can only liken to ghoulish bell-pulling as all the possible changes are rung by the rhetoric when the

---

[6] In sober French, it goes like this: 'Pour commencer, j'ai envie de célébrer ce que fut mon bonheur; mes malheurs inspireront ainsi plus de pitié.' (Parmentier p. 48.)

three bereaved ladies sit down to a regular session, and Queen Margaret begins:

> If sorrow can admit Society,
> Tell o'er your woes again by viewing mine:
> I had an *Edward*, till a *Richard* kill'd him:
> I had a Husband, till a *Richard* kill'd him;
> Thou hadst an *Edward*, till a *Richard* kill'd him:
> Thou hadst a *Richard*, till a *Richard* kill'd him . . .

And the Duchess replies:

> I had a *Richard* too, and thou did'st kill him;
> I had a *Rutland* too, thou holp'st to kill him.

And so it goes on until Queen Margaret leaves the stage exhausted, and the Duchess is left to remark:

> Why should calamity be full of words?

and the other Queen replies:

> Windy Atturnies to their Clients Woes,
> Ayery succeeders of intestine ioyes,
> Poore breathing Orators of miseries,
> Let them haue scope, though what they will impart
> Helpe nothing els, yet do they ease the hart.)

I return to Hecuba, who now braces herself to strike the plangent, pathetic note:

I was a queen once, and had a king for husband by whom I had children of a superior sort. Indeed they had no equals among the people of Troy. No woman in the world could feel so proud as I was. Every male among them I saw killed by the Greeks. So, as you can see for yourselves, I had my hair cut off and I distributed it over their corpses. I was forced to stand by and watch the father of all these children having his throat cut at the central hearth-altar, while the enemy was taking possession of the city. As for the girls I was bringing up to make brides for aristocratic bridegrooms, they were all taken away from me and given to foreigners. I don't expect that I shall ever set eyes on them again, or that they will ever come to visit me.[7]

---

[7] J'étais reine et devins l'épouse d'un roi; j'eus de lui des enfants, excellents entre tous; car leur nombre serait un vain mérite, s'ils, n'avaient été les meilleurs de Phrygiens. Nulle femme, troyenne, grecque ou barbare, ne pourrait se vanter d'en avoir enfanté de pareils. Ces fils, je les ai vus périr sous la lance des Grecs, et

I come now to what the French would call the *comble* of my misfortunes. I am about to enter slavery in my old age, and be deported to Greece. Greeks will put on me tasks too hard for such an old woman as you see I am to bear. They will make me a sort of *concierge* or nightporter, me, the mother of Hector. Or I may have to grind corn to make Greek bread. All my life I have been used to lying in a royal bed; now Greeks will force me to lay my crooked old bones on the bare earth. I shall have to dress my ragged body in matching rags and tatters, hardly the proper wear for one born to the purple. O, how wretched I am! O, how much more wretched I shall soon be! And all this is the result of one miserable case of adultery![8]

A reader who does not believe that Euripides can have wanted his heroine to sound like this, is invited to compare my caricature with a reputable 'crib'. I am confident that he will then admit that in the Greek we have a case of what the French call *délectation morose*. If it might be going too far to say that Hecuba was *enjoying* her suffering, she was certainly making the most of it, and exploiting the pathos to the limit. The facts were as stated, but her tone was such as to prevent our minds being filled with the grandeur of the occasion and the dignity of the chief female representative of the Trojan race. If we hesitated over this verdict, it would be precipitated by a swift comparison with the manner in which Hector rehearsed the same facts in a gloomy forecast to his wife, as we may read it in the Sixth Book of Homer's *Iliad*:

> Not *Troy* it self, tho' built by Hands Divine,
> Nor *Priam*, nor his People, nor his Line,
> My Mother, nor my *Brothers* of Renown,
> Whose Valour yet defends th' unhappy Town,

j'ai coupé mes cheveux sur leurs tombeaux. Et la souche de cette famille, Priam, ce n'est pas sur le récit d'autrui que j'ai pleuré sa mort; je l'ai vu de mes propres yeux égorgé au foyer de l'autel domestique, à l'heure où tombait Troie. Et mes filles que j'avais élevées afin de les donner à des époux du plus haut rang, c'est pour d'autres que j'ai fait leur éducation; on les a arrachées de mes bras. Je n'ai nul espoir qu'elles me revoient jamais, et moi-même je ne les reverrai plus.' (Parmentier, pp. 48–9.)

[8] 'Enfin, pour mettre le comble à mes cruels malheurs, on fait de la vieille femme que je suis une esclave qui doit partir pour la Grèce. Les travaux les plus intolérables à mon âge sont la tâche que l'on m'imposera: je devrai, servante à une porte, en garder les clefs, moi, la mère d'Hector, ou bien faire le pain; la terre nue servira de couche au dos rugueux de celle qui dormait dans un lit de reine; la guenille qu'est mon corps n'aura pour se couvrir que des lambeaux de vêtement, marques honteuses de ma déchéance. Ah malheureuse! à cause du mariage d'une seule femme, que de maux j'ai soufferts et je souffrirai encore!' (Parmentier, 49.)

Not these, nor all their Fates which I foresee,
Are half of that concern I have for thee.
I see, I see thee in that fatal Hour,
Subjected to the Victor's cruel Pow'r:
Led hence a Slave to some insulting Sword:
Forlorn and trembling at a Foreign Lord.
A spectacle in *Argos*, at the Loom,
Gracing with *Trojan* Flights, a *Grecian* Room;
Or from deep Wells, the living Stream to take,
And on thy weary Shoulders bring it back.
While, groaning under this laborious Life,
They insolently call thee *Hector's* Wife;
Upbraid thy *Bondage* with thy Husband's name;
And from my Glory propagate thy Shame.
This when they say, thy Sorrows will encrease ⎫
With anxious thoughts of former Happiness; ⎬
That he is dead who cou'd thy wrongs redress. ⎭
But I opprest with Iron Sleep before,
Shall hear thy unavailing Cries no more.[9]

Some of the admirable pathos in Hector's farewell speech comes as a result of, as it were, hearing two voices. There is the voice of the dramatic hero confined to the particular occasion, inside his play. He may well be doubting the success of his fight with Achilles, and feeling misgivings about the gods who supported the Trojan side in the war. But there is a second voice, of a man with second sight, who knows that the days in which he will have a vent for action are numbered, and knows, too, that he will soon become a helpless victim. He foresees with certainty the truth of Hecuba's remark in the *Aeneid*:

non tali auxilio nec defensoribus istis
tempus eget; non, si ipse meus nunc adforet Hector.

These times want other aids: were *Hector* here,
Ev'n *Hector* now in vain, like *Priam* wou'd appear.

To bring out what a difference this makes to the argument, I am forced to return to the passage in Plato which was my starting-point. A further law for distinguishing true from false pathos may be derived from a consideration of *divisions within the soul*. Yet rather than use the vocabulary of the *Republic*, which might, in the long run, prove more of a hindrance than a help, I fall back on an article by F. R. Leavis,

[9] John Dryden, *Examen Poeticum*, 1693, pp. 464–5.

entitled *'Thought' and Emotional Quality*, first printed in the Spring 1945 number of *Scrutiny*. It is much to be regretted that Leavis never published the whole book (of which this article is part of a chapter) on what he called 'the analysis of poetry', for then he would have had to adjust his notes into a scheme in which I believe that the two main terms 'thought' and 'feeling' might have received a more satisfactory definition.

Nevertheless a valuable lead can be extracted from this article. If we allow the formulation that in the expression of powerful feeling the 'whole soul' is present, then, whatever words we choose for that experience, we can never call it all of one quality, it can never be *all*, never be pure, *feeling*. There is always another side to such experience which involves what Leavis called 'the constating, relating and critical' work of the mind. He therefore desiderates the simultaneous presence, first, in the speaker, of an attitude towards the feeling he is expressing, and, in us, the listeners, a sense that to be *inward* with the experience necessarily involves our feeling *outside* it. (My own efforts to introduce the French term *dédoublement* into the vocabulary of English literary criticism have not met with success.) In Shakespeare's play Hamlet advised the Player:

in the very torrent tempest, and as I may say, whirlwind of your passion, you must acquire and beget a temperance, . . . (Q2 text.)

Just as the speaker must be in the whirlwind as intimately as Eliot thought of the listener to music:

> you are the music
> While the music lasts . . .

and at the same time in a region of eternal calm outside it, an unmoving Empyrean beyond the spheres, for otherwise the pain expressed would pass the limits of the bearable, and tragedy would be destroyed, so it is this co-presence of the Near and the Far in our response which makes the greatest art.

A legitimate objection here might be that, while I have developed an argument in favour of the 'whole soul' as containing more than pure feeling, I have somehow missed the definition of the greatest pathos. My argument tells rather in favour of *strong feeling* than of pathos. It is also an argument which appeals more to the philosopher, the critic, and those theologians who place a high value on the rational, thinking, side of the mind. It is a legitimate claim that there is a higher tribunal than that constituted by such intellectuals. The greatest poets have always found the greatest pathos by taking away from the hero's mind what we call the rational faculty and giving him a greater hold over us by making him *mad*. Not, of course, accidentally mad, but mad because the hero is called on to bear suffering that proved too much for him. The poignancy is increased if the hero's helplessness does not lie in the collapse of the unconquerable will to resist, but in the overmastering of the mind in the attempt to stand up to the blows of Fortune.

Great poets have seized the opportunity offered by popular superstition about the mad that their minds are haunted by superior spirits, about the folk hero known as the 'wise fool', to present us with figures in whom the poets have shuttered down the normal waking faculties in order to open the windows of the soul on truths otherwise inaccessible to mortals. The 'whole soul' thus presented by the poets often strikes us as greater than the well-balanced mind of a Hector in lucid possession of his head and his heart. I shall therefore select examples of this kind of pathos in an attempt to distinguish genuine pathos from *tragic* pathos. In order to keep within the scope of my earlier examples, I shall resist the temptation to revel in mad figures in other plays by Shakespeare and in other examples of Greek tragedy in favour of Ophelia in *Hamlet* and Cassandra in *The Trojan Women*. Let me remind you of a moment in Shakespeare's play:

> *A noise within. Let her come in.*
> *Enter Ophelia.*
>
> LAER. How now? what noise is that?
>> Oh heate drie vp my Braines, teares seuen times salt,
>> Burne out the Sence and Vertue of mine eye.
>> By Heauen, thy madnesse shall be payed by waight,
>> Till our Scale turnes the beame. Oh Rose of May,
>> Deere Maid, kinde Sister, sweet *Ophelia*:
>> Oh Heauens, is't possible, a yong Maids wits
>> Should be as mortall as an old mans life?
>> Nature is fine in Loue, and where 'tis fine,
>> It sends some precious instance of it selfe
>> After the thing it loues.
>
>> OPHE. *They bore him bare fac'd on the Beer,*
>> *Hey non nony, nony hey nony:*
>> *And in his graue rain'd many a teare,*
>> *Fare you well my Doue.*
>
> LAER. Had'st thou thy wits, and did'st perswade Reuenge,
>> It could not moue thus.

OPHE. You must sing a downe a downe, an you call
    him a-downe-a. Oh, how the wheele becomes it!
    It is the false Steward that stole his masters daughter.
LAER. This nothings more then matter.
OPHE. There's Rosemary, that's for Remembraunce.
    Pray loue remember: and there is Pancies, that's
    for Thoughts.
LAER. A document in madnesse, thoughts & remembrance
    fitted.
OPHE. There's Fennell for you, and Columbines: ther's
    Rew for you, and heere's some for me. Wee may
    call it Herbe of Grace a Sundaies: Oh you must
    weare your Rew with a difference. There's a
    Daysie, I would giue you some Violets, but they
    wither'd all when my Father dyed: They say, he
    made a good end;
       For bonny sweet Robin is all my ioy.
LAER. Thought, and Affliction, Passion, Hell it selfe:
    She turnes to Fauour, and to prettinesse.
                        (based on Folio Text.)

Ophelia's 'mad' scenes in *Hamlet* are one of the moments which have made Shakespeare a figure in 'world literature'. No human being can remain aloof or refuse to acknowledge, in the limited particulars of the condition presented in the play, a general truth about what is specifically human in human nature and in the human condition when faced with suffering. Although all men find themselves here, I have no doubt that the experience carried away from these scenes may vary considerably, and may contain experiences of one man which might disgust another. There might even be a debate whether one man's pathos was another man's bathos. The target Shakespeare presents to our sensibility is certainly as wide as a barn-door. I should like to pay my tribute to the width of range that a legitimate response may take before pressing home my argument that here we have true pathos but not the truly *tragic* pathos inherent (potentially) in the position of an innocent victim of an appalling blow.

My chances of winning this argument are most hopeful with people who at first sight might seem my most obstinate opponents; those who are most deeply moved by the insight they think they gain into the unconscious workings of Ophelia's mind, people who trace the path back from the effects to the cause, and believe they read the document in madness to the point where they come to share imaginatively in the actual shock Ophelia suffered on learning of a 'deere Father murthered'. These people, I take it, would not accept the line I have been following, that such a shock occurring in a fiction is more bearable than that which a 'real' Ophelia could have undergone in like circumstances. Indeed they might believe that the route Shakespeare has taken has had the effect of increasing the horror to the point where it is sober truth rather than typically Shakespearean overstatement to say we contemplate *Hell it selfe*.

My line would be to reply, 'granted that this is a pathway open to a sensitive reader, and even more to a sensitive spectator in the audience, are you sure that this is the path along which the author is actually guiding us?' And I could point to the far greater stress being laid on the fact that it is a *beautiful young girl* who is suffering than that she is a feeling daughter. I do not say that thereby *all* the disagreeables are made to evaporate, but that the intolerable is converted into the bearable by Shakespeare's emphasis, as he gives it through Laertes' mouth:

> Thought, and Affliction, Passion, Hell it selfe:
> She turnes to Fauour, and to prettinesse.

Nevertheless I could not hope to prevail if I had not to hand the contrasting example of *Cassandra*, another beautiful, young, female victim. To make my point in a striking but superficial way, I should first like to contrast the impression made when both die. Here I am not thinking so much of the horrors of death as of the manner in which it is put before us to stir our feelings. The Queen in *Hamlet* seems intent on transforming the horrible into a beautiful, touching picture:

> *Enter Queene.*
> *Quee.* One woe doth tread vpon anothers heele,
> So fast they follow; your Sisters drownd *Laertes*.
> *Laer.* Drown'd, ô where?
> *Quee.* There is a Willow growes ascaunt the Brooke,
> That showes his hore leaues in the glassy streame,
> Therewith fantastique garlands did she make
> Of Crowflowers, Nettles, Daises, and long Purples
> That liberall Shepheards giue a grosser name,
> But our cull-cold maydes doe dead mens fingers call them.
> There on the pendant boughes her cronet weedes
> Clambring to hang, an enuious sliuer broke,
> When downe her weedy trophies and her selfe

Fell in the weeping Brooke, her clothes spred wide,
And Marmaide like awhile they bore her vp,
Which time she chaunted snatches of old laudes,
As one incapable of her owne distresse,
Or like a creature natiue and indewed
Vnto that element, but long it could not be
Till that her garments heauy with theyr drinke,
Puld the poore wretch from her melodious lay
To muddy death.   (Folio text.)

(It may be a mere accident that in the First Quarto we are told that Ophelia's clothes

Dragg'd the sweete wretch to death.)

In Euripides' play Cassandra with her god-given powers of prophecy foresees how she will be united in death with the corpse of Agamemnon when both bodies are thrown into a ravine to be devoured by scavenging animals. Here is the passage in the version by J. -P. Sartre:

Qu'attends-tu?
J'ai hâte de m'unir à mon fiancé
pour le meilleur et pour le pire.
Non: pour le pire, toujours.
Hymen, Hyménée!
Notre mariage sera l'enfer.
Roi des rois,
généralissime,
ne compte pas sur un enterrement au soleil.
La nuit t'avalera; ni vu ni connu.
On jettera ton corps dans un ravin,
Hymen, Hyménée,
près de mon cadavre tout nu,
et les vautours nous mangeront ensemble,
toi, le Roi,
Moi, la prêtresse d'Apollon,
unis dans la mort
par les coups de bec des mêmes rapaces.

There we have a form of hell without the prettiness.

My aim in working round to this episode in *The Trojan Women* was larger than the comparison with Ophelia's 'mad' scenes in *Hamlet*. It was in fact to present a single instance which exemplified all the hints and suggestions about *tragic* pathos which I have occasionally referred to rather grandiloquently as 'laws'. I am certainly relying on this one case to give some body and hence some plausibility to my argument, at least enough to persuade the reader to try my theses out on all the *prima facie* instances of *tragic* pathos in the greatest plays. Let me therefore restate the argument of these two chapters. I began by assuming rather than arguing that the problems of pathos would be found to resemble those which arise when we ask why tragic intensity appears to be the product of a force, which, left to itself, would burst and overwhelm us, being held in by a power fiercely containing and mastering the potential anarchy and disruption. The formula for tragic pathos, I thought, was to restrain an expression of suffering and so make bearable what would otherwise have been too distressing to be admitted into literary art. I played with the analogy offered by Plato, who distinguished 'manly' from 'womanly' behaviour when one is faced with personal calamity. The manly thing to do was to fight grief and find some vent in action. I transposed this by turning to Leavis, where he argued that the form of this fight was to bring the 'whole soul' into play and so to qualify the flood of mere feeling by introducing larger considerations. The ideal form of control consisted in a kind of *dédoublement* in which, while giving way to particular grief, the mind contrived to be outside it. The spectator recognized pathos as tragic when he was thus enabled in one act of perception to feel the particular and the general together and to move outwards and onwards from the normal arrest of the pained mind, which would otherwise develop the expression of pain beyond all limits. My argument was that similar conditions rule when we turn from situations where something, however little, could be done by the 'manly' hero to conditions of utter helplessness where there is everything to be endured and nothing whatever to be done. War seemed to me to provide us with abundant examples of 'passive suffering'. But an even greater degree of tragic intensity is reached when the suffering victim breaks down under the strain and goes mad. In 'real' life we know how frequently this happens and what pitiable wrecks of humanity fill our hospitals and mental asylums. The poet, however, seizes on the condition to present us with victims of a more comprehensive soul with larger insights than are given to normal sane minds. In scenes of *tragic* pathos we are carried far beyond ourselves and see further into the human condition, even though no explanation is provided and no justification given of

> The hart-ake, and the thousand naturall shocks
> That flesh is heire to.

Very little persuasion would be needed if we could go to the theatre and sit through *The Trojan Women*. The emphasis on strong scenic effects is so great that one could easily believe that Euripides had faced the arguments put up by Matthew Arnold, and had decided that, although his play was dedicated to the topic of passive suffering, it would also obey the requirements, the strictest requirements, of drama by possessing an almost breathtaking speed and variety. Second, as if in response to Arnold, Euripides has deliberately played off the merely passive against the extremely active. Let me call to mind the dramatic opening of the *Trojan Women*, an opening which would be enhanced by a curtain rising! For, as we, as spectators, take in the stage-setting of tents of captives in an armed camp, we see prostrate on the ground before them an immobile figure who does not move during the action between the divine figures who set out the plot. It is only when both Athene and Poseidon have retired that Hecuba lifts her head from the earth and likens herself to a ship which has lost anchor and is allowed to drift with wind and tide. She says, as M. Sartre puts it:

> Dérive! Dérive!
> Le destin t'entraîne: laisse-toi porter.

Cassandra's entry is at the other extreme. A fire appears to burst out in one of the tents and Cassandra rushes on to the stage with a burning torch in her hand. In the confusion which follows, so many different impressions occur at once that it is hard to say if they are meant to impress us in any order. Cassandra is clearly deranged and acting out a mad fantasy, but, judging by the words used in her own speech and the comments of the others on stage, she is to be thought of more as a *dervish* than a lunatic. Her speech and movements are those which occurred when women were *possessed*, under the control of Dionysus. A second aspect of this scene is the grotesque. While Cassandra is carrying out her ghastly fantasy (to be described in a moment), she is also dangerously mishandling her torch, and her exaggerated leaps threaten to take her, as it were, over the boundary and through the pavilion! Nevertheless in all this confusion we recognize the peculiar form her delusion has taken. It is horribly painful to see that she is assuming that the time for mourning her dear father's death and the destruction of a precious civilization has passed, and the Trojan situation is now one of perfect bliss. For her the blessed moment has arrived which crowns the young maiden's career, a time to enjoy the celebration of her marriage to Agamemnon with all the proper ritual calls, answers, songs and dances. Cassandra has constituted herself both mistress of this ceremony and its chief celebrant. It is horrible to hear Cassandra repeating the age-old sanctified formula:

Ὑμήν,   ὦ   Ὑμέναι',   Ὑμήν.
(hymēn,   ō   hymenai,   hymēn)

a formula which has left traces in our own language. The effect of these words in this moment of national disaster is as monstrous as it would seem to us if Milton's Eve, after hearing of her expulsion from paradise, had re-enacted the scene of her wedding, when

> in close recess
> With Flowers, Garlands, and sweet-smelling Herbs
> Espoused *Eve* deckt first her nuptial Bed,
> And heav'nly Quires the Hymenaean sung . . .[10]

There is a yet more monstrous feature of this scene which I am still keeping back, for we have first to recognize that Cassandra has another side to her nature, arising from the gift of prophecy or second sight made to her by Apollo. We soon learn that there was method in her madness: she had good reason to celebrate her marriage to Agamemnon because in marrying him she would be bringing ruin down on the whole House of Atreus. So we have to take in a completely different Cassandra when we find her changing to iambics and in this metre opening up all the larger considerations about war and suffering which I thought distinguished the tragic from the merely pathetic. The effect of this switch is as if we were being violently shifted from one part of her soul to another, from her heart to her head, if the shorthand is permissible.

I must confess that I miss the psychological plane which in Ophelia's 'mad' scenes somehow made sense of her abrupt transitions, as a bystander remarked:

> She speakes much of her Father; saies she heares
> There's trickes i'th'world, and hems, and beats her heart,
> Spurnes enuiously at Strawes, speakes things in doubt,
> That carry but halfe sense: Her speech is nothing,
> Yet the vnshaped vse of it doth moue
> The hearers to Collection; they ayme at it,
> And botch the words vp fit to their owne thoughts,
> Which as her winkes, and nods, and gestures yeeld them,

[10]   Milton, *Paradise Lost*, Book Four, ll. 708–11.

Indeed would make one thinke there would be thought.
Though nothing sure, yet much vnhappily.   (Folio Text.)

Euripides has divided the scene into three parts: the first is pure feeling, the second, pure thought, and the last, perhaps a mixture of the two, for both are present. Each 'section' is composed in a markedly different metre. He was able to make the three sections into a unity because he was not wedded to 'realism' or 'psychological probability'. No doubt both Shakespeare and Euripides should be thought of as artists, contriving these effects, yet in Ophelia's madness the illusion of psychology persuades us that the effect is of nature rather than art. I suspect therefore that we are missing something Euripides put in here, and we miss it because of our ignorance of the Greek stage conventions governing the interspersion of sung and spoken passages. I therefore, with great hesitation, offer a parallel which has helped me over a sense of awkwardness in the transitions from metre to metre in this passage of the play. What proved to be Henry Purcell's last song exhibits a mad woman, or a woman driven mad by love. Musically speaking, *From Rosy Bowers* is divided into five parts. The singer passes without a pause from a statement of her love for Strephon to a frisky mood, described as 'mirthfully mad', which gives way to a mood of despair and numb melancholy. After toying with the thought of suicide by drowning, the singer, in the last section, runs stark mad, and hopes to escape her pangs by meeting 'some savage Bear'. If by the time the music stops we have completely forgotten that the singer was a counter-tenor, perhaps the late Alfred Deller, and have accepted the composition as a unified peace, we ought to be able to overcome our dislike of the abrupt transitions Cassandra makes while passing in and out of reason. If we could hear the rhythms of the three metres in an acceptable form, we should, I am convinced, be completely won over.

There are, however, several advantages going with these Greek conditions. Not the least is the possibility of looking at Cassandra's state of mind from two very different standpoints. To a hostile Greek she was simply out of her wits. But she thought of herself as invaded by a god. So when Dionysus left her, Apollo took possession. Seen like this, there is less of a strain in finding a mere girl speaking with the wisdom of old men. In fact most critics have felt that on the topic of the futility of all wars Cassandra became the author's own mouth-piece. If this is so, M. Parmentier's note:[11] 'Euripide met une insistance

---

[11] In the 'Collection des Universités de France', *Euripide*, Tome IV, 1959, note on p. 44.

significative à montrer les conséquences funestes de la guerre pour les non combattants. . . .' is worth retaining. Though, it might be just as significant to note the *religious* terms in which the issue is discussed:

The dead in war never see their children again: they are not wrapped in burial-clothes by their loving wives: they lie for ever in unconsecrated earth. The fate of those they leave back at home is not different: women die as widows: parents are left childless when they need children most: those they bore and bred are not present to pour over their graves the tribute of the victims' blood.

(At this point a remark is made to remind us of a note of *restraint* which governs Cassandra in all her states of mind. She will not allow herself to mention some of the horrors she knows about, and some which are the direct result of her presence. Thus although she is willing to reassure her mother by telling her that she will be avenged, she will not reveal to her the end of her story as known to Juvenal, her final conversion to *Hecuba latrans*, the howling bitch we read about in Book Thirteen of Ovid's *Metamorphoses*:

> Priameia coniunx
> perdidit infelix hominis post omnia formam
> externasque nouo latratu terruit oras,
> longus in angustum qua clauditur Hellespontus. (404–7.)

With Troy Old Priam falls: his queen survives;
Till all her woes complete, transform'd she grieves
In borrow'd sounds, nor with an human face,
Barking tremendous o'er the plains of Thrace.

Cassandra refuses to explain the behaviour of Clytemnestra, and she will not stoop to discuss the adulteries committed in wartime by wives whose husbands were fighting at the front.)

By so standing outside herself, Cassandra is able to enlarge our interest and emerge from the all-too-poignant condition of her own fate (which I am postponing consideration of for a moment longer). She includes, and loses, the Trojan calamity in the calamities of all wars, past, present, and future. And there is one revealing moment which, I think, shows Euripides' understanding of the *tragic* form of pathos. When Cassandra hears that Odysseus is proposing to carry Hecuba off as his slave, she recalls Apollo's words, and feels sorry for the poor devil who has no idea of what the future has in store for him. So she tells the whole story of Homer's *Odyssey*. I put it in that form because, although to the actors on the stage all she gives is a brief *résumé*, she reminds the listening world of the huge epic narrative which is thus poured into our contemplation of the pathos of war:

Odysseus, poor wretch, has no idea at this moment of the mass of suffering in store for him. A day will come when he will contemplate my fate and that of the whole of Troy, and think our troubles happiness compared with his misery. Ten long years more than those he has spent here will go by before he returns home as the sole survivor of his company. He will have had to pass through the dread clashing rocks of Charybdis; he will fall into the hands of that feeder on uncooked meat, the Cyclops. He will visit Circe, who turns men into pigs. He will almost lose his life in a shipwreck, will visit the Lotus isles and slaughter the sacred cows belonging to the Sun God, and hear a bitter prophecy as a result. I have no time for further details. He will descend into Hell, and when he is at last rid of the sea, he will find on the dry land of Ithaca a multitude of sorrows.

If asked to give instances where tragedy appears to me as a super-venient spirit descending with a sudden shock and carrying us off into instant conviction of a tragic universe, I should include the lines 445-61 of this play, which bring the horrors to a climax and as triumphantly dissolve the painful into exquisite delight. Now the text openly refers to something which the spectator would have been shocked by as soon as Cassandra rushed on to the scene. A nun dancing a can-can would not give more offence to modern religious suceptibilities than the sight of Cassandra wearing her *religious uniform* must have given to the Greek audience. The items of her clothing were the badge of an intimacy that I have slighted by referring to its phases only as they were seen by hostile outsiders. The presence of the gods has only been seen as bringing madness. The repulsive lackey of Agamemnon at Troy, who despised Cassandra and would not have married her at any price, dismisses her prophecies as lunatic ravings. He sees two deities simul-taneously at work:

> Ἀπόλλων ἐξεβάκχευεν φρένας. (408.)

The god Apollo has driven your good senses out of you in a Dionysiac ecstasy.

Hecuba, however, reminds us that Cassandra sober had enjoyed inti-macies of a kind hard to categorize since they implied total surrender to the god's lust and complete retention of a sacred virginity. Like M.

Sartre, I was taken with the Budé translation of a phrase for her sacred clothing, *parures des heures d'extase*, but for Cassandra, as for the Greeks, they were a nun's gala dress, things that could only be worn on a ritually pure body, things sacred and untouchable by profane hands, objects which could never be shown at a wedding. The monstrosity of Cassandra's celebration of her mother's role at a daughter's wedding was therefore a double desecration. I think the feeling we are meant to have during this scene is concentrated in the following strange expressions, which are found immediately after the tirade I translated, or mis-translated, at the point where Hecuba misses the two daughters she needed most:

ὦ τέκνον, ὦ σύμβακχε Κασάνδρα θεοῖς,
οἵαις ἔλυσας συμφοραῖς ἅγνευμα σόν. (500–1.)

How terrible a catastrophe has fallen on you, my daughter, to twine you from the holy purity of your ecstasies with the gods!

It is as a ravished *ancilla Domini*, both violated and desecrated, that Cassandra pictures her death when she is carried to Greece. For Cassandra now takes us beyond the sufferings of this life into the realm of death. She identifies herself with the fate she foresees, and virtually wills her ship of fortune to take her down to Hades.

A reader who recalls my remarks on the Erinys as the bringer of death and vengeance in *The Women of Trachis* might find the height of triumphant pleasure coming when Cassandra proclaims that she will cross to Greece as an avenging Erinys, one of three on board. Thus from helplessness and passivity she passes to triumphant activity. She descends into Hell as a victorious captain handing over to her defeated parents all the members of the House of Atreus she has succeeded in killing.

I cannot hope to strike the glorious note of the final words of the scene in a prose translation such as this:

Good-bye then, dearest Apollo. I strip off the ornaments you put on me. I bid farewell for ever to the parties where I shone in your vestments. I use the last moments of my religious purity to remove from my body what must not be defiled. Good-bye, my prophetic master! Good-bye for ever! Show me where the ship rides which holds my new overlord. The wind and the tide cannot come too soon for me. I go on board as a Fury to carry vengeance from Troy to Greece. Do not cry for me, mother, good-bye now! Goody-bye, my fatherland! Good-bye for ever! But you down there, get my reception ready! I'm coming to you soon. To you, my dead brothers, to you, dear father. Prepare a glorious place for me among the dead, for I am bringing you victory over the sons of Atreus who defeated you.

M. Sartre, it seems to me, has risen worthily to meet the challenge of the Greek:

> Qu'attends-tu?
> J'ai hâte de m'unir à mon fiancé
> pour le meilleur et pour le pire.
> Non: pour le pire, toujours.
> Hymen, Hyménée!
> Notre mariage sera l'enfer.
> Roi des rois,
> généralissime,
> ne compte pas sur un enterrement au soleil.
> La nuit t'avalera; ni vu ni connu.
> On jettera ton corps dans un ravin,
> Hymen, Hyménée,
> près de mon cadavre tout nu,
> et les vautours nous mangeront ensemble,
> toi, le Roi,
> Moi, la prêtresse d'Apollon,
> unis dans la mort
> par les coups de bec des mêmes rapaces.
> Adieu mes voiles,
> adieu mes bandeaux et ma robe,
> parures de mes extases;
> je vous arrache de ce corps
> pendant qu'il est encore pur.
> Porte-les, brise rapide,
> à mon Dieu d'amour,
> au Soleil.
> Où dois-je embarquer?
> Je suis la mort,
> mettez un pavillon noir
> au mât du vaisseau qui m'emporte.
> Adieu, ma mère,
> Sois calme: tu vas bientôt mourir.
> Et vous, frères couchés sous la terre,
> Père qui me donnas la lumière,
> je viens,
> vous ne m'attendrez pas longtemps.
> J'arriverai chez vous

Victorieuse
à la tête du cortège damné
des Atrides qui vous ont tués
et qui vont s'entr'égorger.
Hymen, Hyménée!

(*On l'entraîne.*)

Iou! Iou!
Hymen, Hyménée!
(*Elle s'en va. Hécube s'écroule.*)[12]

I have now reached the permanent dilemma for all those who assert that they have been visited by a spirit.

I saw Eternity the other night

is a remark which makes us gasp and want to reply, 'prove it!', though we cannot imagine any conceivable way in which such a remark might be verified or falsified. I have certainly found myself speaking of entering a tragic universe and being carried beyond myself to a point where one could see further into the human condition. But it is very difficult to get beyond the *deictic*. If this moment in the play does not produce instant conviction in the reader, there is little I can do. (And candour demands from me the confession that it was not until I first came across M. Sartre's version that I was so bowled over as to be able to make such a claim.)

In this difficulty I fall back on an experience which has left a permanent mark on me, and guided me whenever I needed to make that fundamental extension from 'the whole mind' to 'the whole soul' which I require in positing that with Ophelia and Cordelia we are in a vaster region than that embraced in Plato's rational picture of the soul in the *Republic*. It was in 1928 that I first took in the shock E. M. Forster underwent when he contrasted a scene in George Eliot's *Adam Bede* with a scene in Dostoevsky's *The Brothers Karamazov*. In his *Aspects of the Novel* (1927) he makes the very remarks about the latter episode that I would like to make about the lines I have selected in *The Trojan Women*.

Now contrast with it the following scene from *The Brothers Karamazov* (Mitya is being accused of the murder of his father; he is spiritually though not technically guilty).

'They proceeded to a final revision of the protocol. Mitya got up,

---

[12]   Jean-Paul Sartre, *Les Troyennes*, 1965, pp. 54–5.

moved from his chair to the corner by the curtain, lay down on a large chest covered by a rug, and instantly fell asleep.

'He had a strange dream, utterly out of keeping with the place and the time.

'He was driving somewhere in the Steppes, where he had been stationed long ago, and a peasant was driving him in a cart with a pair of horses, through snow and sleet. Not far off was a village; he could see the black huts, and half the huts were burned down, there were only the charred beams sticking up. And as they drove in, there were peasant women drawn up along the road, a lot of women, a whole row, all thin and wan, with their faces a sort of brownish colour, especially one at the edge, a tall bony woman, who looked forty, but might have been only twenty, with a long thin face. And in her arms was a little baby crying. And her breasts seemed so dried up that there was not a drop of milk in them. And the child cried and cried, and held out its little bare arms, with its little fists blue from cold.

'"Why are they crying? Why are they crying?" Mitya asked as they dashed gaily by.

'"It's the babe," answered the driver. "The babe weeping."

'And Mitya was struck by his saying, in his peasant way, "the babe," and he liked the peasant calling it "the babe." There seemed more pity in it.

'"But why is it weeping?" Mitya persisted stupidly. "Why are its little arms bare? Why don't they wrap it up?"

'"Why, they're poor people, burnt out. They've no bread. They're begging because they've been burnt out."

'"No, no," Mitya, as it were, still did not understand, "Tell me, why is it those poor mothers stand there? Why are people poor? Why is the babe poor? Why is the steppe barren? Why don't they hug each other and kiss? Why don't they sing songs of joy? Why are they so dark from black misery? Why don't they feed the babe?"

'And he felt that, though his questions were unreasonable and senseless, yet he wanted to ask just that, and he had to ask it just in that way. And he felt that a passion of pity, such as he had never known before, was rising in his heart, that he wanted to cry, that he wanted to do something for them all, so that the babe should weep no more, so that the dark-faced dried-up mother should not weep, that no one should shed tears again from that moment, and he wanted to do it at once, at once, regardless of all obstacles, with all the recklessness of the Karamazovs. . . . And his heart glowed, and he struggled forward towards the light, and he longed to live, to go on and on, towards the new beckoning light, and to hasten, hasten, now, at once!

'"What! Where?" he exclaimed, opening his eyes, and sitting up on the chest, as though he had revived from a swoon, smiling brightly.

Nikolay Parfenovitch was standing over him, suggesting that he should hear the protocol read aloud and sign it. Mitya guessed that he had been asleep an hour or more, but he did not hear Nikolay Parfenovitch. He was suddenly struck by the fact that there was a pillow under his head, which hadn't been there when he leant back exhausted, on the chest.

'"Who put that pillow under my head? Who was so kind?" he cried, with a sort of ecstatic gratitude, and tears in his voice, as though some great kindness had been shown him.

'He never found out who this kind man was, perhaps one of the peasant witnesses, or Nikolay Parfenovitch's little secretary had compassionately thought to put a pillow under his head, but his whole soul was quivering with tears. He went to the table and said he would sign whatever they liked.

'"I've had a good dream, gentlemen," he said in a strange voice, with a new light, as of joy, in his face.'[13]

But Forster's *comment* has also stuck with me through more than fifty years. For instance, this: 'In Dostoevsky the characters and situations always stand for more than themselves; infinity attends them, though they remain individuals they expand to embrace it and summon it to embrace them; one can apply to them the saying of St. Catherine of Siena that God is in the soul and the soul is in God as the sea is in the fish and the fish is in the sea. . . .' and this:

The world of the Karamazovs and Mysshkin and Raskolnikov, . . . is not a veil, it is not an allegory. It is the ordinary world of fiction, but it reaches back. Mitya . . . does not mean anything (symbolism), he is merely Dmitri Karamazov, but to be merely a person in Dostoevsky is to join up with all the other people far back. Consequently the tremendous current suddenly flows – for me in those closing words: 'I've had a good dream, gentlemen.' Have I had that good dream too? No. Dostoevsky's characters ask us to share something deeper than their experiences. They convey to us a sensation that is partly physical – the sensation of sinking into a translucent globe and seeing our experience floating far above us on its surface, tiny, remote, yet ours. We have not ceased to be people, we have given nothing up, but 'the sea is in the fish and the fish is in the sea.'

The honesty of these remarks makes it easier for me to fall back on the perhaps flippant observation that a countable number of my chickens have now come home to roost. The most secure position, I feel, is that reticence and restraint in the most passionate outburst are

[13] E. M. Forster, *Aspects of the Novel*, 1927, pp. 168-71.

necessary conditions for the *tragic* note in pathos. Ophelia and
Cassandra move us more because they do not resemble Hecuba or
Hamlet protesting:

> ô cursed spight
> That euer I was borne to set it right.

We lose the tragic if we try to exploit pathos to the limit. It is the mark
of a superior poet to make the listeners do all the work. I should reply
to Horace that it is far more effective to make the audience *think* you
have been crying than to present them with streaming tears.

Second, the episode gives solid body to the thought implied in the
word *dédoublement*. The devices of restraint, reticence, and indirection
keep the pain of our sympathetic participation within the limit that art
can stand. We care for the particular in all its particular features. But,
as Forster wrote, the particular 'reaches back'. In the case of Cassandra
we have to leave the Near for the Far. She is *limited* by her enveloping
vision of revenge. Revenge is not an ultimate value for us. This limitation
helps to make her plight bearable. It also helps the mind *to move on*.
But the ultimate question for me is, where do we move to? and, where
do we land? It seems to me that we are carried far beyond the 'moral'
or the 'lesson' of the play, which we know well in the Biblical formula:
'He that leadeth into captivite, shall goo into captivite: he that kylleth
with a swearde, must be kylled with a swearde. Heare is the pacience,
and the fayth of the saynctes.'[14]

The aspect of *dédoublement* I find governing me at this point in the
play is the one I tried to express in the phrase, 'To be *inward* with the
experience necessarily involves our feeling *outside* it'. First, as we are
drawn into the plight of Ophelia and Cassandra, we cannot think of
them as primarily Revenge-Goddesses. (Ophelia, of course, never willed
the deaths she caused.) Their similarity, however, helps me to see that
both figures matter to me as helpless victims, and force me to ask,
'victims, ultimately, of what?' and to reply, 'not, ultimately, of war'.
Second, the sudden opening of the perspective which occurs when
Cassandra is able to see her troubles as nothing compared with the
future suffering of Odysseus, moves my mind on to the widest general
thought. I am left with a conclusion like Hopkins's: 'It is the blight man
was born for.'

There is, however, a necessary particular in Cassandra's fate. I have

[14] *The Reuelacion of S. Iohn*, The .xiii. Chapter in William Tyndale's translation of 1534.

referred in an earlier chapter to a remark by Heracles about his mother at the crisis of *The Women of Trachis:*

> A quoi lui a servi d'avoir été à Zeus?
> What good did it do her to have Zeus for a husband?

The total abandonment of the victim is greater for one who, like Alcmene, had been in such intimate contact with the gods. Paradoxically, I end by seeing the pathetic tragic victim as a true tragic agent, and therefore return with an enriched sense of its significance to a passage in M. Vernant I made much of when trying to define the tragic act:

The tragic act has two aspects. On the one hand, it is the work of an agent shrewdly taking thought and weighing the pros and cons and doing his best to fit means to ends. On the other hand, he is playing a blind game of chance with the unknown and the unknowable. He is venturing out into a Tom Tiddler's ground where he will never be able to make headway, however long he tries. He is submitting to the play of supernatural powers about which there is no knowing whether they are joining with you to help you or to ruin you. For be he never so far-sighted, still the tragic agent in his most deeply-considered act will always be at best drawing a bow at a venture, making a desperate random shot aimed heavenwards in the hope of a reply, and only when the answer comes will he know, often to his cost, the import and true meaning of his act. It is only at the end of the play that this truth about the act emerges. Its real face is then revealed to the actors, who then, and only then, learn what they have unwittingly brought about by their acts. Until the last word is spoken, the tragic act remains a mystery, a mystery which is deepest and darkest for those who are most confident that they know what they are and what they are doing.

The mystery of 'how' and 'why' is even more complete when we travel away from these two girls to contemplate all mankind in its fundamental helplessness, and inevitably see ourselves as totally implicated.

It is Margaret you mourn for.

8
THE PLACE OF RELIGION IN TRAGEDY

For reasons which will become apparent as the argument develops, this chapter must open with an anecdote. On one fine, one of the rare fine days, of the now distant summer of 1979, when I had been invited by a friend to take a stroll in his garden and expound to him the scheme of what has now taken shape in the present work, and, in particular, he asked me to justify the plan of treating one essential constituent of all Tragedy in each chapter of the book, and I mentioned that I had thought of proposing *religion* as my closing topic, he pulled me up, and said, 'you can't do that', and when I asked, 'why not?' he brought out as a self-evident proposition a truth he said he had gleaned from Bowra and Bradley, which would rule religion out *a priori*. The name of Bowra was introduced on the strength of his book entitled *Sophoclean Tragedy* (1944), where we learn that Sophocles' plays are religious in a sense that Shakespeare's are not, and the Bradley was the A. C. Bradley of 1904, who, in the introduction to his lectures on Shakespearean Tragedy, declared: 'In this tragic world . . . where individuals, however great they may be, and however decisive their actions may appear, are so evidently not the ultimate power, what is this power?' and gave as his first answer:

that this question must not be answered in 'religious' language. For although this or that *dramatis persona* may speak of gods or of God, of evil spirits or of Satan, of heaven and of hell, and although the poet may show us ghosts from another world, these ideas do not materially influence his representation of life, nor are they used to throw light on the mystery of its tragedy. The Elizabethan drama was almost wholly secular; and while Shakespeare was writing he practically confined his view to the world of non-theological observation and thought . . .[1]

To counter this I fell back on the authority of Kitto, the author of *Form and Meaning in Drama* (1956), where he found Shakespeare's *Hamlet* to be in all important respects a religious drama, a kind of

---

[1] The patient reader will recall that I could equally well have cited Santayana's essay entitled, *The Absence of Religion in Shakespeare* (1896).

drama that only a student of Greek drama could understand. I was just beginning a summary of Kitto's essay on *Hamlet*, and making much of a topic which will occupy me in this chapter, what constitutes the essence or the 'real focus' of a tragedy? I was just dwelling on the importance of Kitto's claim that in religious drama the real focus is not the Tragic Hero but the 'divine background', in Kitto's own words: 'the Tragic Hero, ultimately, is humanity itself; and what humanity is suffering from, in *Hamlet*, is not a specific evil, but Evil itself . . .[2] (p. 335.) which allowed him to conclude that Shakespeare's *real* theme in the play is the corroding power of sin, when my friend burst out with, 'Haven't you forgotten what Leavis said about Kitto? and gave me the gist of what the reader can find on p. 162 of *The Clark Lectures 1967*: 'The use of Kitto, the classic who feels himself at home in modern criticism, is monitory; it is that he offers to solve the "problem of *Hamlet*" by telling us that it is "religious drama", and lays such a burden of work on the word "religious" that it does nothing at all.'[3]

I won't say that all this ruined the only enjoyable day of that summer, but it served to bring home to me how little preparation we have if we persist in raising the topic of the *essential* connection of religion and tragedy or the relation of religion to the *essence* of tragedy. Actually, the conversation with my friend took an even more uncomfortable turn when he went on to press the question, 'why do you want to bring religion in at all? I should have thought there were many more obviously essential ingredients warranting prior attention'. When I probed into my own motives, I found this an awkward question, all the more so because I had in my mind put the very same question to Kitto himself. What we all have to ask ourselves, I reflected, when religion comes up in this connection, is, are we free souls? Can we, for instance, bear the conclusion that religion is not *essentially* connected with tragedy? I mentally asked this of Kitto because it seemed to me that he had *willed Hamlet* to be a religious drama in spite of his professed determination to approach the play as a free soul. Here are some of his words: '. . . if we would know what he [Shakespeare] did think, there is nothing to do but to study the play, and to be very careful neither to bring anything

---

[2] This view was once widely accepted, and drew L. C. Knights's admiration. On p. 171 of *Some Shakespearean Themes* (1959) we can find him endorsing it with only verbal modification: 'The world with which Hamlet has to deal is indeed evil, and the play shows convincingly the logic of corruption . . .'

[3] *English Literature in our Time & the University*, 1969.

into it which its creator did not put there, nor to leave out anything that he did.' (p. 248.)

The question must, of course, be put in a second form, 'Are we deeply reluctant to *allow* religion to be considered part of the essence of tragedy?' I challenged my friend to meet the accusation that he was embarrassed and offended by my attempt to include religion in tragedy. He countered with an observation which could not be ignored, that during the Middle Ages, when Christianity was thought to pervade every side of life, the world had no tragedies. There may have been religious plays, but they were certainly not tragedies. And I recalled from Santayana the remark: 'Where Christianity was strong the drama either disappeared or became secular.'

A serious-minded reader might wish to protest at my opening a chapter in this manner. I can imagine a rebuke on these lines. 'Why are you inflicting on me an account of a private conversation? Religion and Tragedy are topics of such depth and importance that there is something flippant in treating them on the level of a dispute between two private figures strolling about in a suburban garden.' A fair question, even if I immediately counter by saying, 'wasn't there something flippant in Bradley if he thought he could dispose of the religious element in Shakespeare's tragedies in the few lines I have quoted?' I shall try to justify the particular *entrée en matière* I have chosen for this chapter in the course of my argument. It will then become clear why I had to begin on this rather helpless note. For it was as a consequence of what I next went on to attempt that no better course seemed open to me. My first step after the conversation I have reported was to look round for the strongest case I could find for the evidence that religion had ever figured in a tragedy in such a way that it would be hard to deny that it was an *essential* feature. I tried to find an instance where it would be clear that the presence of religion was just what was making the play a great tragedy. For I didn't think it a strong line to apply the term 'religious' merely to the 'background'. If religion is ever of the essence of a tragedy, it must be manifest where our attention is manacled by the action.

Although, immediately after his slighting reference to Kitto, Leavis went on to remark of 'religious': 'it is a very important word for the intelligent discussion of Shakespearian tragedy', I thought it tactically safer to start from what is less disputed ground, that the essence of *Greek* tragedy is religious. It will not surprise a reader who has followed me to this point to find me once again stopping and breaking off just when I seemed to be promising to get going. It is characteristic of the topic of tragedy that, the moment you advance any proposition, you put your foot in it, and if you do not notice what you have done, you plunge even further into a morass – or, if that is too strong, you move into an area where you lose touch with an intelligent opponent. In particular, it is impossible to make any opening remark about tragedy without an implication which goes to the heart of the topic. So here I must stop to clarify what is implied in my claim.

The first difficulty meets a reader once he consults those critics who are convinced that religion *is* of the essence of Greek tragedies. For he will invariably find that they resemble Kitto in dwelling on what is sung by the chorus, and often find this religious essence in a single sentence uttered in a 'lyric' portion, using the word 'lyric' in the narrow, technical sense of non-iambic verse. If such a reader has been impressed by, for example, the writings of Hugh Lloyd-Jones, he will have noticed that the Oxford professor obtains his weightiest evidence for the religious significance of the plays from the parts sung by the chorus. My contention is that these portions can never be singled out as giving us the *heart* of the tragedy. They are constituent parts, but never the *focus*. Almost everybody who has bothered to read Bowra's book has afterwards made fun of his *procédé* of discovering the meaning of the play in the closing remarks, where the chorus utter a few platitudes before leaving their arena, remarks which, in fact, could be transposed from any one Greek play and tagged on to another without appearing irrelevant.

This is merely a particular case. The general vice of all the commentators on Greek plays known to me, that of trying to extract from what is marginal a clue to what is central, met me in a painfully defeating form when I read through all the essays available to me on the Greek play which seemed to be universally regarded as a pre-eminent example of a religious tragedy, the *Oedipus at Colonus* composed by Sophocles at the end of a long working life. It seemed to me that all the commentators failed to define a centre, and so make clear what was specifically tragic in the play, and that instead they filled the ensuing central vacuum with a dummy substitute. What this substitute is may be discovered by putting two questions to a fair-minded beginner who has taken up a book purporting to handle what is tragic in the 'Theban' plays. The first question is, 'If you have just finished one of these books on the Greek plays, do you now suppose that the Greeks had available to them a large volume or roll in which huge chunks of what I must call history – but I will say more about that in a moment – were presented in a coherent form? That is to say, if you had no other lights on these plays than what is supplied in your commentary, were you not led to believe that everybody in the Greek audience when the plays were first put on had at home something in written form which might be given the title, *The House of Cadmus*, a connected tale something like Galsworthy's *The Forsyte Saga*? I mean by this a narrative in which the vicissitudes of a family were chronicled and a period of history was covered from the sowing of the dragon's teeth out of which soldiers sprouted down to the various warlike expeditions to replace rulers on the throne of Thebes? Would it come as a surprise to learn that such a connected history was not available to the three great Greek writers of tragedies?'

If my beginner replied that his commentator had not so misled him, I should put a second question, 'Did you not get the impression that Sophocles made up for himself such a connected story, and thought of the period covering the birth and death of Oedipus as a real stretch of events all interconnected in a thousand ways as are events in real life, from which he cut out two slices separated only by the dates, the earlier play treating Oedipus in his prime, the later dealing with the same man twenty years on? Were you not led to believe that for Sophocles this seamless web of connected events was the central thing, the thing he kept constantly in mind as being the heart of his tragedy, and that therefore it is to this we should return when after reading the play we ask ourselves what was tragic in it?'

Encapsulated in this fundamental heresy is another: that what is essentially tragic in any play is the individual myth. The truth is, I believe, that the Greek myths are not tragic, but some of the plays based on them are. For all the larger considerations about human nature, man's relation to the forces inside and outside him, the conflicts between what we deeply desire and what we have to submit to, all, in a word, that is treated of in the tragedies we call great cannot be found in any one myth, even if we had it in all the variations known to any Greek dramatist. Myths in their original shape do not present even by implication a world-belief embracing all the activities of man. Some are little more than fragmentary stories connected with annual religious observances. It is what the poets put into these myths which made the plays tragic.

Although in previous chapters I have tried to establish a sense for an 'orthodoxy' which is violated if we expect a tragedy to be closely related to the external world of cause-and-effect that we loosely call 'history', I have still to justify the strong language of 'fundamental heresy' for the, to me, monstrous attempt to synthesize myths into connected histories and make them the focus of tragedies. What is heretical is every attempt to find the essence of Tragedy in anything outside it which is *fixed and systematic*. The worst form of this heresy is the result of a desire to attach Tragedy closely to any form of *systematic theology or cosmology*. This heresy is so commonly held that I must demonstrate orthodoxy before raising the question of the relation of *Oedipus at Colonus* to any kind of religion.

Among those who have perforce to read Greek tragedies in English versions the commonest form of this heresy is to suppose that Fate is a governing notion in Greek tragedies. The truth is that the Greeks of the fifth century before Christ had no such understanding of the word Fate as we have to-day. Since his book is highly relevant to the topic of this chapter, I gladly refer the reader to *Oedipus at Thebes* (1957) by Bernard W. Knox for an authoritative statement of the facts. In the course of an attack on the commonly-held view that *Oedipus the King* is 'tragedy of Fate', he pointed out that the English word *fate* does not correspond exactly to any particular Greek word,[4] and that it is used by English translators as a stock translation equivalent for, among others, the following Greek words: *moira, moros, morsimon, heimarmenē, peprōmenon, aisa, potmos, anangkē, chreōn, daimōn* – all of which have different connotations. None of these Greek words has the resonance we properly give to Fate as it appears in Roman versions of Greek philosophical systems.

It is of the very essence of Greek tragedy and of all great Tragedy known to me that nothing on the universal scale is fixed, definite, cut-and-dried. You cannot make any such thing stick. It is quite impossible therefore to stage a philosophical contest in a tragedy between the claims of free will and determinism. It is my conviction that Tragedy can only exist so long as such matters cannot be settled. In fact what is *sublime* about Tragedy is the affirmation by mere mortals of convictions that no god will open the heavens to support and justify. At the risk of blasphemy I will give a flash – and all my convictions are never more than flashes – a one-second vision of what for ever separates the tragic from the religious vision. The reader is invited to consider first the grandeur of and the satisfaction given by the following episode in the New Testament. I shall reserve to Matthew the honour of the word, but I am willing to admit into our consideration of the passage all that can

[4] p. 33 and note on p. 204.

be known of John the Baptist to help construct an image of a brave hero who has the conviction which only a mortal man can have that there is a world of the spirit which he can affirm but not see:

I baptise you in water in token of repentaunce: but he that cometh after me is myghtier then I, whose shues I am not worthy to beare. He shall baptise you with the holy gost and with fyre: which hath also his fan in his hond, and will pourge his floure, and gadre the wheet into his garner, and will burne the chaffe with vnquencheable fyre.

Then cam Iesus from Galile to Iordan, vnto Ihon, to be baptised of hym. But Ihon forbade hym, saynge: I ought to be baptysed of the: and commest thou to me? Iesus answered and sayd to hym: Let it be so now. For thus it becommeth vs to fulfyll all rightwesnes. Then he suffred hym. And Iesus assone as he was baptised, came strayght out of the water. And lo heuen was open over hym: and Ihon sawe the spirite of God descende lyke a doue, and lyght vpon hym. And lo there came a voyce from heven sayng: Thys ys that my beloved sonne in whom is my delyte.[5]

(A reader who finds this allusion somewhat far-fetched and off the main line of the argument must be warned that in this quotation I have been presenting what many people see as the essence or the real meaning of the close of *Oedipus at Colonus*.) But to give my one-second flash, I must ask the reader, while he has the Christian scene before him, to fly off to one of the places which make it such a joy to read Greek plays. There we have another lonely figure – and we may enjoy the contrast between her appearance in *Oedipus at Colonus* and in the play I am thinking of, where for a good half she is the undisputed heroine. She is raising her voice in a claim that the principles she is acting on have divine sanction. To appreciate the chosen extract from the *Antigone*, we must imagine Oedipus' brother-in-law, Creon, newly installed in power in Thebes, just having had Oedipus' daughter brought before him, whom a guard had captured in the very act of defying Creon's express order not to bury one of Oedipus's sons, Polyneices, who had failed in his attempt to conquer the city by force:

> – You – yes, I mean you – look up! Do you admit
>   You did all this or say you're innocent?
> – I do admit I did it. He told the truth.
> – In that case, fellow, you can go, you're clear

[5] *The Gospell of S. Mathew* The .iii. Chapter from *The Newe Testament*, translated by William Tyndale, 1534.

> Of what might have been á very serious charge.
> And now, no speeches, mind you. Yes or no,
> Did you hear my trumpeters giving out the edict?
> — How could I help it? They made enough noise.
> — And so you dared to break the laws I made?
> — Yes, it was neither Zeus who blew your trumpet, nor the
> Justice who inhabits with the gods below.
> They never drew up laws like those you made,
> Nor can what you have trumpeted succeed
> In forcing men to break the limits set
> By what the gods have laid down without words.
> The ink is scarcely dry on your decrees:
> Their laws run everlasting. No one knows
> When they began . . .

But no heavens open to assure the girl than Zeus *was* supporting her. Nor did the earth gape to let her see that she had the approval of the gods down below. My contention is that Sophocles' play, *Antigone*, would cease to be a tragedy if we treated the heroine's words as we do those of John the Baptist and Matthew the Gospeller, as standards of unquestionable truth.

A lesser difficulty arises if we consider the proposition that it is part of this same heresy to pronounce the verdict, 'Aristotle must go!' The reader of this book will have noted various passing remarks denouncing Aristotle, which I have taken from J. -P. Vernant and P. Vidal-Naquet. The special consideration I had in mind here is the absence in Aristotle's *Poetics* of anything which could be taken to support all those who turn to Greek tragedies in the hope of finding there the essence of Tragedy bound up with the activity of the gods. Nowhere is this absence more striking than in those passages of the *Poetics* where Aristotle speaks with approval of Sophocles' play, *Oedipus the King*.[6] If it *is* a heresy to declare that Aristotle was incapable of understanding the nature of Tragedy, I have myself been as guilty as any man alive. For years I found myself able to assume that I was a better reader of that play than he was. I felt I had some support in the claims of modern students of the history of religion that they know more about Greek religion than Aristotle did. But as I look back on my declarations, repeated year

---

[6] It is pure pedantry to insist that Sophocles himself wished us to think of his hero as specifically a 'tyrant', that is to say, a king who did not succeed to the title by virtue of being the son of his predecessor, when the whole point of the play is that Oedipus actually became a king in that sense even though he learned the fact at the moment when he tried to relinquish the position.

after year, that Aristotle could not see that Sophocles was asking us in every line of the two plays about Oedipus to notice that the gods were at work, full of passion and self-will and a desire to punish and avenge, I now wonder that it did not bother me to be saying that Aristotle proved unable to catch even a whiff of such a powerful gale.

I shall not now proceed to defend the counter-claim that in rejecting Aristotle we are also rejecting Sophocles, but instead I shall take up some general considerations concerning the two Oedipus plays which at the very lowest must, in my opinion, qualify the verdict that they are both religious plays. The reader is invited, after he has measured how great these qualifications will have to be, to decide for himself whether Aristotle then must be rejected as a critic of Sophocles. A claim to set-tle the matter once and for all against Aristotle is made by many dis-tinguished critics who simply point to the role of *oracles* in these two plays. Santayana, for example, thought that the fact of superhuman control 'is emphatically asserted in those oracles on which so much of the action commonly turns'.[7] Maurice Bowra will once again serve as a representative figure:

Aristotle . . . missed one vitally important element in *King Oedipus*. He says nothing about the part taken by the gods in the rise and fall of Oedipus. His omission is understandable since he was, apparently, not interested in this aspect of tragedy and did not discuss it in his *Poetics*. But it seriously impairs his view. For though Oedipus' mistake in killing his father leads to other disasters, it is itself foreordained by the gods. The tragic career of Oedipus does not begin with it. His doom is fixed before his birth.

The activity of the gods is an essential part of *King Oedipus*. Oedipus is their victim. They have ordained a life of horror for him, and they see that he gets it. He is even the instrument by which their plans are fulfilled. The prophecy that he will kill his father and marry his mother leaves him no escape. He fulfils it in ignorance of what he is doing, but he must fulfil it. . . . More even than the *Women of Trachis*, the play shows how human life is at the mercy of the gods.[8]

There is an even more extreme expression in F. Allègre:

La fatalité y est représentée par des oracles – un oracle se réalise tou-jours fatalement – et par des faits: l'arrivée et la mort d'Œdipe à Colone

---

[7] From the essay entitled 'The Absence of Religion in Shakespeare' in *Inter-pretations of Poetry and Religion*, 1900, p. 158.
[8] *Sophoclean Tragedy*, pp. 166–7.

font partie de sa destinée fatale, et il ne pourrait se soustraire ni à l'une ni à l'autre.[9]

The action of Fate in tragedy is to be seen in the oracles. What is prophesized in these oracles is always fulfilled as part of the action of Fate. Oedipus arrives at Colonus as part of his fate. It is his destiny to die there. He cannot escape either aspect of his fate.

Although I am expecting to have trouble in striking the exact mean between the contending opposites in this debate about the role of religion in tragedy, I feel sure that these last two critics are well out, first, by minimizing the amount of *liberty* Sophocles has given to Oedipus, and, second, by attributing to Sophocles a systematic presentation of the author's intention in the various references to oracles — and they *are* various — in these plays. What both critics are failing to do justice to is the odd, haphazard, piecemeal introduction of oracles and similar pronouncements by the gods into our two plays. What finally persuaded me to desist from the modern habit of dismissing Aristotle when searching for the essence of Tragedy was a general consideration which applies to all plays, and indeed to all works of art offered to a general public. A literary author could never hide his light under a bushel. If he has anything striking or new to say, he puts it where it cannot be missed or overlooked. If, for Sophocles, oracles had been the principal thing to focus on in an attempt to grasp his whole meaning, I am convinced that he would have made far more of them than he has done in these plays. In fact his practice would have been closer to that of Greek historians, who, when they come to a moment when an oracle played a decisive part in historical events, give the circumstances in detail and quote the oracle *verbatim*.

A second general consideration is that the behaviour of the other people on the stage will always tell us how seriously we are in fact to take any remark made by the hero or heroine. That is to say, what they do or do not do, what they say or do not say, immediately after any remark we might be tempted to focus on as a certain authorial tip. This law may be used to dispose of the view that a Greek oracle referring to a future event implies a doctrine of predestination or determinism. For whenever such a prediction occurs in our plays, the hero who has heard his 'fate' pronounced by the gods tries to avoid the consequences. He

---

[9] *Sophocle: Étude sur les ressorts dramatiques de son théâtre et la composition de ses tragédies*, 1905, p. 318.

never thinks he is powerless. The fact that in the end he proves incapable of avoiding these consequences cannot make us change our minds.

Our attempts to discover the middle way will be helped by a glance at the other extreme, of which the most vigorous spokesman is Ivan M. Linforth. Here are a few excerpts:

... an oracle may arouse hope of good or fear of evil, and a wise man will heed it in his conduct; but he cannot be sure that his hope will not fail or his fear prove groundless. This is the prevailing and characteristic Greek attitude in which are combined a notion of predestination, some shrewd skepticism, and a conviction that man's will is free. The Greeks were too strong-minded to be fatalists, even though they receive communications from the gods which might seem to have the authority of fate. They treated oracles, not as pronouncements of fate, but as wise and presumably sound advice, like the advice given by a physician or lawyer of high repute, which a sensible man follows though he is free to disregard it with possible peril to himself ...

When Sophocles invents oracles and uses them in the structure of the play, he does not do so in order to present a dramatic vision of man's impotence in the hands of fate and destiny. He uses them, for his purpose, because they are a familiar part of the life which he and his audience know, and because they will be accepted as a natural element in the human experience of Oedipus himself.

... the oracles are used solely as a dramatic device. They are never made the occasion for discourse on the power of fate, the helplessness of man, or any other topic of religious or philosophical import. Once disclosed with sufficient clarity, they go almost unheeded in the great scenes of conflict.

... They are totally disregarded by the chorus in the lyric portions of the play.

... The play was not written as a vindication of the truth of oracles.[10]

That is as far as I can go on the subject of oracles at this level of generality. I should therefore like to return to the question of 'heresy' in a slightly different form. A fair-minded reader who noticed the scorn I was pouring on the view that Sophocles was composing if not two *tranches de vie*, two slices from a connected *history* in his two Oedipus plays, might well have protested that I had been carried away by my passion and had forgotten the obvious truth that the two plays are

---

[10] *Religion and Drama in 'Oedipus at Colonus'*, 1951, pp. 90-2.

nevertheless connected by having the same figure as the chief personage in both. The form the heresy takes here is to claim that the identity of the two Oedipuses is such that, when we consider the role of religion in the later play we are forced to believe that the general outlook we detect there on guilt-in-innocence and on the part played in man's predicament by the gods was also a governing preoccupation in the earlier play. The form orthodoxy takes, I suggest, is that, on the former question of guilt-in-innocence, we should distinguish the two plays, and, on the question of the role of the gods, we should find a similarity, but, if we are to connect the two plays, the emphasis should be laid on the *ambiguous* and *limited* role played in both tragedies by the gods, such a role, in fact, as they play in every great tragedy.

What must on all counts be avoided is to take for granted that the two plays are as closely related as we suppose the links binding the two 'parts' of Shakespeare's *Henry the Fourth*. Here a consideration arises so simple that it is often forgotten. Sophocles is thought to have composed at least 130 plays. I do not know how many of those were written in the interval between the two Oedipus plays, but in the *seven* extant tragedies I should regard it as miraculous if we could find so close a link binding any two. It is nevertheless a general defect of all the books I know which discuss these seven plays to overstress what the seven have in common and to pronounce that to be characteristic of the lost 123! There are some influential names among those guilty of this unconsidered acceptance that the two Oedipuses are one. Maurice Bowra, for instance, wrote (p. 308): 'This hero is the same person whose hideous misfortunes Sophocles had already presented in *King Oedipus*. His *Oedipus at Colonus* is in some senses a sequel to the earlier play.' Bernard Knox, who is a powerful advocate of the view that 'in the second play Oedipus is made equal to the gods, he assumes the attributes of divinity', regards this as the culmination of a process begun in the earlier play: 'Oedipus is turning into something more than man; now he knows surely, sees clearly, the gods give Oedipus back his eyes, but they are eyes of superhuman vision. . . . The rebirth of the young, confident Oedipus in the tired old man . . .'.[11] How influential these two critics must have been may be estimated by the fact that the distinguished French scholar, Gilberte Ronnet, in her book on Sophocles had to protest in 1969: 'On voit qu'*Œdipe à Colone* n'est pas exactement, comme on le dit trop souvent, la suite d'*Œdipe-Roi*.' ('It becomes

---

[11] 'Sophocles' Oedipus' in *Tragic Themes in Western Literature*, 1955, p. 24.

obvious that *Oedipus at Colonus* is not, as is too often said, in any strict sense the sequel to *Oedipus the King*.') She makes the distinction explicit on a later page:

Quelle différence en effet entre les deux Œdipes! L'un, épris d'absolu, avide de perfection, sacrifie tout à la poursuite de son idéal, et, quand il comprend que l'irréparable a été accompli malgré ses efforts, refusant à la fois et la vie et la mort, s'isole dans une cécité volontaire, qui est à la fois châtiment et libération,—l'autre, servilement soumis à la fatalité, se cherche des excuses en accusant les autres, et regrette un geste qui pour lui n'a pas de sens. L'un soucieux d'assurer le salut de sa cité, accepte de se perdre pour la sauver,—l'autre consacre ses dernières forces à fortifier contre elle la cité voisine. L'un, au plus profond du désespoir, s'arrache à lui-même pour penser aux autres, à sa mère-épouse, 'la malheureuse' qui avait dû sacrifier son enfant avant d'être déshonorée par lui, et à ses filles, dont il déplore d'avance la vie sans époux,—l'autre accepte d'Antigone une abnégation qui ruine sa vie de femme, et condamne ses fils à une mort horrible. Quoi de commun entre ces deux hommes? . . . On ne peut croire que Sophocle ait considéré ses deux héros comme un même homme à deux âges de sa vie. . . . (p. 306.)

In fact the difference between the Oedipuses of these two plays is immense. In the earlier play we find him wildly in love with the Absolute, eager for perfection and willing to sacrifice everything for the sake of his ideal, and when he finally realizes that in spite of all his efforts the irreparable has occurred, refusing either to live or to die and withdrawing into a self-inflicted blindness, which is at one and the same time both his punishment and his escape; in the later play, we see him servilely subject to the action of Fate, trying to find excuses for his crime by accusing others. He rejects the act of self-blinding, which now appears pointless. In the earlier play he is concerned for the safety of the city, and is willing to die to save it, in the later play he devotes the last ounce of his energies to strengthening a neighbouring city against the assault of Thebes. In *Oedipus the King*, even when the hero is plunged in the depths of despair, he is able to tear himself away from his own troubles to think of others, his wife-mother, the poor wretch, who was forced, first to sacrifice her own child and then to find herself brought to shame by him, and his daughters who would never have husbands. The Oedipus of the later play is willing to allow Antigone to sacrifice her chance of marriage and ruin her life to serve him. He condemns his sons to a horrible death. Have these two Oedipuses anything in common? . . . It is impossible to believe that Sophocles ever thought of these two characters as those of one man at different moments of his career.

And in pointing out the difference between the Creons of these two plays she seems to me to state the law that applies to Oedipus in these plays:

Il ne sert de rien de comparer des personnages qui portent le même nom, mais qui appartiennent à des pièces séparées par des dizaines d'années, et sont par conséquent indépendants l'un de l'autre.[12]

When two plays are found to have been written at an interval of at least ten years and, consequently, have no connection, there is no advantage to be gained by treating any characters in them who bear the same name as if they referred to one and the same person.

An altogether deeper consideration arises from remarks about *Oedipus at Colonus* of which this is a fair specimen: 'The play is a worthy last will and testament . . . it is as if Sophocles were summing up a lifetime of thought and feeling.'[13] For English people a comparison of this play and Shakespeare's *The Tempest* is irresistible. The almost certain fact that we have in both cases the last of a long series of plays has led many people to expect (as some have done with Euripides' *The Bacchae*) that the poets have put more of themselves than usual into their last wills and testaments, and, in particular, have finally delivered the key to unlock their most precious thoughts on the meaning of life. For critics more interested in the poet than in his works it was natural to suppose that as the poet grew older he also became wiser. They were therefore bound to conclude that he must at the end of his life have *improved* on his tragedies, and somehow left them behind. For some of these people the watchword for Shakespeare's late plays became *reconciliation*, because in them the bitterness of the unsmiling tragedies had been allayed. Shakespeare was thought to have moved into a region where 'grace' and 'harmony' were the appropriate words for his state of mind. I haven't found anybody pushing the thought so far as to say that the ending of the perfect tragedy ought to resemble the close of Dante's *Paradiso*, nor can I name a critic who has accepted the note of Browning's *Pippa Passes*:

> God's in his heaven —
> All's right with the world!

as the last word in a religious tragedy, though this is the implicit general conclusion. But I have found an ideal mouthpiece for the generous

---

[12] *Sophocle, Poète Tragique*, 1969, p. 294.
[13] Bernard M. W. Knox, *The Heroic Temper*, 1964, p. 144.

sentiments governing those who have found both plays rising above the rest of the plays by Sophocles and Shakespeare. The comment arises directly from these lines, spoken by Gonzalo at the close of *The Tempest*:

> I haue inly wept,
> Or should haue spoke ere this, looke down, you gods,
> And on this couple drop a blessed crowne;
> For it is you that haue chalk'd forth the way
> Which brought vs hither.

In the light of earlier plays this is not difficult to interpret. Alonso, like Lear, like Leontes, has come through penitence to realize his errors and to ask his child forgiveness, and Prospero replies that the time has come to cast off the burthen of past memories and to look forward to a harmony that long and often bitter experience has gained. And, apart from them both, the faithful Gonzalo is given for a moment a dignity that he has not so far reached in the play, a dignity that makes him at this stage — rather even than Prospero — the mouthpiece of Destiny. In his words the gods are invoked to 'crown' the new-born vision of humanity with a symbol of royalty: the gods who have unwound the whole plot and brought it at last, through the actions of Prospero, to its harmonious conclusion.[14]

The difficulty of this is, as I remarked earlier in the chapter on the Tragic End, that 'although there *is* much talk of forgiveness and reconciliation in the winding up of the play, everybody notices that there is no hint of permanent change. Once back in Europe, we feel, things will take their old course, evil remain potent, human weakness perennial.'

With *Oedipus at Colonus* everybody agrees that if the play has religious point, it becomes most apparent near the close. The great question here is, do we find Sophocles showing us a man leaving mortality and putting on immortality? Do we discover that the gods who punished Oedipus in the earlier play are now reconciled, and, wishing to make amends for their former injustice, agreeing to receive the suffering old man and make him one of them? (It is quite amusing to watch the more scrupulous of the critics who would answer 'yes' to these questions shying away from downright *apotheosis*, but, like Knox with his 'he assumes the attributes of divinity', coming as near to the thought as they dare.) I am not alone in contending that the text of the play shows that these critics have been imposing on the play something they want

---

[14] Derek Traversi, *Shakespeare: the Last Phase*. 1954, p. 271.

to be there, but isn't, and blinding themselves to something they don't want to be there, but is.

There is no doubt, however, that the ending of the play contains a magnificent dramatic moment. It is a rare instance where a *coup de théâtre* is also a triumph of dramatic art, where our attention is manacled by the action. Throughout the play the Oedipus we have been seeing might have been called by an unsympathetic observer 'Old Stiff-Rump', for his hams are so weak that his daughter has to help him either to sit or to stand. In fact it is quite incredible that both were able to foot-slog it along the rough and tangled ways between Boeotia and Attica. Physically, then, Oedipus has shown himself to be a decrepit Lear, and blind like Gloucester. Yet almost without warning we see him at the end starting up like a hypnotic and leading the very people who had been leading him, and leading them straight to the goal. So dramatic is this moment that a modern reader could be forgiven for bringing into the experience another episode from the life of John the Baptist. He is now in prison and sending out his spies to find out from Jesus what he had been doing: 'When Ihon beinge in preson hearde the workes of Christ, he sent two of his disciples and sayde vnto him. Arte thou he that shall come: or shall we loke for another. Iesus answered and sayde vnto them. Go and shewe Ihon what ye haue hearde and sene. The blynd se, the halt goo, the lepers are clensed: the deef heare, the ded ryse ageyne, and the glad tidinges is preached to the povre.'[15] I take it that the man who spoke and the two disciples of John all understood here a reference to the prophecy in Isaiah of the coming of the Lord to reward the good and punish the wicked: 'Say to them that are of a fearful heart, Be strong, fear not: behold, your God will come with vengeance, even God with a recompense; he will come and save you. Then the eyes of the blind shall be opened, and the ears of the deaf shall be unstopped. Then shall the lame man leap as an hart . . .'.[16]

At l. 1450 in our text a change in the tempo comes about as thunder is heard from a blue sky. All on stage are terrified by the successive claps or rolls. But Oedipus at once recognizes what has happened. 'Zeus is sending his winged messenger to conduct me down to Hades. This is the promised end. There is no turning back.' Something of the grandeur now acquired by Oedipus can be detected in the stage version made by

---

[15] The Gospell of S. Mathew, The .ix. Chapter, as translated by Willyam Tindale in *The Newe Testament* of 1534.

[16] Isaiah 35: 4–6, in the Authorized Version.

W. B. Yeats.[17] I begin at the point where the hero is giving his last instructions to Theseus, the king of the region, and follow it, as a 'control', with the version by Paul Mazon.[18]

Son of Aegeus, I shall expound a mystery and give your city that which time shall never take away. First, I shall lead you to my place of death, and though blind I shall need no guiding hand. But that place you must never show to any living man, for it shall be, while it stays hidden, more protection than a multitude of Athenian shields or than the borrowed might of an ally; and there by that place mysteries shall be revealed, revealed to you alone, things that I dare not speak to my own daughters, much as I love them, things it is not lawful to put into words; and these you must guard in your heart and reveal to your successor, and then only upon your death-bed, that they may be revealed to his successor in turn and so through all time. So shall this city and countryside be kept unharmed from the dragon's teeth and from the men of Thebes . . . Now let us hurry to that place, for the heavens call and I dare not linger. Follow me, children, though but for a portion of the way. It is my turn to guide these that long have been their father's guide; come, but lay no hand upon me; all unhelped I shall discover my predestined plot of ground, my sacred tomb. Come this way, this way; Hermes guides and the Goddess of the Dead. O light bathing my body for the last time; O light, my light long ago, I tread the road to Hades, blessed be this land, blessed be its people, you, best of friends, be blessed, and when your fortune mounts, remember me in the tomb.

Je vais donc, fils d'Égée, t'apprendre quel trésor vous conserverez, toi et ta cité, à l'abri de l'âge et de ses soucis. L'endroit où je dois mourir, je vais t'y mener moi-même sur l'heure, sans qu'aucun guide me tienne par la main. Mais toi, ne l'indique à nul autre, ne révèle ni où il se cache ni l'endroit où il se trouve, si tu veux qu'un jour je te vaille une aide égale à mille boucliers, voire à une armée de renfort accourue d'un pays voisin. Mais le pieux mystère que la parole n'a pas le droit de remuer, tu l'apprendras, toi, une fois là-bas – toi seul, car moi je ne le peux révéler à personne, ni à nul de ces citoyens ni à mes propres enfants, malgré l'amour que je leur porte. Garde-le, toi seul, toujours, et, quand tu atteindras le terme de ta vie, confie-le au plus digne, pour que celui-ci à son tour et ainsi de suite, le révèle à son successeur. C'est de cette façon que tu maintiendras ton pays à l'abri des ravages que lui infligeraient les Enfants de la Terre. Partons, et sans tarder – l'appel du dieu me presse – partons pour l'endroit que j'ai dit. Mes filles, suivez-moi

---

[17] *Sophocles' Oedipus at Colonus. A Version for the Modern Stage*, 1934. *Collected Plays*, 1972, pp. 570–1.
[18] *Sophocle*, tome III, Paris, 1960, pp. 140–2.

— ainsi; c'est moi qui cette fois m'affirme votre guide, guide étrange sans doute, mais pareil à celui que vous étiez pour moi. Venez, sans me toucher, et laissez-moi tout seul trouver la tombe sainte où le Destin veut que je sois enseveli en ce pays. Par ici, — ainsi — par ici! avancez. Oui, c'est bien par ici que m'emmènent ensemble et Hermès, le guide des morts, et la déesse des enfers. Lumière, invisible à mes yeux, depuis longtemps pourtant tu étais mienne, et mon corps aujourd'hui éprouve ton contact pour la dernière fois. Je m'en vais de ce pas cacher dans les Enfers mon dernier jour de vie. A toi, le plus aimé des hôtes, à ce pays, à tous ceux qui te suivent, je souhaite d'être heureux; mais, au milieu de ce bonheur, ne m'oubliez pas, même mort, si vous voulez que la prosperité reste votre lot à jamais.

Nothing could be more explicit. The positive facts are clear, and the rest of the play confirms them. Oedipus dies and goes into a grave, or rather, his body lies in the grave, but his spirit joins the spirits of all the dead in Hades. Gilberte Ronnet puts this well:

Comme n'importe quel mortel, il dit adieu à la lumière qu'il va fuir dans les ténèbres. Il n'attend aucune autre immortalité que celle de tous les hommes, la pâle survie de la ψυχή dans l'Hadès.' (p. 310.)

Like every other mortal being, Oedipus bids farewell to the light of day he is going to lose when he goes into the dark. He looks forward to no other form of after-life than that of all men in the pale survival of the soul in Hades.

Negatively, the facts are just as clear. There is no mention of gods relenting or of gods making Oedipus one of them. Gilberte Ronnet is equally firm on this point:

Are we not putting words into Sophocles' mouth if we say that Oedipus is summoned to any kind of familiar intercourse with the gods? Bowra writes on page 344, 'The god who summons him regards him as a companion and wishes him to come with him on their common errand. Oedipus is not only at peace with the gods, he is almost of their company', and on page 354, 'We do not know precisely what his state will be, but we can be sure that he will be conscious and active.' Knox strikes the same note on pages 161–162, 'The last of the Sophoclean heroes . . . is here recognized by the gods as their peer'. Sophocles does not think that gods and men have anything in common. The idea that a man could become a peer or a companion of the gods is radically alien to his way of thinking.

Oedipus will not become an immortal voice. It is the *corpse* in the earth which will preserve Attica from enemy attacks. The lines to retain are these, where Oedipus makes clear to Theseus what the value of his dead body will be in days to come when Thebes becomes an enemy. Then he says:

ἵν' οὑμὸς εὕδων καὶ κεκρυμμένος νέκυς
ψυχρός ποτ' αὐτῶν θερμὸν αἷμα πίεται,
εἰ Ζεὺς ἔτι Ζεὺς χὠ Διὸς Φοῖβος σαφής.   (621-3.)

Alors mon froid cadavre, endormi sous la terre, doit boire leur sang chaud, si Zeus est toujours Zeus, et si Phoebos, son fils, est toujours véridique.

Then my chill corpse will, though sleeping in burial underground, receive their hot blood. That is, if Zeus is still Zeus, and Phoebus, his son, is a true prophet.

I cannot believe that on a first reading anyone would be prepared to call this 'material' and 'primitive' explanation given by Oedipus a touch of the real religious thinking of the play. So, in my Polonius fashion, I shall take a round-about route via the question, 'Is *Oedipus at Colonus* the most tragic of Sophocles' plays?' To answer this, we must have an answer to a prior question, 'What is the essentially tragic element in the play?' As we have seen, some critics do not regard the play as a tragedy. They classify it along with Shakespeare's *The Tempest*, and call it supreme because it *transcends* tragedy. Such a way out is not available to those who think of tragedy as the supreme form of drama. My winding line must take the form of going behind these questions and comparing *Oedipus at Colonus* and *Oedipus the King* in order to provide grounds for answering the first question as follows: '*Oedipus the King* is a great tragedy but *Oedipus at Colonus* is no tragedy at all.'

The 'mystery' I stumble upon in making the comparative judgement comes in finding the tragic in an attitude to guilt and responsibility which the Greek nation grew out of, and in calling untragic an attitude to guilt and responsibility which is much nearer our own ideas of right and wrong. Since, so far as I know, nobody has deduced a law for all tragedy from this 'backward' feature of *Oedipus the King*, let us return to the basic facts. Let us in the sketchy way provided by a crude translation attempt to re-create in our imagination what the original may have been like. Let us so reconstruct the central scene of *Oedipus the King*. I call it central, for it is in this scene that for me the essence of all tragedy is revealed. This 'horror-scene' (*deinos* in every sense) occupies a little more than a hundred lines (1297-1415) of the Greek text, and covers only a moment, when Oedipus reveals his mutilated eyes to the Chorus and tells them what it more concerned him to say than them to hear.

— How could you bring yourself to destroy your eyes? What the god that pushed your arm?
— Apollo. My friends, I want you all to know that it was Apollo who willed these troubles on me and brought me low. But it was my own hand alone did the horrid deed. I had nothing left my eyes could bear to see. All was bitterness.
— It was indeed.
— Yes, friends, there was nothing to give me joy, seeing or hearing. Take me away as quick as you can. Get rid of a man, the worst of wretches, the most accursed, the most hateful to Gods and men.
— When I think of what you did, and of what was done to you, I wish I had never known you.
— My curse on the man, whoever he was, in those pasture lands, who took the clamps off my feet and saved my life. Little good did he do me. If I had died then, I should not now be giving pain to myself and my friends.
— Amen to that.
— I should never have killed my father. I should never have married someone from whom I am descended. As it is, I have lost my connection with the gods. My parents have desecrated religion. I am the child of sin. No sin can be greater than mine when I shared the defiled bed.
— There is no action of yours I can say was well done. You ought to have killed, not blinded yourself.

[Here there must have been a change of tone. The metre is now iambic.]

— Don't preach at me! Don't tell me *now* that I did not do all for the best! It had to be my eyes. I couldn't bear to die and go down to Hades and look my father and my poor mother in the face after the things I had done. Can you suppose I want to go on seeing my children, got as they were? Or go on seeing the sights of our beloved city, all its palaces and temples, now that I, once the finest man in all Thebes, am excluded from worship, *and* by my own decree, when I gave orders to expel the godless creature, the man the gods themselves had pronounced impure, the son of Laius? If you think I could have borne to witness a dishonour of that magnitude with open eyes, you are very much mistaken. I would have made myself deaf as well as blind if I could have had my way. The only form of happiness open to me now is to shut the world out.

Why were you so kind to me Cithaeron? You could have killed me on the spot, and nobody would have known I had existed. What an ugly sore was festering under my fair skin when I was a boy in the Corinth I took to be my true fatherland, and you my true father, Polybus! Now everybody has seen me exposed as a bad son of bad parents.

Are you still dreaming of my fine doings, you three roads, you secret glen, you coppice and narrow way where those three roads meet? Do you still remember how you supped up my blood, the blood I poured out for you from my father's veins? And did you ever hear of the sequel – what transpired elsewhere? The bed on which I was got with sperm and brought into the world had to know me delivering the same sperm and having *that* turned into children – a dreadful mix-up in the blood of our tribe, father and son, brother and sister, boys and girls, daughter and mother, all wrongly blood-related – there is no fouler nor unholier deed a man can commit.

This, with its repeated and insistent personal pronoun, 'I', coupled with an active verb of doing, committing, abominations, used to strike me as ethically backward. I used to find enlightenment in the later play, *Oedipus at Colonus*, where the accent falls rather on being sinned against than sinning, and I used to applaud this later Oedipus when he tried to persuade the Chorus that he was totally innocent: 'My life has been suffering, not doing. I need not tell you that story of my father and mother, you know it already. It has put the fear of god in you, I know well. But why should you think ill of me? I only gave as good as I got. Even had I known all the circumstances, I didn't do wrong. But contrast my behaviour with theirs. Those who caused me to suffer knew exactly what they were doing. I was acting all the time in the dark.' Looking back, I can see that what induced me to this belief was the whole argument of *Merit and Responsibility*[19] and in particular the following passage from the fifth chapter, entitled 'Pollution':

We left Oedipus in the *Oedipus Tyrannus* incestuous and a parricide, condemned by his acts. Even had Sophocles the will, he had no means of acquitting Oedipus of his unintentional crimes. Nor did Oedipus expect it. But a far different Oedipus appears in the *Oedipus at Colonus*, written in or just before 406 B.C. As soon as he appears on the stage he rebukes the Chorus [in the words just given] .... Later the point is put succinctly, and forced home to the audience, in an exchange between Oedipus and the Chorus:

[19] The title of a work by Arthur W. H. Adkins, first published in 1960.

Cho: You have suffered.
Oed: I have suffered things not to be forgotten.
Cho: You have 'done'.
Oed: I have not 'done'.   (p.105.)

My task is now to vindicate the change that has come over me and to give reasons for thinking that we have the essence of all tragedy in the scene from *Oedipus the King*. When faced with a task of this difficulty, it is often easier to begin by dismissing what can be shown to be a wrong view. At least I would claim that we totally miss the tragic centre and go off at a tangent if we follow the commentary by J. C. Kamerbeek.[20] To my mind he is offering us an example of what I can only call a lightning-conductor, a device to make the shock of tragedy run harmlessly into the ground, when he says of Oedipus in his remark about Apollo: 'he recognizes the divine agency (i.e. the forces by which the cosmic order is maintained) by which his existence has been governed and his fate sealed.' (p. 244.) For I am bound to report that, if we search for an emphasis in this scene on 'the forces by which the cosmic order is maintained', we find nothing of the sort, and if we ask where the hero's tongue goes to meet the aching tooth, we must answer that it is into a different area altogether. This 'lightning-conductor' is what I shall in a moment be calling a 'sunlight' thought. Our scene, to my mind, is predominantly one where something dark and horrible, which has been lurking in the depths, is dragged up to the hero's troubled consciousness.

A reader of the so-called *Poetics* by Aristotle may have wondered whether I lacked the courage to tackle him rather than the Dutch scholar over his account of his favourite play. For Aristotle, too, found the essence of all tragedy in this play. But not in the scene I have been trying to present. What Aristotle admired was the *plot*. Although 'whizzkids' in our universities can find minute faults in this plot, when one is in the theatre the play works like a good detective story, better, in fact, for we continue to enjoy the manner in which it is worked out even when we know 'who dunit'. But is this the quality which has made the play one of the world's best tragedies? My answer is 'no'. Although I have no trouble in rejecting Freud's version — for I do not think the tragic plane is the psychoanalytic — I am sure that what places this tragedy among the best is the vision uncovering the roots beneath all society, a vision in which we consequently accept Oedipus as guilty, though we would acquit him in any 'daylight' court of law.

[20] *The Oedipus Tyrannus*, Leiden, 1967.

The *absence* of moral and metaphysical speculation about guilt and innocence is what strikes me most in this scene, particularly the absence of the considerations raised by the Oedipus of the later play. Oedipus in the earlier play is evidently too disturbed to bring the top of his mind into play. Just because of the trouble he is in, whatever finer feelings he may have had are swallowed up by his confrontation with all that is holy in the bonds which bind *philoi*. This explains the deep ambiguity in Oedipus' language here. If ever the tragic act was performed in a mist, this blinding is an instance. For this reason I find Gilberte Ronnet too French and clear-cut when she offers the terms *châtiment et libération* – punishment and escape. In this scene both aspects of the act of blinding are blurred and covered over by inexpressible feelings.

We are helped to travel in the direction in which Sophocles is sending our thoughts if we consult authorities on the origins of Greek speculation about the horrors of pollution.[21] But if it is true that Oedipus is here calling up the oldest and most precious acquisitions of centuries and centuries of experience of the formation of humanity, it may be more illuminating to have recourse once again to our imagination, as suggested in the chapter on Tragic Bonds. This scene provides further illustration of some comments on an earlier page:

It would be pure *fumisterie* if I did not confess how like the religious our approach to the few very great tragedies must be. For it is not only that we are asked to rise high above our normal selves and begin to think and feel on a plane we do not habitually frequent, our difficulties lie just as much with the necessity to confront terrors and desires we think of as belonging rather to our heritage from the distant days when our ancestors had not yet emerged from the jungle.

The horror felt by Oedipus is ultimate horror; its depth is in direct proportion to the values placed on what he has desecrated. In the search for religion we have to plunge down as well as soar up. We must dig deep to come upon what is most precious.

A similar plea is in place once we begin to appreciate the horror of Oedipus's position. He has been put out of the universe. Now although enlightenment can be obtained from learned treatises on the meaning of the Greek word for a scape-goat, *pharmakos*, and from the works of

---

[21] The reader who is unfamiliar with the ancient Greek notions of 'pollution' might obtain light by consulting the index of Louis Moulinier's *Le pur et l'impur dans la pensée des Grecs, d'Homère à Aristote*, Paris, 1952.

anthropology, which inform us that the idea was both ancient and widespread, it is still more important to sink ourselves dramatically into the precise situation of the hero, which is both more and less than that of a scape-goat. I also find it helpful in getting below the habitual surface of our thoughts to contrast this inarticulate, deeply ambiguous cry made by Oedipus with the most heart-rending *articulate* expressions of the state of the outcast in other great literary works. Everyone will have his own passage of special significance. I propose one dear to me in Racine's *Phèdre*.

> Le Ciel, tout l'univers est plein de mes aieux.
> Où me cacher? Fuyons dans la nuit infernale.
> Mais que dis-je? Mon père y tient l'urne fatale . . .

especially if I am allowed to re-think her position like this: 'The heavens, the universe itself, is full of my blood-relations. I must hide from them, but where? The depths of darkest hell? My father stands there at the seat of judgement . . .' and then link the classical imagery with the Hebrew:

Can any hide himself in secret places that I shall not see him? saith the Lord. Do I not fill heaven and earth? saith the Lord . . . . Whither shall I go from thy spirit? or whither shall I flee from thy presence? If I ascend up into heaven, behold, thou art there: if I make my bed in hell, behold, thou art there . . . . If I say, Surely the darkness shall cover me . . . . the darkness hideth not from thee . . .[22]

But even more heart-breaking are those words where Dido expresses her sense of having no everlasting arms underneath to prop her when abandoned by Aeneas:

> iam iam nec maxima Iuno
> nec Saturnius haec oculis pater aspicit aequis.
> nusquam tuta fides.
> What shall I doe? for now alasse I see
> that neither Juno Deignes to favour mee
> nor Jove himselfe lookes downe with equall eyes
> the earth is faythlesse, faythlesse are the skies . . .[23]

But these passages are all instances of what I still have to characterize as belonging to the 'sunlight' world. When the religion to be discovered is both dark and deep, we are blocked off if we are offered rhetorical

---

[22] The Authorized Version, *Jeremiah* 23, and *Psalms*, 139.
[23] *Aeneid* IV, 371–3 S. Godolphin *The Passion of Dido for Aeneas*, 1658.

skill. While I am helped in feeling into the mystery of this passage in the Greek play by recalling the mystery in Shakespeare's *Macbeth* when the hero feels cut off from humanity by his crimes, I am rebuffed when rhetoric closes the gate to the dungeon. Shakespeare was significantly indebted to some lines in Seneca:

> quis eluet me Tanais aut quae barbaris
> Maeotis undis Pontico incumbens mari?
> non ipse toto magnus Oceano pater
> tantum expiarit sceleris . . . .

when he wrote:

> Will all great *Neptunes* Ocean wash this blood
> Cleane from my Hand? no; this my Hand will rather
> The multitudinous Seas incarnadine
> Making the Greene one Red.

I find this magnificent rhetoric taking my mind away from the horror of the deed. The blood ceases to stick to the fingers.

Oedipus sees himself in the hands of the god, and is to that extent a religious figure, but we come nearer a deeper sense of religion in the scene I have singled out when we find Oedipus indulging in what I can only call *blood-thinking*. He is obsessed by the blood in the place where those three roads meet. Whose blood is it? Mine, he cries in the same breath with which he admits that it is his father's. Clearly, the important thought for Oedipus is that it is the same blood, the blood of the whole tribe. Sophocles has a word for it — *haima emphylion*. Oedipus thinks of this blood as life-blood, transmitting life from generation to generation. Hence his two abominations are linked. He did the unforgivable thing in shedding his father's blood; he did a further unforgivable deed in re-channelling the precious fluid generated from the blood which secures the transmission of life from generation to generation. This forcing back of the generating act is the ultimate wound. It destroys the family, the tribe, all society. It destroys all forms of life, of creation in plants and animals. Oedipus thought that the whole universe cried out in horror: it was the foulest, most dreadful deed a man can perform.

By following my nose, as it were, I have landed myself in a quagmire, if in fact I am obliged to assert that the place where religion and tragedy *coalesce* is in this obscure case of 'blood-thinking'. It is bad enough to have found this passage in *Oedipus the King* expressing the essence of all tragedy. But what hope have I of making good the claim that all the deepest moments in plays, moments which finally 'send' us, convince us beyond question that we stand in the presence of the mystery of Tragedy, resemble this chosen moment? No hope at all with a reader who will not allow the existence of religion *below* the public forms we all recognize. Even if such a reader allows the proposition that tragic religion in the Greek plays can only be felt when the fictional reality of the gods is dismissed, when we feel them no longer as persons but purely as forces – in this context, only when we have lost the truth of 'It was Apollo who blinded me' in the wide absorption of the hero's vision of the place where three roads meet – can we imagine such a reader allowing that in comparable moments of great tragedies composed in the Christian era the tragic depths will be found *below* surface references to the numinous?

I would not despair of carrying a student of Shakespeare's plays with me in directing his attention once again to the bonds which dominate *Macbeth, King Lear,* and *Othello,* and in asking him to connect the tragedies with the spilt blood involved in the breaking of these bonds. But to go further and find *religion* in that blood would be beyond my capacity. For such a religion could not be grasped by a modern mind. We are therefore driven to try what fancy could do. My fancy is that thought-patterns similar to those I have been attributing to Oedipus can be detected under the all-enveloping, all-concealing drapery of the Christian religion. I shall not attempt to specify what it is that is so hidden. But we know that it was the habit of the first Christians who 'converted' Britain to erect their altars over pagan shrines. I then ask, 'What came before those pagan shrines? Is it relevant to this query to recall what is popularly known as the Corpus Christi Carol?

> Lully lulley, lully, lulley,
> The fawcon hath born my mak away.
> He bare hym vp, he bare hym down;
> He bare hym into an orchard brown.
> In that orchard ther was an hall,
> That was hangid with purpill and pall.
> And in that hall there was a bede;
> Hit was hangid with gold so rede.
> And yn that bed ther lythe a knyght,
> His wowndes bledyng day and nyght.
> By that bedes side ther kneleth a may,
> And she wepeth nyght and day.
> And by that beddes side ther stondith a ston,
> *Corpus Christi* wretyn theron.

There we have what might be called the 'orthodox' version of the poem. The extant variants are sufficiently various to encourage the fancy that the body of Christ is here an after-thought covering the thought for the sake of which the poem was originally composed. It is hard to believe that, if the bird was the thought out of which the poem was made, this falcon was called up to introduce a *Christian* mystery. How the original bird poem might have gone is suggested by the following variant from Scotland, which might be given the title, *What the heron saw*:

> The heron flew east, the heron flew west,
> The heron flew to the fair forest;
> She flew o'er streams and meadows green,
> And a' to see what could be seen:
> And when she saw the faithful pair,
> Her breast grew sick, her head grew sair;
> For there she saw a lovely bower,
> What a' clad o'er wi' lilly-flower,
> And in the bower there was a bed
> With silken sheets, and weel down spread;
> And in the bed there lay a knight,
> Whose wounds did bleed both day and night;
> And by the bed there stood a stane
> And there was set a

[Here the poem falls into apparent confusion. There must have been a rhyming word which would reveal that the *stane* had other words written on it than *Corpus Christi*. Our recorded version goes back to the preliminary item of the *kneling may* and ends as follows:

> leal maiden
> With silver needle and silken threde
> Stemming the wounds when they did blede.[24]

We may well ask, what was the sight which sickened the heron? but I won't go on save to confess that I can't help wondering about the lovers, Paolo and Francesca, in Dante's *Inferno*, and a thing the girl said:

> noi che tignemmo il mondo di sanguigno.
> we who dyed the world blood-red.

[24] Texts taken from *The Early English Carols*, ed. Richard Leighton Greene, 1935, pp. 221–2.

I am sure of one thing, that the tradition Dante was in – a tradition so well imagined in the fancy of Denis de Rougemont in his *L'amour et l'Occident* – overlay and concealed older connections between love and blood. I am tempted to fly off to the forests of Scandinavia to search for the 'true' story behind the ballad which begins:

> Why dois your brand sae drap wi bluid,
> Edward, Edward.

But the flight would only provoke the thought: *obscurum per obscurius*.

Returning now to the consideration from which I started – the 'material' and 'primitive' explanation given by Oedipus in the later play of the effect of his corpse when buried in the earth – I should be sorry if any reader were to think, even for a moment, that I had allowed the 'blood-thinking' by Oedipus in the earlier play to rush to my head. Aristotle was not mistaken in saluting the intelligence both of the hero and the author of this play. What I deplore, however, is the suggestion that Sophocles had come down in the world by giving place in his tragedies to such instances of 'blood-thinking'. Gilberte Ronnet's regret that Sophocles should have ended his *Oedipus at Colonus* with an attri- bution of 'magical' powers to a corpse strikes me as typically French:

. . . pourquoi ce recours aux formes les plus primitives de la religion? On a peine à imaginer qu'un Sophocle ait partagé avec les plus humbles de ses contemporains ces antiques croyances . . . (p. 311.)

Why does Sophocles here revert to the most primitive stages of religion? It is difficult to believe that Sophocles shared these antiquated views with the least enlightened of his contemporaries.

And she adds in a foot-note:

Sans aborder ici l''énigme' des *Bacchantes,* on peut tout de même re- marquer l'étrange coincidence qui fait qu'en plein 'siècle des Lumières', les deux grands tragiques terminent leur carrière par la représentation des formes les plus irrationnelles de la religion grecque.

Without attempting to touch on the so-called 'riddle' of the *Bacchae*, we may still take note of the strange coincidence created by the fact that in the glorious century of Greek Enlightenment its two great composers of tragedies closed their artistic careers with representations of the most irrational forms of Greek religion.

In such a dark area as that I have been peering into I hope I may be allowed a pictorial image. I suppose that at great depths the world's oceans are full of strange fish which, like the coelacanth, may be thought of as remote ancestors of the known species of fish. I further suppose that if we attempted to bring one of these primitive monsters to the surface, it would disintegrate in our atmosphere. I am helped in the application of this supposition by the passage in Eliot's poem *The Dry Salvages*, where he speaks of a sea which tosses on the beach

> Its hints of earlier and other creation
> and of fishermen who find that they have made
> a haul that will not bear examination.

It is not because I am near the end of my book that I am unwilling to say more on this topic. For, if I am right, we cannot drag to the light and inspect whatever is making the horrible into the tragic, the tragically horrible. But I can toss out an experiment a reader might try who was willing to go back to Eliot's notorious account of Shakespeare's *Hamlet*. In an article he contributed to the *Athenaeum* for 26 September 1919, Eliot accepted the view that this tragedy turns on a mother's guilt and the feelings of a son towards a guilty mother. Eliot thought that Shakespeare had failed to handle the subject: 'It is not merely the "guilt of a mother" that cannot be handled as Shakespeare handled the suspicion of Othello, the infatuation of Antony, or the pride of Coriolanus. The subject might conceivably have expanded into a tragedy like these, intelligible, self-complete, in the sunlight. *Hamlet*, like the sonnets, is full of some stuff that the writer could not drag to light, contemplate, or manipulate into art.' Eliot glossed this by saying: 'Hamlet (the man) is dominated by an emotion which is inexpressible, because it is in *excess* of the facts as they appear.'[25] This leads me to wonder whether Eliot could have mistaken the nature of tragedy if he thought of it as occurring *wholly* in the sunlight. But I like the phrase 'in the sunlight', because the tragic mystery must not lie in some hole or corner of the play, in something mumbled by a chorus, but must be manifest in a conspicuous action on which the whole play turns. My experiment would be for the reader to try out the thought that a mystery like that I have attempted to describe in *Oedipus the King* lies at the heart of every great tragedy. Isn't it for want of such a mystery that we cannot class that beautiful and moving play, *Bérénice*, among the very greatest tragedies?

If compelled to sum up my views on the questions raised in this

---

[25] Re-printed in *The Sacred Wood*, 1920.

chapter, I should have to answer that, if asked whether religion lies at the heart of tragedy, my answer would be, yes — and no! The moment you deny religion such a place, you are forced to concede it. The moment you try to make tragedy essentially religious, you lose tragedy altogether, and substitute an illusion for a glorious reality. I shall always be found siding with those critics who declare that tragedy is, ultimately, an affair of men, not of gods. But as soon as the company begins to overstress what is nowadays called a 'humanist' position, I leave that company in the secure conviction that the men who have the last word on the tragic stage are interpenetrated with the divine. Similarly, whenever we are forced to concede that the world's greatest tragedies are soaked in religion, I would suggest that we must recognize that everything in them we could call religious has suffered

> a Sea-change
> Into something rich, & strange.

In entering tragedy, religion loses its absolute rights, and submits to the laws of poetry. It is in this sense that I concur with those who, like W. B. Yeats, deny that tragedy states truth, but declare that tragedy *embodies* truth. Any truth there is in tragedy arises exclusively from the convictions which are *dramatically* constructed. Which means that we are never finally referred outside the play for falsification or verification. The terms for entry into fiction are absolute. I therefore conclude that religion so transformed enters as an essential consituent but does not constitute the essence of Tragedy. That is an instance of what the French call *esprit de l'escalier*. It is what I should *like* to have said on that memorable summer day of 1979.

INDEX OF PRINCIPAL NAMES AND TOPICS